MW00809775

AMERICAN AIRPOWER STRATEGY IN KOREA, 1950-1953

MODERN WAR STUDIES

Theodore A. Wilson
General Editor

Raymond A. Callahan
J. Gary Clifford
Jacob W. Kipp
Jay Luvaas
Allan R. Millett
Dennis Showalter
Series Editors

AMERICAN AIRPOWER STRATEGY IN KOREA, 1950-1953

CONRAD C. CRANE

 UNIVERSITY PRESS OF KANSAS

The views expressed herein are those of the author and do not purport to reflect the positions of the United States Military Academy, Department of the Army, or Department of Defense.

Published by the University Press of Kansas (Lawrence, Kansas 66049), which was organized by the Kansas Board of Regents and is operated and funded by Emporia State University, Fort Hays State University, Kansas State University, Pittsburg State University, the University of Kansas, and Wichita State University.

Library of Congress Cataloging-in-Publication Data

Crane, Conrad C.
  American airpower strategy in Korea, 1950-1953 / Conrad C. Crane.
    p.   cm. — (Modern war studies)
  Includes bibliographical references and index.
  ISBN 0-7006-0991-1 (alk. paper)
  1. Korean War, 1950-1953—Aerial operations, American. 2. United States. Air Force—History—Korean War, 1950-1953. I. Title. II. Series.
  DS920.2.U5 C73 2000
  951.904'248—dc21   99-35874

British Library Cataloguing in Publication Data is available.

Printed in the United States of America

10 9 8 7 6 5 4 3 2 1

CONTENTS

PREFACE

When I was finishing my previous book, *Bombs, Cities, and Civilians: American Airpower Strategy in World War II,* I closed with a couple of chapters that tried to analyze the legacies of that experience for American air forces in the limited wars that followed. Some critics were dissatisfied with that section, and it was apparent to me as I wrote it that the Korean War especially deserved more detailed treatment. In that previous volume I dealt with the temptations that lured American airmen down the path toward Tokyo and Hiroshima; this book is concerned with how they responded to the challenges of a different kind of conflict where their options were severely curtailed. My proposed title for my study of World War II airpower was "The Temptations of Total War," and for this book it could be "The Frustrations of Limited War." In Korea the new U.S. Air Force was forced to conduct an unexpected type of war in an unexpected place. It acquitted itself well, but for a number of reasons afterward it returned to its focus on a general war in Europe, much to its detriment in Vietnam. The Korean conflict is worth looking at again not just because we are approaching its fiftieth anniversary. Policy makers today are again wrestling with the proper use of military force in an era typified by unclear threats and resource constraints. The flexibility and destructive potential of airpower make it an attractive option, as has recently been demonstrated in the Balkans, and studying its accomplishments and limitations in a similar previous scenario can better inform us about its best application today. If in the process this analysis also acquaints readers with the hardships and heroism involved in the air war over Korea and increases their respect for the veterans of the "Forgotten War," then so much the better.

This book could never have been completed without the assistance of many people. The encouragement of Noel Parsons of Texas A&M University Press and Michael Briggs of University Press of Kansas was essential in keeping me motivated to maintain high standards yet finish the project in a timely manner. It was considerably enriched by thoughtful comments from Mark Grandstaff,

David Mets, Walt Moody, and John Sherwood. Not only did Allan Millett provide many important suggestions to improve the manuscript, but he and his student Kelly Jordan furnished me with a number of key documents. Eduard Mark gave me the benefit of his expertise on interdiction, and Gian Gentile provided documents and many lively discussions about the evolution of American bombing doctrine. Barton Bernstein offered useful suggestions and essential documents concerning biological warfare issues.

I am also grateful for the assistance of archivists at a number of locations. Wilbert Mahoney and his colleagues at the National Archives II were very helpful, as were 1st Lt. William Butler and Dr. Joseph Caver at the Air Force Historical Research Agency. Terry Keenan helped me greatly in Special Collections at Syracuse University, as did David Keough at the U.S. Military History Institute. Alan Aimone and Suzanne Christoff worked with me to obtain pictures from the United States Military Academy (USMA) Special Collections. Christian Ostermann and Nancy Meyers of the Cold War International History Project were very tolerant and cooperative when I badgered them for advance copies of new material. Richard Bancroft and Walter Nelson dug old reports out of RAND Corporation's historical files. Anne Lamb and Melissa Mills of the USMA History Department administrative staff provided invaluable help in keeping some of my research trips straight, and Frank Martini assisted me with maps.

Two people in particular made special contributions to this book. I feel honored to have been able to interview Gen. Jacob Smart, retired, one of America's great air warriors. He deserves a biography of his own one day. And I was privileged to have Sharon MacDonald share her father's letters with me, along with the results of her own research into the circumstances surrounding his death. She should write a book about it sometime.

Last but not least, I again must give credit to my wife and sons for providing me with support or quiet when I needed it during a rather tumultuous time in our lives. I could not have completed this without them. Life, like war, does not always happen the way you expect.

ABBREVIATIONS

AAF	Army Air Forces
AFHRA	Air Force Historical Research Agency
AFR	Air Force Regulation
ATC	Air Training Command
BW	biological warfare
CAS	close air support
CCAF	Communist Chinese Air Force
CEP	probable circular error
CIA	Central Intelligence Agency
CINCFE	commander in chief, Far East
CINCPAC	commander in chief, Pacific
CINCUNC	commander in chief, United Nations Command
CW	chemical warfare
FAD	Fighter Air Division
FEAF	Far East Air Forces
FOF	fear of flying
FRUS	*Foreign Relations of the United States*
GHQ	General Headquarters
GMU	Guided Missile Unit
ICRC	International Committee of the Red Cross
IFF	Identification Friend or Foe
IG	inspector general
ISCC	Inter-Service Coordinating Committee
JAAF	Joint Action Armed Forces

JCS	Joint Chiefs of Staff
JFACC	joint air forces component commander
msg	message
NATO	North Atlantic Treaty Organization
NKPA	North Korean People's Army
NSC	National Security Council
OSI	Office of Special Investigations
PIO	Public Information Office
POW	prisoner of war
RAAF	Royal Australian Air Force
RAF	Royal Air Force
ROK	Republic of Korea
ROTC	Reserve Officer Training Corps
RPV	remotely piloted vehicle
SAC	Strategic Air Command
SHORAN	short-range navigation radar
TAC	Tactical Air Command
UN	United Nations
USAF	United States Air Force
USAMHI	United States Army Military History Institute
USGPO	United States Government Printing Office
USMA	United States Military Academy
USSBS	United States Strategic Bombing Survey
WHO	World Health Organization

INTRODUCTION

I think this is a rather bizarre war out there, and I think we can learn an awful lot of bad habits in it.

MAJ. GEN. EMMETT O'DONNELL, JR.[1]

The conflict that raged up and down the Korean peninsula between 1950 and 1953 has been called by many different names. Various historians have referred to it as the Korean civil war or the first limited war of the Nuclear Age or just as the "Forgotten War" as it has faded from our collective memories. Some airmen have emphasized the advent of new technology in the confrontation between United Nations (UN) and Communist forces by calling it the "First Jet Air War." It was also the first war for the new United States Air Force (USAF), though, as General O'Donnell's remark to a Senate committee in May 1951 implies, this was not the type of conflict that that organization expected or wanted to fight.

For readers unfamiliar with the course of the seesaw war in Korea, it can be roughly divided into five phases. The first began on 25 June 1950 when the North Korean People's Army (NKPA) attacked poorly prepared Republic of Korea forces and swarmed southward over the thirty-eighth parallel. Over-confident American units deployed from Japan were also driven back, and UN forces were soon bottled up in a perimeter behind the Naktong River defending the key port of Pusan. But the NKPA's lines of communication were over-extended, and it had suffered tremendous attrition from constant combat. It was therefore very vulnerable to counterattack. The second phase of the war began on 15 September, when Gen. Douglas MacArthur landed a strong force at Inchon in the enemy rear and the surrounded U.S. Eighth Army broke out of the Pusan perimeter, along with South Korean forces. The NKPA collapsed, and the quick turn of events forced leaders on both sides to make strategic decisions of great importance on short notice. The United States and its UN allies gave MacArthur permission to cross the thirty-eighth parallel and reunite the two Koreas, and as UN forces headed for the Yalu, it was their turn to become vulnerable and overextended. The war turned again and began its third phase as a massive Chinese intervention in late November

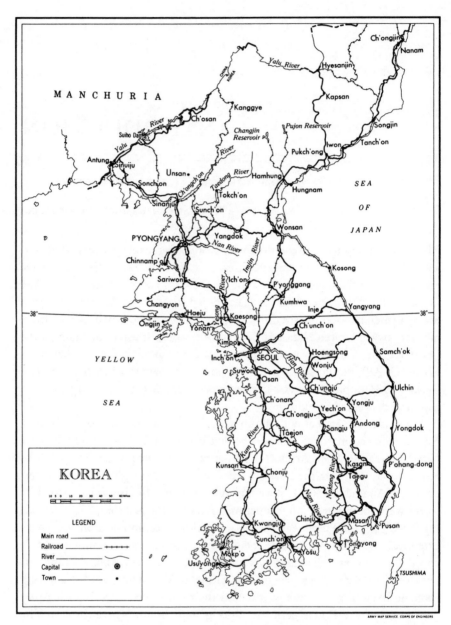

(Army Map Service Corps of Engineers)

caught the American Eighth Army and Tenth Corps with their allies in North Korea by surprise, and they were lucky to escape without even heavier losses. The Chinese armies rolled over the parallel again and retook the South Korean capital of Seoul, but because of long supply lines, harsh weather, and growing UN resistance, the Chinese reached their culminating point in early 1951. The fourth phase began when the Eighth Army, rejuvenated by the dynamic leadership of Matthew Ridgway, spearheaded a counteroffensive that could not be slowed even by President Truman's relief of MacArthur in April for insubordination. By June, UN forces and firepower had recaptured Seoul and restored the battle line to the vicinity of the thirty-eighth parallel. At that time armistice talks began, and for the next two years, the war settled down to its fifth phase—a bloody stalemate in the mountainous Korean terrain.

The peninsula's topography features jagged mountains, deep valleys, and one main transportation corridor following the generally north-south axis Pusan-Taegu-Seoul-Pyongyang-Sinuiju. Lateral communications in 1950 were poor, and land transportation depended primarily on railroads built by the Japanese during their brutal occupation from 1910 to 1945. These usually followed the coastal plains and river valleys. The prevalent ridgelines and rice paddies made target identification from the air very difficult. Weather also played a key role in shaping combat operations. Summer is a season of heavy rains, especially in July. Cloud cover, fog, and haze can wreak havoc with air missions. But it is a common joke among those who have served in Korea that the country has only three seasons: summer, early winter, and late winter. Temperatures in winter can be extreme, and "the Hawk" that blows down from Siberia exacerbates the cold while creating strong winds at higher altitudes. However, the dry winter air makes it the best season for aerial operations. Predicting actual flying conditions was still difficult, since warm currents in the surrounding oceans and the fact that weather patterns generally flowed down from enemy territory made weather forecasting for UN forces an inexact science. Even in winter, airmen could sometimes be surprised by unexpected overcast. One experienced pilot described a November training flight to his wife by writing, "The new boys were thoroughly indoctrinated on flying in Korea—they never saw the ground." One of them popped out of the clouds as visibility dropped, landed too fast, and skidded sideways within ten feet of a cliff at the end of the runway. The commentator noted, "Needless to say, he went to church a few hours later."[2]

Despite such problems with terrain and weather, American airpower played a major role in UN operations, and the way it was employed depended on the attitudes and experience of a number of key leaders. Most important were the three Army generals who filled the dual position of commander in

"I don't care how accurate it is, get rid of it!"

This cartoon by T. Sgt. James Mabry from the 20 April 1952 Pacific edition of *Stars and Stripes* parodies the lengths that the FEAF weather service would go to provide accurate forecasts. It did the best it could, but Korean geography produced fickle and tricky weather patterns. Some of the most useful sources for American forecasters were international meteorological observations broadcast by Russian weather stations throughout the war, but the Chinese provided no such information. (Pacific edition of *Stars and Stripes*)

chief Far East (CINCFE) and commander in chief, United Nations Command (CINCUNC) during the war. MacArthur had used his Far East Air Forces (FEAF) adroitly to achieve great success against the Japanese as commander of the South West Pacific Area in World War II and had also seen the devastation wrought by B-29s against the enemy homeland. Ridgway, his successor, had commanded the Eighty-second Airborne Division and Eighteenth Airborne Corps in the European theater and had been a witness to the impact of overwhelming Allied air superiority on German forces and cities. Gen. Mark Clark, who became CINCFE in May 1952, had been involved in a more frustrating campaign during World War II, commanding the Fifth Army and Fifteenth Army Group in Italy, where airpower had been effective but not enough to significantly speed the Allied advance through difficult terrain. His attitudes were also shaped by two years negotiating with the Soviets as American high commissioner for Austria.

These theater commanders all received advice from the subordinate leaders of their air components. A number of USAF officers had roles in shaping the application of airpower during the Korean War, and they were also influenced by their World War II experience. When the North Koreans launched their invasion, the commanding general, FEAF, was Lt. Gen. George Stratemeyer. From 1943 to 1945 he had commanded American air units in Burma and India, and he finished the war in charge of the Army Air Forces in China. Stratemeyer was succeeded at FEAF in May 1951 by Lt. Gen. Otto P. Weyland, one of the few senior USAF leaders who retained his faith in tactical airpower after World War II, and who would have a significant impact on its resurgence during and after the Korean War. No one influenced the conduct of air operations during the conflict more than Weyland. He had made his mark while in charge of the Nineteenth Tactical Air Command supporting Gen. George Patton's Third Army in its drive across France into Germany. Weyland had been directly under Gen. Hoyt S. Vandenberg, the commanding general of the Ninth Air Force, which provided tactical support to all American units in the European theater, and former deputy commander of the Allied Expeditionary Air Forces. In 1950, Vandenberg was chief of staff of the USAF. More important than his combat experience was the fact that he was the nephew of a U.S. senator and proved very adept at peacetime political maneuvers in Washington.

One other airman back in the United States had significant impact on the men and machines that applied American airpower in Korea. He was Lt. Gen. Curtis LeMay, commander of the Strategic Air Command (SAC) in 1950. Gen. Carl Spaatz, the first USAF chief of staff who had led the U.S. Strategic Air Forces in Europe in 1944 and 1945, called LeMay the greatest air combat commander of World War II. While leading a bomb group in Europe, LeMay had developed combat formations that provided maximum defensive firepower; the nonevasive action bomb run, which improved bombing accuracy; and lead crews who were experts on specified targets. As commander of the Twenty-first Bomber Command of the Twentieth Air Force in the Marianas, he had initiated the incendiary raids that devastated so many Japanese cities. He had applied his leadership and problem-solving skills to organize the Berlin Airlift and was the obvious choice to revitalize SAC and turn it into the world's premier aerial striking force. His faith in the war-winning capacity of strategic airpower and focus on general nuclear war were shared by most Air Force leaders. When he was promoted to full general in 1951, he became the youngest four-star general in American history since Ulysses Simpson Grant.[3]

LeMay was particularly known for his innovation and willingness to try new ideas. This trait was shared by another airman who would help shape the American air campaign in Korea once he was assigned as FEAF deputy for operations in January 1952. Brig. Gen. Jacob E. Smart was known for his intellect but had exhibited plenty of courage during World War II as well. As one of the bright young officers selected to provide fresh ideas to the Army Air Forces' commanding general Henry "Hap" Arnold as a member of his Advisory Council, Smart had developed the concept and written the plan for the mass raid on the Ploesti oil refineries in Romania in August 1943. He later commanded the Ninety-seventh Bomb Group of the Fifteenth Air Force in Italy. While leading his unit on a bomb run in 1944, a flak hit disintegrated his B-17. Everyone thought he had been killed, but he had actually been blown from the aircraft, unconscious. He revived just in time to pull his rip cord, and though badly wounded, survived a year as a prisoner of war.[4]

One of the problems that Smart encountered in Korea was that too many ground commanders and political leaders expected "miracles" from airpower. In an interview, he asserted, "Few people other than experienced Air Force people appreciate the limitations of airpower." Air forces "have only destructive power," and while it may be substantial, it might not always be the best means to an end. Additionally, in Korea, FEAF sometimes lacked the resources or competence to carry out assigned missions or those requested by supported units. This was especially applicable to aerial interdiction. However, Smart also admitted, "We Air Force people don't advertise our limitations to demagogic politicians, and we certainly don't advertise our limitations when we're talking to the members of the press, who are looking for the opportunity to denigrate the speaker or his service."[5]

As a result of these shortcomings in USAF resources and capabilities, and the service's reluctance to reveal them to politicians or the press, American leaders and the public, as well as some generals, entered the Korean War with inflated expectations of what airpower could accomplish. These high hopes influenced decisions reached in Washington and on the battlefield early in the conflict and led to some disillusionment as the war dragged on. At the same time, everyone remembered the destruction wreaked by American bombers on German and Japanese cities, and this especially shaped perceptions of USAF bombing around the world and in the United Nations. Throughout the war, the State Department was sensitive about air operations that might be exploited by a skillful enemy propaganda campaign focusing on the "barbarism" exercised by American technology against civilian populations. The primary purpose of this book is to examine the image and reality of American airpower as it struggled to meet high expectations with limited resources and to apply its destructive power in acceptable and effective ways in a limited war.

Although the narrative follows a generally chronological sequence, it does not repeat the thorough coverage of day-to-day air operations provided by

Robert Frank Futrell in his three USAF historical studies or his superb *The United States Air Force in Korea, 1950-1953*.[6] Richard Hallion has done the same for the Navy in *The Naval Air War in Korea*.[7] The book instead focuses on broader themes dealing with the strategic application of airpower to achieve victory in Korea, or at least to produce a favorable armistice as speedily as possible. Since the USAF was the only American service with a true doctrine and capacity for strategic airpower and controlled the way the aerial instrument of force was applied in Korea, this book focuses primarily on its operations. Air Force leaders entered the conflict hoping to quickly achieve air superiority and then gain victory with a bombing campaign to destroy enough economic and military targets to eliminate the enemy's capacity and will to wage war. Instead, they found themselves with a nagging problem neutralizing surprisingly effective MiG-15 interceptors, and, unable to strike the true source of enemy war-making resources, they were forced to look for alternative methods to achieve decisive results in a limited, non-nuclear war. Some of these required innovative targeting concepts; others focused on thorough and effective execution of more traditional tactical support roles such as interdiction. All were designed to somehow use airpower to force a stubborn enemy to agree to a political settlement meeting U.S. war aims.

Some readers may feel that the contributions of close air support (CAS) have been slighted in this analysis, but those have been covered well elsewhere and were not as important in influencing enemy decision makers.[8] Still, the many disputes over the conduct of CAS are examined to shed light on interservice relations in the USAF's first war, as well as on differing service attitudes about airpower. Weyland once remarked that he expended as much effort fighting the Navy as he did the Communists, and Smart, who kept systematic records of how he spent his time, discovered that he spent 40 percent of it "countering Army and, to a lesser extent, Navy proposals for the use of our air forces."[9] Navy–Air Force relations had been poisoned by the controversy over the B-36 bomber program and the "Revolt of the Admirals" in the late 1940s, and it was well into the war before the personalities of the leadership of each component in the Far East meshed enough to overcome that legacy and their technical differences to allow effective joint air operations. The situation with the Army was more complicated. It was not uncommon during World War II for ground commanders to justifiably suspect that airmen in heavier bombers preferred to hit strategic targets "and had to be dragged, kicking and squealing all the way, to any tactical targets."[10] Now the USAF had a recognized primary mission of launching a devastating assault against the enemy homeland, further increasing Army fears that CAS was a low priority. Ground commanders desired a specialized aircraft for CAS that would attack any target no matter how heavily defended, and they considered long loiter time an essential trait, but with limited resources, the Air Force preferred multirole planes that could get in and out of the target area quickly and valued survivability at least as much as accuracy. The presence of Marine aviators in the theater heightened interservice tensions, as Army leaders often looked wistfully at the air wings dedicated solely to the tactical support of each Marine division. Air Force reaction to accusations about inadequate CAS was magnified by the service's insecurity about its independence, especially fears that it might lose the tactical mission and the resources that accompanied it.

FEAF believed that ground forces asked for too much CAS, especially when the enemy was dug in during armistice negotiations, and that airpower was better applied against targets off the battlefield that would have a greater impact on ending the war. Before the war, the Air Force had invested much thought and resources into fashioning an instrument that could destroy an enemy nation's war-making capacity, but Communist forces in Korea drew their support from areas off-limits to strategic bombing. FEAF had to develop another way to employ airpower to influence enemy decision makers, and its campaigns of aerial interdiction and "air pressure" through destruction were attempts to solve that problem.

Despite these efforts to adapt to the reality of limited war in Korea, the specter of atomic weapons always loomed over the theater. Whenever actions on the battlefield or at the peace talks took a bad turn for UN forces and U.S. interests, the nuclear option came up in Washington. Whereas there was virtually universal agreement early in the war that atomic bombs had utility only as a last resort to avert disaster, as concerns about the buildup of Communist forces and frustrations over the deadlock in armistice negotiations grew, so did the possibility of using weapons of mass destruction. Although the role that their threat had in ending the war remains open to dispute, by 1953, there were plenty of signs that the conflict might intensify if it continued much longer, including expansion beyond the borders of Korea.

Within those borders, however, it could not have been much more brutal. Although most authors estimate that more than a million civilians died on each side during the conflict, there is no reliable figure for civilian casualties caused by bombing.[11] Air attacks on North Korean cities and towns, and some South Korean ones as well, contributed to the widespread destruction on the peninsula. Although MacArthur and Stratemeyer, in keeping with traditional U.S. precision doctrine, initially tried to limit bombing to specific military and economic targets, they responded to Communist Chinese intervention by unleashing American airpower in a campaign reminiscent of LeMay's incendiary campaign against Japan. Later Ridgway and Weyland sometimes tried to restrain their forces and limit excessive destruction, but Smart remembered one of his superiors commenting, "Looking for morality in war is like looking for a virgin in a house of ill-fame." Smart qualified that remark himself, adding, "But of course there is morality in war. But it takes a lower priority than surviving. It takes a lower priority than winning." One of the great tragedies of warfare, and the Korean War especially, is that the people being destroyed are rarely the ones responsible for the war. In Smart's words, "The innocents suffer far more than the perpetrators." And one of the most difficult tasks for FEAF and Air Staff planners was devising some kind of air strategy to influence the minds of those "perpetrators," even when no one was really sure who they were or how they thought.[12]

The ending of the war was ambiguous enough to allow the U.S. Air Force to believe that it had indeed been successful in bringing about an acceptable armistice. This contributed to its inability, and lack of desire, to draw many useful lessons from Korea. The war had changed the service considerably. It had weathered the transformation in technology brought by the jet engine. More nimble jet fighter-bombers had replaced the venerable B-29 in daylight missions against all manner of targets, and the news media were dominated by images of Sabre aces downing enemy MiGs. Increasing service resources were committed to a resurgent Tactical Air Command. The Air Force also survived the personnel turbulence caused by worldwide commitments that were expanding even faster than its force structure. During the war, it more than doubled in size and had become an even more effective deterrent for the Cold War as the cornerstone of President Eisenhower's "New Look" defense policy. But another limited war in Asia would again highlight American airpower problems with doctrine, technology, and joint operations in that type of conflict. The United States currently faces an era of declining defense budgets and unknown threats similar to the situation in the late 1940s. The flexibility and destruction that airpower provides can be a potent and agile tool for policy makers. The Korean War offers many insights about its capabilities, and limitations.

1
PRECEDENTS AND
PRECONCEPTIONS

Symington—
Do you realize that in accepting our new jobs and in the event of war with Russia,
we will be hanged as war criminals if we lose?

There had better be some honest to God thinking about what we need to avoid being
on the losing side.

The U.S. has already set the pace for the atomic bomb, strategic bombing and hang-
ing war criminals.

This is no time to temporize very long with old established prerogatives of the Ser-
vices, nor to tolerate inter-Service rivalry, friction, jealousy. Whoever does not cooperate
should be obliterated.

GEN. CARL SPAATZ, 1947[1]

The strategic objective of air power is the elimination or reduction of the enemy's
power and power potential. The technique employed by air power in accomplishing this
objective is to attack directly the power and sources of power of the enemy state. The tar-
gets may be selected segments of his industrial establishment, his communications or
transportation system, the source of his governmental or social control, or his military
forces in being.

MAJ. GEN. ORVILLE ANDERSON, 1949[2]

The atomic attacks of SAC's war plan . . . are not area attacks with the connota-
tion which is usually associated with the type of bombardment laid on by the RAF dur-
ing all except the latter part of World War II. The SAC attacks when they come will
be precision attacks with an area weapon.

DAN DYER, 1951[3]

Brig. Gen. Thomas Power, commander of the 314th Bombardment Wing, and his intelligence officer, Harry Besse, circled over Tokyo in a B-29 early on the morning of 10 March 1945. They had been assigned by Maj. Gen. Curtis LeMay, commander of the Twenty-first Bomber Command of the Twentieth Air Force, to record the results of new tactics he had instituted to attempt to revive the disappointing strategic bombing campaign against Japan. Like giants "pouring a big shovel full of white hot coals all over the ground," each Superfortress dropped firebombs covering a rectangular area of approximately 2,500 feet by 500 feet. Power later remarked, "The air was so full of incendiaries that you could not have walked through them." The observers made their first sketch of the resulting fires at 0146, noting sixteen burning areas of about a quarter mile in length. By 0237, the largest visible fire area was over forty blocks long and fifteen wide, and it was becoming increasingly difficult to see through thick smoke rising to 25,000 feet. Their last sketch was drawn exactly one hour after their first, showing a confused mass of smoke and flame. They noted, "It is difficult to describe a conflagration ignited so swiftly and spreading so far. At least a score of separate areas from fifty to a thousand city blocks were burning at the same time." They closed their report with, "The glow from the fires was clearly visible 150 miles away."[4]

Plagued by problems with technology, training, and weather, B-29 precision attacks against Japanese industrial targets in accordance with normal Army Air Forces (AAF) bombing doctrine had been dismal failures through February 1945. The mass incendiary bombing of urban areas inaugurated that night over Tokyo resuscitated the flagging strategic bombing effort and restored the hopes of AAF leaders that the Very Heavy Bombers could prove the worth of independent airpower by defeating an enemy nation without the need for an invasion. Many members of LeMay's command took credit for the new tactics, but he was the driving force behind an air campaign that eventually destroyed 178 square miles of some sixty-six built-up urban centers.[5]

Mission reports emphasized that the objective of the incendiary attacks was the destruction of "industrial and strategic targets concentrated in urban areas" and "not to bomb indiscriminately civilian populations." But as the terrible impact of the fire raids on residential areas around those targets became apparent, LeMay initiated a psychological warfare campaign in late June to take advantage of the resulting "destruction bonus." His aircraft dropped leaflets designed to inspire inhabitants to flee Japanese cities, thereby increasing disruption of industry and the social infrastructure while creating a massive refugee problem. The front page of the document depicted a B-29 dropping incendiaries, with the names of eleven cities printed around the plane. The text on the reverse side emphasized that air attacks were aimed only at military installations, but "unfortunately, bombs have no eyes." Accordingly, to avoid injuring "innocent people," the AAF advised everyone to evacuate the cities named. The warning was not very specific, however; it concluded with a promise that at least four of the named cities would be attacked, but noted that unnamed others could be hit as well. At the height of the campaign, more than 8.5 million Japanese were fleeing urban areas, and one-seventh of the population eventually fled to the country.[6]

B-29 Superfortresses of the Twentieth Air Force are silhouetted against Mount Fuji on their way to deliver deadly incendiary cargo to another Japanese city in 1945. (USAF Pre-1954 Official Still Photography Collection, Record Group 342, via the National Air and Space Museum, Smithsonian Institution)

Although a study done for Gen. Douglas MacArthur in 1944 concluded that Japanese civilians were too adaptable and inured to hardship to be affected by bombing, and he and his staff abhorred bombing civilians, his own airmen soon copied LeMay's tactics when they finally got into position to mount air attacks on the Japanese homeland in force. MacArthur gave his capable and trusted air commander, Gen. George Kenney, a free hand and probably knew few details about the three incendiary attacks launched by his Far East Air Forces in August against towns in Kyushu with industrial targets. After dropping a series of leaflets exploiting the impact of LeMay's B-29 campaign, Kenney's airmen issued warnings to target cities of their own raids seventy-two hours before bombing, proclaiming to the inhabitants, "We want you to see how powerless the military is to protect you." While urging civilians to evacuate, the message also demanded that they overthrow their military government to "save what is left of your beautiful country." A follow-up leaflet compared the American air onslaught to forces of nature and again urged the Japanese to replace their leaders and seek peace. It stated bluntly, "The military forces of Japan can no more halt the overwhelming destruction by the United States Air Force than the people can stop an earthquake."[7]

This campaign to warn cities and exploit the effects of bombing on civilian morale had been proposed and rejected in Europe, another sign of the intensification of the war in the Pacific. Yet it must be noted that airmen considered these leaflets humanitarian gestures as well. LeMay sincerely believed that the warnings would "convince the Japanese people and certain articulate minority groups of our own people that our Air Force policy is aimed at destruction of the war-making industrial capacity of Japan and not at the Japanese people." Although the area bombing methodology used by the Royal Air Force (RAF) Bomber Command and the Twentieth Air Force against enemy cities was similar, their primary objectives were not. The American campaign focused mainly on the destruction of Japanese war-making capacity. Psychological warfare against civilian morale was a secondary effort. While the British campaign also aimed to overwhelm the enemy's war economy, from 1942 on, its main goal was to undermine the morale of the German populace, especially industrial workers.[8]

Accordingly, LeMay's urban incendiary raids fit into the pattern of American bombing doctrine that emphasized the destruction of key military and industrial targets. Area tactics and weapons could be employed to take out strategic objectives just as well as precision attacks, though obviously there would be more widespread "collateral damage." Once this approach was accepted, it could also be applied to the atomic bomb. Air Force leaders in Washington thought that by displaying a photomap of Hiroshima emphasizing the military and economic targets covered by "the aiming point and the general area of greatest damage," they could refute any claims that the atomic bomb involved "wanton, indiscriminate bombing."[9]

POSTWAR LEGACIES

Airpower played a key role in Japan's surrender. LeMay's incendiary campaign, the dropping of the atomic bombs, and even mines laid by B-29s in harbors and waterways were important components of the series of shocks that finally motivated Japanese leaders to end the war. LeMay himself believed that his bombers alone could have ended the war without the atomic bomb and without an invasion, a position generally echoed by the findings of the United States Strategic Bombing Survey (USSBS), a supposedly objective study of the accomplishments of strategic airpower during World War II conducted by scientists, economists, and military representatives. However, the reports were shaped by the individual biases of their writers and were more an advocacy of the positions of various division directors and military services than a balanced assessment of the decisiveness of airpower. Gen. Haywood Hansell, LeMay's predecessor as commander of Twenty-first Bomber Command and an important contributor to the development of precision bombing doctrine, remarked that "the Survey was much like the Bible in one respect. If you reach deeply enough you can find substantiation for almost any preconceived notion or prejudice." For airmen involved in the process, the survey was an opportunity to justify their cherished dream of service independence, which was finally realized with President Truman's signing of the National Security Act of 1947 on 26 July of that year.[10]

The beginnings of the new National Military Establishment, which would eventually become the Department of Defense, occurred during a tumultuous period of Air Force reorganization and doctrinal disputes that would continue into the early 1950s. The new service came into existence with a revised structure installed by the new chief of staff, Gen. Carl Spaatz. Combat forces in the continental United States were organized into the Strategic Air Command (SAC), Tactical Air Command (TAC), and Air Defense Command; air units overseas were controlled by theater air commands. Support commands in the continental United States included Air Materiel Command, Air Proving Ground Command, Air Training Command, Air Transport Command, and Air University. Congress approved a goal of seventy air groups for the service, but rapid demobilization and budget cuts kept the force well below that level until the rearmament sparked by the Korean War. On V-J Day, the Army Air Forces possessed 2,253,000 men, but by the end of May 1947, its total strength was down to only 303,614. Spaatz's successor, Gen. Hoyt Vandenberg, proved himself adept at garnering support from Congress and the public for Air Force programs, despite administration reluctance to spend money on defense. By spring 1950, however, force modernization still lagged, and the Air Force director of programs was outlining plans for only forty-two groups in fiscal year 1952.[11]

The new service, and the new National Military Establishment, also needed new doctrine. Interservice disputes prompted by battles over scarce budget dollars, as well as genuine differences of opinion, were exacerbated by a lack of a coherent national military strategy, making joint doctrine almost impossible to write. The Navy even questioned the whole raison d'être of the Air Force, portraying plans to drop atomic bombs in an air offensive against an enemy homeland as immoral and ineffective. During the debates about the Air Force B-36 bomber connected with the "Revolt of the Admirals" in 1949,

Rear Adm. Ralph Ofstie told the House Armed Services Committee, "We consider that strategic air warfare as practiced in the past and as proposed for the future, is militarily unsound and of limited effect, is morally wrong, and is decidedly harmful to the stability of the postwar world." His accusations inspired a spirited defense by Maj. Gen. Orville Anderson of the Air University, who argued that the United States "was not only morally justified but morally obligated to develop our maximum strength to provide for our security" from the aggression of totalitarian nations that would have "little to worry about in a war with us fought according to traditional patterns." This was not the first time Ofstie and Anderson had disagreed over airpower issues. They had first clashed while assigned to the USSBS, where they had been the most strident spokesmen for their respective service viewpoints. The Navy conveniently forgot its arguments about the immorality and ineffectiveness of strategic bombing when it got its own nuclear striking forces, an irony that was gleefully highlighted by Air Force supporters.[12]

The new service also had great difficulty writing its own doctrine. War Department Field Manual 100-20, *Command and Employment of Airpower*, had been written in 1943 and emphasized the coequality of land and air forces. It needed to be replaced by a new basic doctrinal manual for the air service that would also serve as the foundation for a series of supplementary publications detailing strategic air, air defense, theater air, and air transport operations. Attempts to centralize doctrinal responsibilities at Air University were resisted by some field agencies, especially Tactical Air Command, and significant disagreements arose within the service about the content, style, and format of Air Force manuals. Opinions were particularly divided over the differentiation between strategic and tactical air missions and the proper role for theater air forces. Because of these problems, plus a slow review process when drafts reached the Air Staff in Washington, the new capstone Air Force Manual 1-2, *United States Air Force Basic Doctrine*, was not published until 1 April 1953.[13]

Although it took over five years to publish a basic doctrinal manual, there was agreement within the U.S. Air Force from its inception about the basic principles regarding the proper employment of American airpower. In October 1945, AAF commanding general Henry "Hap" Arnold convened a board consisting of Spaatz, Vandenberg, and Lauris Norstad to determine how the atomic bomb would affect the United States and the Air Force. Their report never questioned the validity of World War II precision methods and asserted that the atomic bomb just enhanced the effectiveness of current strategic bombing doctrine. Many targets were not appropriate for scarce and expensive atomic weapons anyway, and a requirement would continue for conventional bombing forces. The three influential officers (Spaatz and Vandenberg would become USAF chief of staff, and Norstad became the only airman to command the armed forces of the North Atlantic Treaty Organization [NATO]) concluded that the atomic bomb "does not at this time warrant a material change in our present conception of the employment, size, organization, and composition of the post-war Air Force." Perhaps desensitized by the extensive destruction wreaked by LeMay's fire raids, many airmen did not grasp the real impact of nuclear weapons on warfare until they witnessed the phenomenal power of the hydrogen bomb. When the Air University was established in 1946, its faculty board emphasized the basic principles of American precision bombing doctrine by declaring that all curricula would incorporate the concept that "the ultimate objective of air power is to force the capitulation of an enemy nation by air action applied directly against the vital points of its national structure." The devotion of airmen to this concept was also evident in the Joint Chiefs of Staff (JCS) general war plans in the years leading up to the Korean War. Although the avowed purpose of such operations was "to destroy the will of the USSR to resist"—a vague joint strategic concept that gave all services a role—the primary mission of the Air Force was always "to initiate a powerful U.S. air offensive against selected vital elements of Soviet war-making capacity."[14]

The objective of the USAF to destroy the enemy's war-making capacity seemed to be the same as that of the old AAF, which had gone after ball-bearing plants at Schweinfurt and oil refineries at Ploesti, but the new service's methods had been expanded by the experience against Japan. Trends that had begun with the acceptance of LeMay's urban incendiary raids as another way to destroy strategic targets culminated in the emergence of two targeting approaches to exploit Soviet vulnerabilities. A "vertical" school focused on eliminating key systems such as electric power and transportation; a "horizontal" school wanted to take advantage of the mass of suitable military and economic targets in cities, which also seemed a more efficient use of atomic weapons. These methods complemented each other in the JCS war plans. Within the Air Force, with its lack of a formal written service doctrine, individual preferences for the different approaches generally reflected World War II experience. As the atomic stockpile grew, war plans developed by SAC under LeMay's command targeted more and more urban industrial complexes in the USSR. The Air Staff in Washington tended to favor the vertical approach against key systems, particularly Gen. Charles P. Cabell, USAF director of Air Intelligence and former director of plans for Spaatz's U.S. Strategic Air Forces in World War II. During the war, he had consistently opposed any "baby-killing plans" aimed at civilians, and now his division developed targeting folders focusing on Soviet liquid fuel and electric power industries, along with atomic energy plants. His boss, General Vandenberg, had commanded a tactical air force in Europe supporting American ground forces in their drive into Germany and had no enthusiasm for city bombing, either. When some target planners in the Directorate of Intelligence suggested that atomic attacks might be directed against Soviet cities to destroy governmental control and industrial mobilization potential instead of specific industrial targets, they encountered resistance from the State Department as well as other airmen. George Kennan and Charles Bohlen were especially adamant that an atomic campaign that concentrated on wiping out Soviet cities would spark hatred and guerrilla war and endanger any chances for postwar peace.[15]

Although LeMay's staff continued to focus more on urban area targets, neither SAC plans or those of the JCS exploited the effects of their attacks on civilian morale, a fact that appalled civilian analysts at the RAND Corporation such as Bernard Brodie. His work on the subject would have a major influence on nuclear strategy, but it also had implications for conventional bombing. Often engaged in targeting studies for the Air Force, RAND commissioned a project in 1949 on psychological warfare from Yale University, where Brodie was a member of the Institute of International Studies. A paper entitled "The Morale Factor in STRAP Planning" appears to have been Brodie's contribution to that effort. In it, he criticized RAND and the Air Force for neglecting to consider the military worth of the morale effects of mass bombing. After studying the USSBS report, *The Effects of Bombing on German Morale,* he argued that "the significance in World War II experience with respect to the active consequences of depressed morale" was being neglected. Planners were "giving an unduly low estimate of the pure shock and confusion effects of devastating attacks highly concentrated in time."[16]

By the end of that year, the Social Science Division at RAND had completed a preliminary study, "The Warning of Target Populations in Air War," that relied heavily on a thorough evaluation of LeMay's leaflet campaign against Japan. The project was inspired by W. Philip Davison, who found a German report describing the effects of rumors about the impending British bombing of a Czech town. Despite official attempts to suppress the rumor, almost everyone evacuated the town and abandoned their work. This suggested to Davison that warning populations before bombing might be not only humane but also very effective, perhaps creating enough disruption that the bombing would not even be necessary. The "Warbo Study," as it was known, concluded that warnings had many uses. They could instill fear, provide evidence of friendly strength and enemy weakness, increase enemy populations' resentment of their government while minimizing resentment about bombing, and improve the reputation of friendly propaganda for truthfulness. However, to achieve the strongest effects, and the dispersal of a panicked population, the stimulus and threat of large-scale area bombing were necessary. Extrapolating from that data, the report assumed that the possibility of atomic bomb attacks would cause inhabitants to flee their cities just as LeMay's threats of incendiary destruction had. Brodie's ideas eventually came to the attention of Vandenberg in Washington, and as a special consultant to the chief of staff, Brodie provided his expertise and copies of the Warbo Study to USAF and SAC headquarters in the latter half of 1950. By then, the issues of strategic targeting and population warnings had already arisen in Korea.[17]

REVITALIZING STRATEGIC AIRPOWER

While the effects of the fire raids mounted by Twentieth Air Force were being studied by RAND, their originator was working diligently to develop an even more powerful striking force. Curtis LeMay became commander of Strategic Air Command in 1948. Eventually his dynamic leadership would again turn a group of underachievers into an elite force. In his typical fashion, he quickly identified organizational shortcomings and developed solutions. He always tended to view a new command assignment as being far below his acceptable standards, but in this case, a simulated radar bombing mission LeMay scheduled against Dayton, Ohio, demonstrated to everyone in SAC just how woefully unprepared they were. After that, he had full cooperation in overhauling the organization. He intensified training and emphasized high standards. Since atomic tactics utilized dispersion of aircraft at night instead of formation flying by day, this put more responsibility on individual crews to accurately deliver their valuable weapons on target by radar. Visual bombing was not neglected, but radar bomb scoring became a crucial indicator of crew proficiency. LeMay improved facilities such as family housing, as well as airfields. He instituted standard operating procedures for every position in the command and enforced safety standards that considerably reduced accidents. He even persuaded USAF headquarters to allow him an extra allocation of temporary promotions, which he used to reward his best crews. He realized that these "spot promotions" were an important incentive to motivate performance and sustain morale during eighty-hour workweeks in peacetime, not only for airmen who wanted the recognition but also for wives who appreciated the extra pay. LeMay also liked to hand-pick key subordinates and brought into SAC many of his most trusted veterans from the World War II air campaign against Japan. These included Power, who became deputy commander of SAC, and

Lt. Gen. Curtis LeMay with his trademark cigar at Tempelhof Air Base in Berlin, Germany, in October 1948. As commander of the U.S. Air Forces in Europe, LeMay had recently organized the massive aerial resupply of the city in response to a Russian blockade. That operation has gone down in history as the Berlin Airlift but was called "the LeMay Coal and Feed Company" by many of his airmen. It was a typical example of his problem-solving ability, involving the gathering and management of large resources, coordination with numerous American and Allied agencies, and even some "extralegal" actions to circumvent the peacetime rules of Belgium and France. (USAF Pre-1945 Official Still Photography Collection, Record Group 342, National Archives II)

Emmett "Rosie" O'Donnell, Jr., who had commanded the Seventy-third Bombardment Wing of LeMay's Twenty-first Bomber Command and took over SAC's Fifteenth Air Force. In addition, LeMay grabbed one of the key architects of the fire raids, Brig. Gen. John B. Montgomery, from the Office of the Secretary of the Air Force to head SAC Plans and Operations.[18]

In his efforts to improve SAC, LeMay profited not only from the Air Force's emphasis on his mission but also from the support of the Joint Chiefs of Staff. During the hearings about the B-36, newly appointed chairman Gen. Omar Bradley stated that the JCS "all believe that the No. 1 priority for the Air Force must be strategic bombing ability." As budget cuts reduced the Air Force from an overall group strength of sixty to forty-eight in 1949, SAC's strength actually rose from eighteen to nineteen, with six medium bomb groups approved to maintain a wartime level of forty-five aircraft instead of the usual thirty. Its 60,000 personnel in June 1950 made up 15 percent of total USAF strength. SAC also got the biggest chunk of USAF modernization efforts. The massive B-36 dwarfed the Very Heavy Bomber of World War II, the B-29, which was now classified as medium. Although the old aircraft was still the most common bomber in SAC, it was slowly being replaced by the B-50. The new model resembled the old Superfortress but was an upgraded design about 75 percent changed from the original, with a speed advantage of about sixty miles per hour at an increased maximum altitude of 40,000 feet. The B-50 was also capable of carrying atomic weapons without the modification required on a B-29. Like the B-29, however, the B-50 had many engine failures when it was initially fielded, and these problems, along with a shortage of parts, would restrict the new aircraft's utility during the Korean War. New jet B-47 and B-52 bombers were also in the developmental stages but still a few years away from active service.[19]

Although a number of new jet fighters had appeared since 1945, by 1950, overall modernization for tactical airpower lagged far behind strategic forces. In contrast to the expansion that SAC had experienced, by December 1948, TAC had been stripped of its units to become just an operational and planning headquarters under Continental Air Command. Disappointment with this action contributed to the retirement of the Air Force's most outspoken supporter of tactical airpower, Gen. Elwood Quesada. The new commander of this downgraded TAC was Maj. Gen. Robert M. Lee, and he tried his best to keep the doctrine and mission for his organization alive. The Army was also very dissatisfied with the USAF deemphasis on tactical aviation, and the Air Force convened a Board of Review for Tactical Air Operations in 1949, in response to growing criticism from the other services. The board consisted of Quesada, who had good relations with the Army, and Maj. Gen. Otto P. Weyland, who also believed in the need for tactical air capabilities but supported the service emphasis on strategic forces. They produced a report that discounted Army concerns about jets in close air support and the need for a special aircraft dedicated to the mission but was still strongly critical of current Air Force policies. Eventually, the results of the board, continuing complaints from the Army, the Navy's emphasis of USAF tactical deficiencies in congressional hearings, bad press coverage, and increased confidence in its own viability convinced Air Force leaders to restore TAC to its status as a major command in July 1950. Although its defenders had managed to maintain and promulgate a theater tactical air doctrine based on World War II that emphasized descending priorities of air superiority, interdiction, and close air support, it would take a while to restore TAC's capability to execute it.[20]

Even some officers within TAC doubted its utility and hindered efforts to upgrade its resources. Col. William Momyer, assistant chief of staff at TAC in 1949, concluded in a study that his organization would not become involved in hostilities unless the atomic offensive failed, and that would probably be two years after the outbreak of war. This finding supported Air Force contingency plans projecting that tactical air units could be mobilized and built up along with the ground forces. Momyer did not even see a need for his jet fighters in escort duties, calling that mission "an obsolete concept of the last war." Because of disparities between the range and speed of bombers and fighters, TAC, as well as the service as a whole, saw the main role of jet fighters as interceptors to protect airfields and the continental United States. The Air Force's primary light bomber remained the two-engine propeller-driven Douglas B-26 Invader (known as the A-26 in World War II), and jet fighter-bomber designs and tactics were still being perfected. The defense budget for fiscal year 1950 allowed for the procurement of 81 B-47s and 709 jet fighters, and American airmen looked forward to the retirement of their propeller-driven combat inventory before the nation's next major conflict.[21]

But wars rarely come when or how you plan for them. The new independent Air Force was about to find itself relying on old World War II bombers to support an unexpected type of war in an unexpected place.

2
OPENING MOVES

Rhee and other Korean officials will look to US for air assistance above all else.
Future course of hostilities may depend largely on whether US will or will not give ade-
quate air assistance.

U.S. AMBASSADOR JOHN J. MUCCIO[1]

It was my intention and hope . . . that we would be able to get out there and to cash
in on our psychological advantage in having gotten into the theater and into the war so
fast, by putting a very severe blow on the North Koreans, with advanced warning, per-
haps, telling them that they had gone too far in what we all recognized as being a case
of aggression, and General MacArthur would go topside to make a statement, and we
now have at our command a weapon that can really dish out some severe destruction,
and let us go to work on burning five major cities in North Korea to the ground, and to
destroy completely every one of about eighteen major strategic targets.

MAJ. GEN. EMMETT O'DONNELL, JR.[2]

The somber group of representatives from the State and Defense Departments who had dinner with President Truman at Blair House on the evening
of 25 June 1950 spent much of their time discussing the proper application of
airpower. Meetings at the beginning of the Korean crisis revealed that civilian
leaders especially had high expectations of what it could accomplish, while the
Joint Chiefs tended to be more cautious. Considering their mind-set that the
Russians were behind the North Korean invasion of the South, and contem-
porary views about the proper role of the Air Force, it is not surprising that
the first order the president issued to General Vandenberg was to make plans
to destroy all Soviet air bases in the Far East. However, North Korean air
strikes had already hit Seoul, and Ambassador Muccio's first pleas requesting
American air support for Republic of Korea forces had arrived early that
morning. Vandenberg was confident that his planes could knock out enemy
tanks, but he warned that taking out Russian bases, even with atomic weapons, would "take some time." At the moment, Truman would authorize only
air cover for the evacuation of civilians from the capital, but the next night he
waived all restriction on Air Force actions south of the thirty-eighth parallel.
Army Chief of Staff J. Lawton Collins cautioned that "it was impossible to say
how much our air can do" to salvage the situation, but Secretary of State Dean

Acheson argued "it was important for us to do something even if the effort were not successful." B-26s carried out the first American bombing missions on the evening of 27 June. The Far East Command advance party arrived the next day and requested extensive aerial support, including special B-29 strikes, to be concentrated on targets around Seoul, justifying them as "essential from South Korean morale standpoint as well as destruction desired."[3]

These early air efforts did little to repair the rapidly deteriorating ground situation, and they were not allowed to target vulnerable enemy bases or communication lines outside South Korea. In a meeting with his principal advisers on the afternoon of 29 June 1950, President Truman, bolstered by UN resolutions condemning the North Korean aggression, approved the conduct of air operations north of the thirty-eighth parallel "to provide the fullest possible support to South Korean forces." The JCS immediately sent instructions to Gen. Douglas MacArthur, commander in chief, Far East, to considerably expand his air attacks to military targets throughout North and South Korea, with the only restriction being to stay clear of the Soviet and Manchurian borders. By then, he had already directed the dropping of pamphlets containing the UN resolutions over North Korea, along with copies of Japanese newspapers with favorable reactions to them, but now he could deliver explosives as well as leaflets to the enemy. The Air Intelligence Staff of Far East Air Forces had produced a detailed analysis of Korea a year earlier, including targeted ports, industrial and power centers, airfields, and transportation nodes. However, in June 1950, MacArthur's FEAF, under the command of Lt. Gen. George Stratemeyer, had no more than twenty-two B-26s, twelve B-29s, seventy F-80s, and fifteen F-82s available for missions in Korea. Its primary combat force, the Fifth Air Force, was focused mainly on the air defense of Japan instead of on close air support or other bombing missions expected of theater air commands.[4]

Vandenberg immediately began looking for aircraft to reinforce FEAF. For the next three years he would wear himself out struggling with the apportionment of resources among Korea and other worldwide commitments. Building up men and material for a new war would take time. On 30 June, Stratemeyer cabled his aircraft needs to Washington, including 164 F-80 jets, 22 B-26s, 23 B-29s, and 64 F-51 Mustangs, which were considered "exceptionally well suited for long-range, low level missions." USAF was extremely short of F-80s and decided to substitute 150 F-51s instead, some still with World War II markings. The commander of FEAF's Fifth Air Force, Maj. Gen. Earle Partridge, would have preferred P-47 Thunderbolts, "a far better strafing and dive-bombing airplane," but none of those were available, either. Propeller-driven planes had considerable advantages over jets at this stage of the war.

This USAF picture of an F-80 Shooting Star taking off from its base in Japan on a mission to Korea in August 1950 was originally entitled "Rice More Important Than Jets to Japs," and its caption began, "The ancient and ageless Orient is taking the futuristic jet and rocket warfare without a second bat of its eye." The F-80 was the USAF's first operational jet fighter, and its limited time on station over Korea when flying from Japan helped fuel the debate about the utility of jets in close air support. (RG 342 NA II)

One of the most important factors affecting Korean air operations was the availability of airfields, and F-51s had fewer problems operating from rough runways. Any level land in mountainous Korea was usually turned into rice paddies, and there were only five improved airfields in the South, in addition to six primitive, short sod strips. The only two suitable bases for jet aircraft, at Kimpo and Suwon near Seoul, had already been lost. It would take considerable work to upgrade the remaining fields, and even after extensive rehabilitation, jagged steel planking and pebbles kicked up by exhaust would take a heavy toll on jet tires and wing flaps. In order to operate effectively from distant Japanese bases, the F-80s had to utilize improvised wing tanks that reduced performance and often cracked the wing tips. In-country bases were essential to permit the relatively short-range jets adequate time on station. As the battle lines, and targets, moved north later, the fields at Suwon and Kimpo would become crucial, as much for their forward location as their superior surfaces. Besides possessing better range, the Mustangs also used less fuel than the jets. The USAF preference for the F-51s in July 1950 made sense, but the reputation of the F-80 suffered as a result. Ground commanders tended to favor the slower propeller planes because they could loiter longer over the battle area, had more time to pick out and focus on targets during bomb runs, and carried more varied ordnance, but an Air Force concerned with scarce resources favored the better survivability of the faster jets. In 1950, the rate of Mustang losses to enemy action in relation to sorties flown was more than double that of the jets, which also could fly twice the sorties of the F-51 per day because of better parts availability and less required maintenance. The Mustang was especially vulnerable to ground fire because of its liquid-cooled engine. One lucky shot in the radiator could bring the plane down.[5]

These different aircraft preferences would contribute to considerable interservice friction over close air support, and concern about jets in that combat role caused the first perceived public relations crisis in FEAF. By 1 July, USAF Headquarters was already complaining about media coverage of Air Force CAS, and Vandenberg quickly rerouted Col. Bill Nuckols to FEAF to meet Stratemeyer's need for "a fully qualified public relations officer." Nuckols had been heading for Mexico City to be the air attaché there. Vandenberg continued to badger Stratemeyer for pictures and "well reasoned factual reporting" to show the American public "that your air action has been an essential factor in the operations in Korea." He was pleased with Nuckols's initial releases, which "went a long way toward putting the jet fighter in its proper perspective." The Air Staff also was gratified by Lowell Thomas's offer to counter adverse publicity on jets with coverage on his popular radio show, and the Air Force provided him with plenty of information about jets' contributions in Korea.[6]

FEAF also needed propeller-driven bombers. B-26 reinforcements could be obtained only by recalling the Air Force Reserve 452d Bombardment Wing (Light) to active duty, but B-29s were available from SAC. LeMay was reluctant to dissipate his strength by sending aircraft piecemeal to Korea and argued vehemently when notified on 1 July to send ten non-nuclear B-29s instead of a full group "for political reasons." He later told an NBC reporter that "SAC was the USA Sunday punch and that every effort must be made to make sure that it stayed intact and able to strike and not be pissed away in the Korean War." His dissent had some impact, and on 2 July he was ordered to send two full groups of B-29s to the Far East along with O'Donnell, now commander of SAC's Fifteenth Air Force. The feisty LeMay wanted to go also, but Vandenberg forbade it. O'Donnell was to assume control of the FEAF Bomber Command (Provisional), consisting of the FEAF's own Nineteenth Bombardment Group along with SAC's Thirty-first Strategic Reconnaissance Squadron and Twenty-second and Ninety-second Bombardment Groups deploying from the United States. The units chosen were among those select medium bomber units at a wartime strength of forty-five aircraft and crews. On 4 July LeMay met with O'Donnell to develop target lists, and FEAF Bomber Command was activated four days later. LeMay also adjusted his war plans to allow the two deployed bomb groups to attack assigned targets from their new bases in case general war broke out. Instead of heading out for Fourth of July picnics, aircrews found themselves planning to move 8,000 miles to Yokota and Kadena Air Bases in Japan and Okinawa. Although the new facilities were overcrowded and crews at Kadena had to live in tents, specially designed "fly-away" kits with supplies and spare parts enabled the units to quickly achieve operational capability after deployment. The two SAC groups mounted a combat mission against Wonsan on 13 July, only nine days after receiving orders to relocate. FEAF personnel joked that before the new crews went on a mission, they had their navigator draw a line in the direction of Omaha so they could get on their knees and bow to SAC headquarters. Partridge thought that it was ironic to watch Japanese civilians at Yokota loading bombs into the same aircraft that had been blasting their homeland five years earlier.[7]

MacArthur believed that just the announcement that SAC would support the UN might deter Chinese intervention, and the movement of B-29s to the Far East in July 1950 was highlighted in newsreels as a symbol of American commitment and might. Coverage showed "big B-29 bombers" being taken out of mothballs to be deployed, and almost every week until mid-September, movie audiences were treated to footage of the Superfortresses blasting some enemy target. There was no hint in the images or narration, however, of the difficulties involved in shifting the units from U.S. bases to the Far East, or of the disputes over their employment and control that accompanied the move.[8]

OPERATIONAL DISAGREEMENTS

Before the Wonsan mission was carried out, General Stratemeyer had already had his first major battle with MacArthur and his staff about the application of FEAF air assets. Bothered by what he considered excessive and often misguided direction of the air campaign by Army officers from Tokyo, on 10 July Stratemeyer felt compelled to compose a memorandum to CINCFE asking for the same trust and responsibility that MacArthur's previous air commanders such as George Kenney had enjoyed. CINCFE agreed and told Stratemeyer that he "was to run his own show as he saw fit." Friction between ground commanders desiring more close air support and airmen who believed that interdiction or strategic operations would be more profitable would continue throughout the war. Stratemeyer quickly assigned his Fifth Air Force F-51, F-80, and B-26 units with the former responsibility and Bomber Command with the latter, although the deteriorating ground situation forced him to concentrate primarily on tactical missions in front-line areas through July.[9]

At the same time, he was struggling to define his command relationship with naval carrier aircraft of Task Force 77 of the Seventh Fleet. The aircraft carrier *Valley Forge* struck airfields around Pyongyang on 3 and 4 July before it was diverted to protect Formosa. When it returned two weeks later, some of its jets spotted an intact oil refinery at Wonsan, and a strike was launched by twenty-one Skyraiders and Corsairs. The target was set afire, but the Navy had to wait until the actual area was occupied by the UN advance in October to get any bomb damage assessment. They found that earlier USAF raids had motivated an evacuation of most of the oil and workers from the site before 18 July, but the carrier planes had damaged much of the machinery. Mac-Arthur's headquarters had given the *Valley Forge* vague orders to support ground troops but had not coordinated with FEAF beforehand. CINCFE's instructions of mid-July delegated "coordination control" to FEAF when it operated with naval air on assigned missions, but that vague term meant different things to each service and led to considerable misunderstandings. Partridge tried to get the Navy to conform to Fifth Air Force operating procedures, but that proved impossible due to service differences in technology, attitudes, and practices. FEAF ground control for carrier strikes was especially difficult. Naval aircraft had different radios from the Air Force, and Navy personnel did not understand USAF terminology. Because of deck loading, carriers also had to launch their planes in large groups that usually overwhelmed surprised ground controllers who had no idea what was coming. In early August a conference was held at FEAF headquarters to coordinate interservice air operations, and the Air Force claimed that the Navy's assigned priorities were close air support under Fifth Air Force tactical control and then interdiction of enemy transportation. However, the informal agreements were "not promulgated in writing by the Navy," which complained that its ranking representative at the meeting was a captain who had been over-matched by four USAF generals. This all sparked another public relations flap when the Navy's grievances about poor USAF control of joint air operations were expressed in an editorial in the *Baltimore Sun*. Partridge responded to the charges as best he could, but he eventually gave up trying to conduct "cumbersome" coordination with the carriers and just assigned them a "piece of the battlefield" that was their responsibility alone. One historical study of joint air

South Korean Air Force pilots examine a carrier-based Skyraider (on left) and Corsair that landed at a Fifth Air Force fighter strip in Korea in August 1950. Navy and Marine aircraft provided valuable close air support as UN forces established and held the Pusan perimeter, although their presence in the theater also led to interservice friction and disagreements over the control of joint air operations. (RG 342 NA II)

operations in Korea describes accounts of Air Force–Navy cooperation as reading more like "a summary of treaty negotiations between uneasy allies" than a record of sister services working together against a common foe.[10]

The arrival of Marine air units in Korea in August led to more controversy over press coverage and highlighted service sensitivities about close air support. In early August, two escort carriers with the First Marine Air Wing went on station to support the Marine brigade recently assigned to Lt. Gen. Walton Walker's Eighth Army. Normally each Marine division, which had far less organic and supporting artillery than its Army counterparts, had its own air wing, with seventy-five aircraft devoted exclusively to close support of ground operations. In the middle of the month, articles by Robert Miller of United Press and Wayne Thomis of the *Chicago Tribune* trumpeted the superiority of Marine tactics and technology over the Air Force approach to close air support. The writers claimed that jets were inappropriate for CAS and that Army commanders were pleading, "Give us flying Marines!" An angry Stratemeyer called the articles "the most reprehensible pieces of carefully contrived propaganda and untruths that I have read in my military career." MacArthur was concerned that they might undermine interservice coordination in the theater and urged Stratemeyer to get Vandenberg to discuss them with Adm. Forrest Sherman at the JCS level. Many in the Air Force were convinced that the articles had really been written by the Navy in a continuation of the clandestine practices that had contributed to the B-36 controversy and "Revolt of the Admirals" before the war. Stratemeyer quickly gathered supportive statements by Army commanders and made sure that Edward R. Murrow of CBS, who had just flown on six combat missions in the theater, was prepared to devote considerable broadcast time to FEAF contributions to the ground battle. Army commanders such as Walker knew that the nation did not have the resources to build an Air Force that could dedicate seventy-five aircraft to each Army division, but the dispute highlighted ground force suspicions, not completely unfounded, that airmen would completely ignore tactical missions if they could, preferring deep interdiction and strategic bombing instead. Differences between the Army and the Air Force were exacerbated by the lack of a shared doctrine and by the fact that MacArthur's understrength prewar Far East Command forces did not have the resources for training in CAS and were still short of required artillery assets. The incident also revealed continued animosity between the Air Force and the Navy and the sensitivity of the newest service to any accusations that it was not doing its job properly. Airmen were still concerned that bad publicity might be exploited by those who had not favored an independent Air Force and perhaps lead to the reassignment of tactical air assets to the Army. USAF's insecurity in this regard would be evident in a number of its future actions.[11]

FEAF had to coordinate with other national forces as well as other services. Allies such as the South Koreans used American airplanes, but unfamiliar British models caused problems with aircraft identification. In one embarrassing incident on 28 July, a B-29 shot down a Seafire from the carrier HMS *Triumph* operating with the Seventh Fleet, after the British plane had mistakenly been identified as a North Korean Yak. Stratemeyer apologized profusely but also asked that Royal Navy pilots stay out of machine gun range while trying to identify four-engine aircraft. That was not the first time carriers had scrambled to intercept unknown aircraft that turned out to be B-29s. Eventually, Bomber Command learned the markings of British and naval planes, and better electronic identification procedures were established. Stratemeyer warned the Navy, however, that B-29s would still fire on any aircraft that turned toward them on an attacking course, since they "often fly singly and unescorted deep into enemy territory" and could not risk giving an enemy fighter any advantage.[12]

FEAF's disagreements over operational matters were not generated only by other services or allies. General O'Donnell also arrived with his own agenda.

79392AC

Eventually, FEAF had to deal with foreign air contingents from Australia, Great Britain, Greece, the Republic of Korea, South Africa, and Thailand. This F-51 Mustang of the Second South African Air Force Squadron is carrying six rockets, two tanks of napalm, and over 1,500 rounds of ammunition for its six .50-caliber machine guns. Ground commanders liked the Mustang's ability to conduct close air support from rough fields near the front, but it was hard to maintain and vulnerable to ground fire. (RG 342 NA II)

Vandenberg's notification to Stratemeyer that SAC units were coming to the Far East had cautioned that the diversion came "at considerable cost to our overall air capabilities" and that "a primary consideration in making these additional groups available is the vital necessity of destruction of North Korean objectives north of the 38th Parallel." O'Donnell and LeMay considered that task their main mission, and the new commander of Bomber Command arrived with two different approaches to accomplish it, both examples of the "horizontal" targeting school discussed in chapter 1. The SAC director of intelligence had identified five major target areas: Konan (Hungnam), Wonsan, Pyongyang, Seishin (Chongjin), and Rashin. Rather than bombing a single target system, as in the assault on German oil in World War II, these objectives were chosen because of their concentration of different industries, similar to the selection system used in the bombing campaign against the Japanese. Whereas SAC planners preferred destroying the targets with demolition bombs, O'Donnell and LeMay wanted to repeat the urban area firebombing they had executed against Japan.[13]

This became apparent as soon as O'Donnell arrived in Tokyo. When he was introduced to MacArthur, the airman quickly proposed "to do a fire job on the five industrial centers of northern Korea." When CINCFE asked for more details, O'Donnell said that they had learned in World War II that bombing tanks, bridges, and airdromes was useless. Instead of such "infighting," Mac-Arthur should announce to the world that Communist reactions to his pleas for peace forced him to use, "against his wishes, the means which brought Japan to its knees." His declaration of intent to burn the industrial cities of North Korea would also serve as a warning to get all noncombatants out, and systematic attacks would begin after twenty-four or forty-eight hours. Mac-Arthur listened to the whole presentation and replied, "No, Rosy, I'm not prepared to go that far yet. My instructions are very explicit." He did agree to bomb military objectives in those cities with high explosives and added, "If you miss your target and kill people or destroy other parts of the city, I accept that as part of war." MacArthur's sentiments about indiscriminate firebombing would be echoed by later JCS targeting directives. LeMay complained to interviewers in 1972 that his plan might have convinced the Communists that we were serious and ended the war. Instead, the war went on and we destroyed "every town in North Korea and every town in South Korea" anyway. He believed that "once you make a decision to use military force to solve your problem, then you ought to use it and use an overwhelming military force. . . . And you save resources, you save lives—not only your own but the enemy's, too."[14]

After the meeting between O'Donnell and MacArthur, Stratemeyer included instructions in mission directives on 11 July reminding subordinate units that "attacks for the sole purpose of destroying urban centers will not be mounted without authority from CINCFE." Although hitting military targets within cities was allowed, "reasonable care" had to be exercised "to avoid providing a basis for claims of 'illegal' attack against population centers." The FEAF Psychological Warfare Division later provided a memorandum reinforcing the ban on incendiary raids, cautioning that "the propaganda value to the Communists would outweigh the tactical value to the United Nations forces." Meanwhile, on 12 July Stratemeyer proposed his own version of O'Donnell's bombing ultimatum. He recommended that MacArthur warn the North Koreans that it was his "intent to destroy by air bombardment all railroad centers, airfields, heavy industry locations, port facilities, sub bases, POL [petroleum, oil, lubricants] storage facilities, refineries, railroads and highways used by their armed forces." Plenty of warnings would be issued to get civilians out of target areas, with the caveat that the bombing would cease when the North Koreans withdrew back across the thirty-eighth parallel and stopped fighting. Although similar warnings were later used by the Far East Command Special Projects Section, at this time, MacArthur was no more receptive to Stratemeyer's proposal than he had been to O'Donnell's.[15]

Despite MacArthur's reassurances to O'Donnell, it would be a while before Bomber Command could execute any strategic campaign, even with conventional high-explosive bombs. LeMay was concerned about the precedent of having his SAC bombers under the control of the theater commander instead of the JCS, fearing that the Superfortresses would be misused. O'Donnell was soon complaining to Stratemeyer that Bomber Command received too many short-notice changes of mission from Far East Command General Headquarters and that assigned bombing priorities were wrong. Stratemeyer explained to MacArthur on 18 July "that you cannot operate B-29s like you operate a tactical air force. B-29 operations must be carefully planned in advance and well thought out." That discussion solved the problem of last-minute targeting changes, but O'Donnell remained irritated that his broad mission directive of 11 July was changed to make close support his first priority and industrial targets his last. Despite his verbal and written protests, the deteriorating ground situation kept Bomber Command focused on tactical support missions until early August.[16]

The joint command and control situation was worsened by the fact that the Far East Command General Headquarters Target Group was designating B-29 targets based on an obsolete map of Korea and without Air Force representation. Maj. Gen. Otto P. Weyland, diverted from command of the reconstituted Tactical Air Command to become Stratemeyer's new vice commander for operations, decided that something had to be done. Weyland told an interviewer in 1960 that Stratemeyer "adored and respected MacArthur so much that it didn't occur to him to be kind of mean and nasty" with his remonstrances, but Weyland persuaded his boss to send a harsh memorandum to MacArthur complaining about his staff's handling of FEAF assets and suggesting the formation of a new General Headquarters (GHQ) Target Committee consisting of Weyland, a Navy representative, Far East Command Deputy Chief of Staff Maj. Gen. Doyle Hickey, and G-2 Maj. Gen. C. A. Willoughby. Weyland, Hickey, and Willoughby began deliberations on 24 July and agreed on the need for an interdiction program north of the thirty-eighth parallel. MacArthur approved their recommendations on 26 July, after Weyland explained to him that "putting everything in close support is just like trying to dam up a river at the bottom of a waterfall." By 4 August, details of B-29 employment had been ironed out, and O'Donnell was notified that his bombers would no longer be used in the battle area. Instead, Bomber Command could focus on interdiction and strategic targets beginning the next day. The responsibilities of the GHQ Target Committee eventually passed to the FEAF Formal Target Committee, but in the six weeks that the joint GHQ group existed, it established an ordered process of developing B-29 operations that was more acceptable to FEAF and Bomber Command.[17]

Weyland had been in command of TAC for only a week before being assigned to Korea, and he brought a unique combination of leadership and technical skills to FEAF. He had graduated from Texas A&M in 1923 with a degree in mechanical engineering and had served in a number of important staff and combat assignments with the AAF and USAF. George Patton considered him "the best damn General in the Air Corps," but Weyland had the respect of Air Force leadership as well. With all his tactical expertise, he was also known for his support of the service's emphasis on strategic airpower. No one would influence the course of the air war over Korea more than he. He would be reassigned back to temporary duty with TAC in April 1951, but when Stratemeyer was hospitalized with a heart attack the next month, Vandenberg quickly chose Weyland to take over FEAF. He would remain in that position until March 1954, long outlasting all his theater contemporaries from other services. During that time, he advised two different theater commanders; guided the development of the Japanese Air Force; flew combat missions, including one unescorted bomber operation that was jumped by enemy jets; and did much thinking about ways to utilize airpower in a limited war.[18]

MORE B-29s DEPLOY

The plans developed by Weyland and the GHQ Target Committee now covered five B-29 groups, as the 98th and 307th Medium Bombardment Groups were headed for the Far East for thirty days to complete a strategic bombing campaign directed by the JCS on 31 July. Responding to Vandenberg's desire to get some new units in the theater to execute only strategic bombing, and with MacArthur's acceptance of additional bombers, the JCS now considered it "highly desirable to undertake mass air operations against North Korean targets, the destruction of which will assist your future operations, destroy industrial targets in North Korea and reduce the North Korean ability to wage war in the future." A supplemental message on 15 August added more objectives, which now included the five major industrial centers originally selected by SAC, as well as a number of supplementary targets, some of which had also been considered in initial SAC planning. Significantly, the new orders

Lt. Gen. George Stratemeyer, pictured here in his Tokyo office on the eve of hostilities, supervised the restructuring of FEAF to fight the war in Korea. He commanded the organization from April 1949 until he was hospitalized after a heart attack in May 1951. He was a member of the famous West Point class of 1915 that produced so many generals, including Dwight Eisenhower, Omar Bradley, and James Van Fleet. (RG 342 NAII)

did not mention hydroelectric plants along the Yalu and other North Korean rivers, important secondary objectives for SAC that would become the focus of much controversy during the war. The JCS directives also required advance warnings to be given to populations in urban areas to be bombed, emphasizing the military nature of targets to be attacked. The JCS conceded that the warnings could include a number of false locations to be struck, "to avoid the possibility of pin pointing our specific objectives." These notifications eventually became an important, and controversial, part of Far East Command psychological warfare operations.[19]

The first elements of the new bombardment groups launched an attack less than five days after their departure from the United States. Although initially two of the five B-29 groups were diverted to interdiction missions, the mass destruction of specified strategic targets proceeded fairly rapidly. There were some distractions, however. Demands for help by Eighth Army units in the Pusan perimeter desperately trying to hold their line along the Naktong River led to a massive carpet bombing mission by ninety-eight B-29s from all five groups on 16 August. Newsreel footage of the more than 900 tons of bombs was very impressive, showing orderly rows of flashes moving across a landscape soon obscured by heavy black smoke. O'Donnell was not impressed by the results of such missions and advised that they should not be repeated unless for a "truly grave emergency." He thought that the only positive aspect of the operation was the psychological lift it gave UN ground forces in the area. Stratemeyer concurred with O'Donnell, although the FEAF commander also thought that carpet bombing was suitable if ground forces aimed to immediately occupy and exploit the area, such as Operation COBRA in World War II. He took the FEAF arguments to MacArthur that same day and prevented a repeat saturation raid a few days later. Like B-52 ARC LIGHT strikes in Vietnam or similar raids in DESERT STORM, however, the bombs did not necessarily have to kill to be effective. South Korean troops in the area confirmed that the strike had missed the enemy's main force, but North Korean prisoners revealed that it had dealt "a crushing blow" to their morale.[20]

There had been much confusion involved in getting the new B-29 groups to the Far East. Initially, the Air Staff requested two wartime-strength B-50 units, but problems, including parts shortages, made the newer bombers unavailable for a conventional combat role in Korea. Because of the deployment of additional nuclear-capable B-29s to shore up the American air presence in Europe in early July, as well as limitations and commitments of other units, the only groups that could now go to Korea were at a peacetime strength of only thirty aircraft and crews. LeMay finally got the Air Staff to accept this reduced commitment, although promises he received that the reinforcements would not be under the control of the theater commander were not fulfilled.[21]

LeMay also lost his battle to prevent the deployment of ten nuclear-capable B-29s of the Ninth Bombardment Wing to Guam in addition to the 98th and 307th Groups, the first prepositioning of such potential in the Far East. The JCS first examined the use of atomic weapons in Korea in early July. In a foreshadowing of things to come, this initial discussion may have been a result of the prodding of Gen. Dwight Eisenhower. He showed up in the offices of the Army Staff in Washington on 28 June and "stated in most vigorous language and with great emphasis" his feelings about what should be done to resolve the current crisis. He even suggested "the use of one or two atomic bombs in the Korean area, if suitable targets could be found." He wanted to present his views to the chairman, but upon learning that General Bradley was ill and would not be coming into the office, Eisenhower dictated a memorandum for the staff to transmit to Bradley. During a JCS meeting on 9 July discussing a request from MacArthur for support, Bradley remarked that the JCS might want to consider whether A-bombs should be made available to Far East Command. However, the consensus of opinion was against the proposal, and the issue was dropped at the time.[22]

During the month, both the Army and the Air Force Staffs examined the feasibility of employing nuclear weapons in Korea. The USAF Psychological Warfare Division saw no benefit in bombing North Korean targets, since the Soviet Union really supplied and controlled the war. In addition, using atomic weapons on tactical targets would probably be ineffective, demonstrating U.S. impotence and cruelty while doing considerable damage to South Korean territory. It would place us in "the untenable propaganda position of a butcher discarding his morals and killing his friends in order to achieve his end." That study recommended that the United States capitalize on its decision not to use the bomb in an extensive propaganda campaign, including leaflet warnings of any conventional attacks on North Korean cities to allow civilians "to seek refuge from bombs and forced labor in the countryside." The Army study by the G-3 Plans Division also concluded, "At the present time, the use of atomic bombs in Korea is unwarranted from the military point of view, and questionable from the political and psychological point of view." However, it considered that use of the weapon might be necessary "to avert impending disaster" and recommended that preparations be made for that eventuality.[23]

Because they could foresee a possible emergency use of the bomb, the Army G-3 staff thought that some actions could be taken. They sent a cable to

General Collins, then visiting the Far East, and asked him to elicit Mac-Arthur's views on the issue. They also thought that it would be appropriate to secure policy approval from the president for limited nuclear contingencies. The staff section received a memorandum claiming that MacArthur had proposed to the Army chief of staff using the special weapons to take out bridges and tunnels to completely cut off North Korea from supply sources outside its borders, an option that the G-3 thought unsuitable for the airburst bombs available. However, when Collins returned, he denied that he had gotten the cable or had any conversation with MacArthur about nuclear weapons. He directed the G-3 to suspend efforts to generate any policy decisions on the issue, including any move to secure presidential approval. As the executive agent on Korea for the JCS, Collins was the most sensitive of its members concerning the use of atomic bombs there.[24]

In his memoirs, Collins noted that MacArthur had in fact mentioned his ideas about atomic weapons to Vandenberg, who had accompanied Collins to the Far East. By the time they returned to Washington in late July, the military situation in Korea was "a hell of a mess." In his study of atomic diplomacy during the Korean War, Roger Dingman asserts that the JCS added the ten nuclear-configured B-29s to the SAC deployment for a number of reasons. They seemed a prudent response to Chinese threats against Taiwan and met subordinates' and MacArthur's pleas to preposition a nuclear strike force in the region. Truman also had a number of motivations to approve the move of the aircraft with nonnuclear bomb components. It might have seemed the proper response to North Korean actions or a way to deter the Chinese from increased involvement in the war, or it may have been an attempt to demonstrate toughness to Republican critics. The movement of the Ninth Bombardment Wing did not go smoothly, as one B-29 crashed on takeoff in California and killed the task force commander, leading LeMay to speculate about sabotage. The airplanes were ordered back to the United States in September, though the bomb components were left on Guam with supervisory teams. The JCS informed MacArthur in July that this action was in keeping with "previously-approved long-term plans, formulated prior to the Korean incident, for dispersed storage of Non-Nuclear components of Atomic Bombs." The results of the short aircraft deployment were unclear, though it would set a precedent for later actions.[25]

Vandenberg was especially concerned about the possibility of enemy air strikes on crowded FEAF airfields and continually prodded Stratemeyer about neutralizing that threat. His airmen conducted an effective campaign to destroy the overmatched North Korean Air Force and achieve air supremacy over the peninsula. Vandenberg and Stratemeyer were also worried about the possibility of an air attack mounted from Soviet or Chinese territory, and they queried the JCS for permission to reconnoiter Chinese and Soviet bases. The JCS granted CINCFE permission in late July to conduct "periodic reconnaissance flights over the coastal area of China, south of the 32nd Parallel of latitude," although the avowed purpose of those missions was to determine whether an attack on Formosa was imminent. The JCS remained reluctant to allow UN air incursions over the Soviet or Manchurian border.[26]

Vandenberg also pushed Stratemeyer for publicity and results that the chief of staff could use to trumpet USAF accomplishments to the public and JCS. Nuckols and Stratemeyer restrained Vandenberg on the first issue by explaining that they were holding back detailed press releases on air successes until a more "opportune time" when the ground situation had stabilized. They believed that heralding FEAF achievements while the ground forces were being pushed back into a shrinking perimeter around Pusan would cause a detrimental reaction against the Air Force. As for Vandenberg's accusations that FEAF operational rates, especially for medium bombers, were "substantially lower than that of WWII" and did not even meet planning figures, Stratemeyer sent back a testy reply showing that all types of aircraft were exceeding planned sortie rates and that O'Donnell was "driving his force to the limit." Soon UN successes would provide USAF with plenty of opportunity to showcase its accomplishments and give strategic airpower a chance to make a real impact on the war.[27]

3
AIRPOWER GETS ITS CHANCE

I believe that with my air power, now unrestricted so far as Korea is concerned except as to hydroelectric installations, I can deny reinforcements coming across the Yalu in sufficient strength to prevent the destruction of those forces now arrayed against me in North Korea.

GEN. DOUGLAS MACARTHUR, 9 NOVEMBER 1950[1]

I believe that perhaps too much was expected of the air.

GEN. DOUGLAS MACARTHUR, 5 MAY 1951[2]

By mid-August, the stage was set for the new United States Air Force to demonstrate its full conventional capabilities. Attacks on enemy airfields and aggressive fighter sweeps had destroyed most of the small North Korean Air Force, and the UN enjoyed complete air supremacy over the peninsula. With the relative stabilization of the ground situation in the Pusan perimeter and augmentation of FEAF from the United States, American bombers were now available to strike deep into the enemy's rear areas. By night and day, aerial destruction rained down on interdiction and strategic targets, until almost all were destroyed by air attacks or overrun by advancing UN ground forces. However, the appearance of a new enemy would completely change the nature of the conflict and raise questions about the utility and effectiveness of American airpower in this kind of limited war.

The strategic campaign so ardently desired by O'Donnell and LeMay finally kicked into high gear with the arrival of the two new B-29 groups. However, these reinforcements contributed to even more overcrowding at congested Yokota and Kadena airfields. Living conditions were often primitive, maintenance and supply operations required much improvisation, and mission flight times took eight and a half hours from Yokota and an hour longer from Kadena. Nevertheless, B-29 crews maintained about a 70 percent in-commission rate, and morale remained high.[3]

Although O'Donnell continued to ask for permission to conduct incendiary missions in August, MacArthur and Stratemeyer refused to sanction more than preparations. O'Donnell later complained at the Senate hearings after MacArthur's dismissal that if he had been able to execute his fire raids, he could have destroyed "every single thing" in North Korea within three months, but his Bomber Command did a pretty thorough job on strategic targets with high-explosive bombs in less than two. While three groups hit interdiction targets daily, the other two conducted a maximum effort against North Korean industry about every third day. The aging B-29s averaged 8.9 sorties a month between 13 July and 31 October and dropped over 30,000 tons of bombs. The brunt of the damage was wrought in August and early September. The level of destruction for the arsenal and railyards in Pyongyang was 70 percent, for the chemical plants at Konan (Hungnam in JCS directives) it reached 85 percent, and the oil refinery at Wonsan was listed as 95 percent eliminated. One of the targets at Konan was a plant that processed monazite into thorium for the Russian atomic energy program.[4]

The interdiction campaign by Bomber Command and the Fifth Air Force was effective enough to force the enemy to make most movements at night, and in August, Partridge decided to put most of his B-26 effort into night intruder missions. There was no better airman to be in charge of tactical air operations at this stage of the conflict, since Partridge had a unique perspec-

The area around Konan (Hungnam) contained the most extensive basic chemical and light metals production complex in the Far East. FEAF destroyed 85 percent of it during the strategic bombing campaign, including this nitrogen fertilizer plant. The November 1950 photograph highlights the destructive power and accuracy of the American bombing effort. (RG 342 NA II)

tive of the ground war. He had begun his military career as an enlisted engineer with the Seventy-ninth Division in the Meuse Argonne in World War I and often piloted his own aircraft around Korean battlefields looking for targets, with Walker as his passenger. To improve the effectiveness of his night missions, Partridge tried a number of experiments with flares, made technical modifications to aircraft, and even brought in an expert from the RAF who had considerable World War II experience. Vandenberg furnished FEAF with a staff study on night tactical air operations and encouraged the full conversion of the Third Bomb Group to that role. He realized that his service was poorly prepared for night interdiction operations. When the recalled 452d Bomb Wing arrived in Korea, it picked up the responsibility for daylight missions, while the Third, along with the attached 731st Squadron of the 452d, concentrated on night raids. The night intruders had to improvise tactics, avoid enemy flak traps, and work with old World War II ordnance that was inconsistently supplied and sensitive to handle. Low-level strafing runs with the B-26s' fourteen forward firing machine guns in poor visibility over Korea's mountainous terrain were especially risky. Although the night intruders did considerable damage to the enemy, the commander of the Third Bomb Wing noted that "to find answers to certain problems which are peculiar to night attack, we have often groped as we have operated in the darkness." The inability to knock out moving ground targets at night would remain an Air Force deficiency through Vietnam.[5]

CONCERNS ABOUT AIRPOWER EXCESSES

Despite the best efforts of the Air Force to emphasize its desire to avoid civilian casualties, around the world the mention of strategic bombing still conjured up images of the destruction wrought on Germany and Japan a few years before. In accordance with JCS directives, leaflets warning of future bombing raids were dropped on eleven North Korean cities beginning on 18 August. This brought a quick protest from the British, who thought that the promptings to evacuate target areas indicated that "we were preparing to engage in mass bombings of those cities, and that this, if carried out, would produce a feeling in Asia and elsewhere that would be harmful to the West." The State Department complained about FEAF press releases that summarized bomber operations in terms of tonnage dropped and requested more emphasis on accuracy, including special awards for outstanding crews. Stratemeyer responded by furnishing strike photographs of Pyongyang that showed untouched civilian buildings next to destroyed military targets; he declined to recognize individual crews, however, since "practically all are equally skillful and turn in similar results." After numerous FEAF attacks, the enemy capital was still in much better condition than Seoul. South Korean troops who liberated Pyongyang in October were amazed that all its "cultural properties remained intact," though its inhabitants "shared a particular dread of the U.S. Air Force." Even when B-29s had to determine their bomb release points with radar because of poor visibility, collateral damage was generally limited. Despite this record, Russian accusations in the UN of "barbarous and indiscriminate bombing of peaceful towns and civilians" received some sympathetic coverage in the world press, especially in a few British papers and in Asia. Indian reaction included charges of racism and reflected the attitude of Nehru, who "could not keep quiet in the face of suffering brought about by US bombing in Korea."[6]

There were concerns about airpower excesses in tactical missions, also. As the UN counteroffensive surged northward in September, airmen attempted to exercise some restraint in operations south of the thirty-eighth parallel against an obviously beaten enemy. Navy and Fifth Air Force aircraft wanted to keep enemy forces from fleeing, but did not want to endanger refugees. Pedestrian movement toward Seoul was considered harmless, and any people moving away had to be reasonably identified as troops before they could be attacked. Any transportation that could aid the enemy had to be destroyed — even carts — but if civilians were around, they were first dispersed by a warning pass before targets were engaged. Thousands of leaflets were dropped warning civilians to stay off roads and away from Communist facilities that might be bombed. Some British observers, however, thought that the American ground forces were much too quick to call in overwhelming close air support to overcome any resistance in flammable Korean villages. One wrote of the UN counteroffensive, "Few people can have suffered so terrible a liberation." Many airmen also believed that soldiers were misusing airpower in tactical roles. This helped motivate FEAF grumbling about ground force requests for support by medium bombers during this period. O'Donnell believed that he had not gotten very good guidance on how best to support the Inchon landings, and Stratemeyer would not honor Eighth Army requests for B-29 strikes on South Korean cities to assist the advance because such operations were "not desirable for political reasons and are probably not of sufficient military value." He realized, however, that the JCS strategic targets were almost all destroyed, and the B-29s had the power to influence the ground battle, so he had O'Donnell prepare a standard procedure to effectively employ his aircraft against tactical targets.[7]

Stratemeyer's action was timely, because on 26 September, the JCS suspended the strategic campaign due to the success of the UN counteroffensive and ordered MacArthur to concentrate his air forces on targets to assist the tactical situation. Bomber Command was running out of targets anyway and had spent the previous few days attacking North Korean barracks and training facilities. As UN forces drove deeper into North Korea and broken enemy remnants took up positions closer to the Yalu, the need for air interdiction of their supplies, and even an enemy rear area to attack, seemed to disappear. Although CINCFE requested to keep the two reinforcing bomb groups until 8 November, by the end of October, targets were so scarce that a B-29 chased an enemy motorcycle rider down a road with single bombs until one obliterated him. Accordingly, MacArthur authorized the return of the Twenty-second and Ninety-second Bombardment Groups to the United States on 25 October.[8]

The only real disappointment in the strategic air campaign was that facilities at Rashin (Najin) had escaped destruction. This port was in far northeastern Korea, only sixty miles from Vladivostok and less than twenty miles from the Soviet border, and contained key oil storage tanks and railway yards, as well as docks frequented by Russian ships. Headquarters USAF instructed Stratemeyer to bomb the area only visually to avoid an error that could result in an international incident, but FEAF did not pass that information to Bomber Command. Perfect weather was forecast for the first strike on the city on 12 August, but complete cloud cover forced B-29s to drop by radar. O'Donnell called the results "a good, solid, sound, accurate miss," but the State Department was not so sanguine. Fears that raids on Rashin might persuade hesitant Soviets to take a wider role in the war were reinforced by reports in the *Herald Tribune* that the real purpose of the mission was to hinder Soviet submarine operations from the ice-free port. Protests were lodged with the president and Secretary of Defense Louis Johnson, but he argued that the target was still well clear of the Manchurian border, and once war operations had begun, external political decisions should not be permitted "to conflict with or hamper military judgment in actual combat conditions." Although Secretary Acheson decided not to pursue the matter further in August, Vandenberg, aware of the controversy and wanting to avoid any more mistakes, instructed Stratemeyer to hold off attacks on the oil storage site until its importance could be reevaluated. Both Truman and Johnson agreed that the State Department should be consulted before the next mission against Rashin, which General Bradley and Johnson proposed to Truman at a National Security Council meeting on 7 September. By then, two F-51s had strafed a Chinese airstrip near Antung on 27 August, and the Navy had recovered a Russian body from a twin-engine aircraft that had been shot down by Task Force 77 on 4 September. A worried Truman asked the JCS to study the matter more while the Defense and State Departments got together to discuss the risks of bombing so close to Russia so soon after the most recent provocations. Because of the tension caused by those actions and the upcoming Inchon invasion, the JCS decided on its own not to risk another possible incident. It ordered that no further attacks be made on Rashin. MacArthur concurred in that judgment at the time, but the issue would arise again.[9]

The JCS were also concerned about the political implications of an all-out bombing of the North Korean capital of Pyongyang and asked MacArthur on 29 September to consult them before mounting any such operation. The chiefs were concerned that destroying cities might endanger chances for a quick end to the war by embittering the North Korean people, and it would also necessitate considerable American rebuilding and aid programs after victory was won. Stratemeyer was planning a mission with 100 B-29s against the remaining military targets in the capital and had even prepared special warning leaflets for the "citizens of Pyongyang." However, Mac-Arthur assured the JCS that he had no plans to attack the city unless it became a "citadel of defense" and that he was "trying to end the campaign with as little added loss of life and destruction of property as possible." The cessation of the strategic campaign also stopped raids on the North Korean power plants, which FEAF had just begun without clear guidance from Washington.[10]

The hydroelectric complexes soon became the focus of growing international unease about the American bombing campaign and its effects. On 7 October, the day the UN authorized ground operations across the thirty-eighth parallel, Assistant Secretary of State for Far Eastern Affairs Dean Rusk asked that those targets be preserved as possible bargaining chips with the Chinese Communists. There was also growing concern in the UN about the possibility of Chinese intervention to protect their power supply, and on 22 October the JCS asked MacArthur's opinion about a proposal by the State Department to have him report to the UN Security Council that he would not interfere with plant operations or power distribution. He thought that such a unilateral action would be unwise. Although he had no intention of disturbing any peaceful uses of the electricity, he could not sanction maintaining the status quo if resources were being used "for potentially hostile purposes through the manufacture of munitions of war." He advised waiting until the plants were under UN control and such a judgment could be made. The JCS did not push for such a statement again, although pressure for it grew in the UN, fostered to some extent by skillful Communist propaganda that included the announcement of a "Volunteer Corps for the Protection of the Suiho Hydroelectric Zone."[11]

MACARTHUR ESCALATES THE AIR WAR

Whereas initial evidence of Chinese intervention in early November caused increased demands in the UN for military restraint, MacArthur's response was to order an expansion of the air campaign that brought it closer to the image portrayed by enemy propaganda. In World War II he had probably been the commander most concerned with the effects of bombing on civilians, and in his periodic reports to the UN about Korean operations, he had emphasized warnings given to noncombatants about bombing raids, noting that "there remains the capability of the United Nations Air Forces to completely devastate the urban areas of North Korea, but with assiduous care destruction of the civilian population has been avoided and only targets of military significance have been attacked." MacArthur had disapproved of Stratemeyer's September attack on Pyongyang and prohibited strategic incendiary missions, but the threat of open Chinese involvement in the war compelled him to take drastic action. He did not believe that Peiping had made a decision for all-out war, and he hoped to deter or drastically limit any intervention by Chinese forces in Manchuria, which his intelligence on 3 November estimated to be at a strength of 868,000, and growing. In early July he had informed the Army Staff that in case of active Chinese Communist intervention, he wanted to have SAC "destroy the communications facilities into and through North Korea." With the appearance of Chinese Communist "volunteers" in combat against his forces, he now felt obliged to expand the air war accordingly.[12]

With the suspension of both strategic and interdiction campaigns, FEAF medium bomber groups had received stand-down orders on 24 October, but the new Chinese threat brought them back into action with a vengeance. Escalation in the air war was evident with the first major mission of the new campaign, against Kanggye. Twenty-six aircraft loaded with incendiaries tried to hit the town on 4 November, but weather diverted them to secondary targets. Mission summaries stated, "It was felt that the destruction of this town would greatly demoralize and retard Chinese Communist troops entering into the Korean conflict." Twenty-four aircraft returned the next day and destroyed 65 percent of the city. Stratemeyer justified the mission in a message to Vandenberg immediately after the raid by explaining, "Entire city of Kanggye was virtual arsenal and tremendously important communications

This post-strike photograph shows the extensive damage caused by FEAF's 5 November incendiary attack on "the military supply center, communications hub and high command post" of Kanggye. The white arrow points to a hospital area designated by a red cross that was unharmed, although located only 630 feet from the outer edge of the target area. The more concentrated part of the city in the lower part of the picture is heavily burned out, however. (RG 342 NA II)

center, hence decision to employ incendiaries for first time in Korea." This explanation was also offered in press coverage. In reality, CINCFE had ordered his air forces "to destroy every means of communication and every installation, factory, city, and village" in North Korea, except for Rashin and the hydroelectric plants. Stratemeyer justified these orders to Bomber Command and Fifth Air Force by adding, "Under present circumstances all such have marked military potential and can only be regarded as military installations." MacArthur told the American ambassador to South Korea that he intended to turn the narrow stretch of territory between UN lines and the border into "a desert" incapable of supporting Communist troops. When the JCS canceled the next incendiary attack in Sinuiju because of its proximity to

Manchuria, an angry MacArthur persuaded them that the mission was essential for interdiction of Chinese reinforcements, and more than seventy bombers burned down 60 percent of that city. Smoke from the flames rose to 15,000 feet. At least eight more towns shared the same fate in November, highlighted by the 90 percent destruction of Hoeryong. During the month, Bomber Command delivered more than 3,300 tons of incendiaries, constituting about two-thirds of the total effort. After Sinuiju, MacArthur believed that he had JCS approval to strike anywhere in North Korea. He accordingly waived all restrictions on bombing south of the Yalu River and assigned the destruction of international bridges to Task Force 77 and the B-29s as a top priority. In a series of messages with the JCS discussing interdiction of the Yalu and altering UN objectives, MacArthur expressed confidence "that with my air power, now unrestricted so far as Korea is concerned except as to hydroelectric installations," he could deny reinforcements coming into North Korea enough to ensure destruction of enemy forces there. Newspapers speculated that the U.S. government was about to threaten the power plants also, in an attempt to deter further Chinese intervention.[13]

It was not only Red Chinese ground forces that threatened the UN position. Reports of mysterious swept-wing jets on enemy airfields began in early October, and at the beginning of November they entered combat in earnest. The appearance and performance of MiG-15 jet fighters surprised and alarmed commanders in Korea and the United States. It is no coincidence that Air Training Command activated an Aerial Gunnery Training Center right after the MiGs appeared and that SAC soon instituted biannual evaluations for every gunner in the command. On 7 November Vandenberg offered Stratemeyer F-84 and F-86 wings to counter the new threat, and also to test the new American aircraft in combat conditions. Soon images of jet dogfights and jet aces would displace the B-29s in newsreels. Operating from airfields in Manchurian sanctuaries, the MiGs would increasingly challenge UN air superiority in the northern reaches of Korea.[14]

The MiG-15s that attacked UN aircraft in early November came from the 151st and 28th Fighter Air Divisions (FADs) of the Soviet 64th Fighter Air Corps. Stalin had initially furnished Mao with air units to defend Shanghai from Nationalist attacks in February 1950. In July the 151st FAD with its sixty-two jet fighters was ordered to Manchuria to provide air defense for Chinese forces and to begin training pilots of the expanding Communist Chinese Air Force in the new jets. Eventually the Soviets began training North Koreans as well. According to Mark O'Neill, who has done extensive research in Soviet archives, Stalin peformed a "carefully orchestrated ballet," trying to keep his air commitment large enough to satisfy his Chinese allies but small enough to avoid antagonizing the United States. However, as threatening UN forces advanced northward and the Chinese prepared to intervene, the pace of Soviet support quickened greatly. Expecting the worst, the Chinese began evacuating industry from exposed cities and emphasizing civil defense measures in anticipation of American bombing raids.[15]

The Soviet aerial intervention on 1 November was not planned, however, and seems to have come in response to some perceived UN provocation over the Yalu. The MiG-15s soon set up an effective defense of the key bridges over the river between Antung in China and Sinuiju in Korea, along with the Suiho hydroelectric facilities. They outclassed all UN aircraft then in Korea, flying more than 100 miles an hour faster than the F-80. As the air war heated up, both sides made exorbitant claims. For instance, while the Air Force is proud to proclaim that the first enemy jet fell to one of its Shooting Stars on 8 November, Soviet records actually give that credit to a Navy F9F Panther the next day. In fact, the Navy jets appear to have downed the first three MiGs, as their cannons packed a lot more punch than the machine guns on the Air Force planes. Soviet claims are also hard to reconcile. O'Neill has researched both sides extensively and concluded that "there are probably fewer jet aces than previously thought on both sides of the Yalu."[16]

The determined Soviet defense of key Yalu bridges contributed to the heated exchanges between Tokyo and Washington about conduct of the air campaign. Reacting to Partridge's requests to protect his airmen, Stratemeyer began pressuring MacArthur on 2 November to allow FEAF pilots to chase the MiGs back to their airfields in Manchuria. Although Vandenberg was sympathetic, talks with new Secretary of Defense George Marshall and Secretary of the Air Force Thomas Finletter convinced the USAF chief of staff that adopting a policy of "hot pursuit" over the Yalu was an unacceptable widening of the war. Negative reaction from allies reinforced Defense Department concerns about the dangers of such escalation. Vandenberg's misgivings that the scheduled raid on Sinuiju on 7 November violated directives about bombing within five miles of the Chinese border led to its disapproval by the JCS and the president. MacArthur's passionate retort that enemy reinforcements teeming over the Yalu bridges threatened the survival of his command shocked the JCS. They were unaware that the situation was so serious and, after consulting with Truman, gave permission for the attack. However, they demanded that Manchurian airspace not be violated and limited attacks to only the Korean side of the spans. Twists and turns in the Yalu made such an approach difficult, and bombers were vulnerable to the Soviet MiGs. Stratemeyer advised MacArthur that it could not be done. FEAF did its best to meet the intent of its theater commander and the JCS, mounting attacks right up to the Chinese border but making sure that such bombing was conducted in optimal visual conditions to eliminate navigational errors. However, the JCS restrictions and spirited Soviet air defense defeated attempts to destroy the key bridges. A disgusted MacArthur called the JCS orders "the most indefensible and ill-conceived decision ever forced on a field commander in our nation's history."[17]

He was no more successful in getting permission to conduct hot pursuit, even after Stratemeyer complained to Vandenberg in late December that FEAF pilots were "becoming rebellious against being used as sacrificial expendables" and pleaded for a reconsideration of the policy that gave the MiGs a sanctuary in Manchuria. As American planes approached targets near the Yalu, Soviet interceptors would take off from fields in Antung, gain altitude on their side of the river, dive down through the bomber formation, and then scamper to safety. The situation was ideal for the short-range MiGs, which could carry only enough fuel for one hour of flying time. In his report to the UN that month, MacArthur railed against the antiaircraft guns and aircraft based in Chinese territory. The Yalu barrier "imposed by the democracies' desire to prevent expansion of the arena of conflict" worked to nullify the superiority of his flyers. To counter this enemy advantage, he announced, "Command, communication and supply centers of North Korea will be obliterated in order to offset tactically the handicap we have imposed upon ourselves strategically by refraining from attack of Manchurian bases." He admitted that UN air supremacy was being seriously challenged for the first time "by modern high performance type jet aircraft." No one in his command or the U.S. Air Force was prepared for the difficulties the enemy interceptors were giving FEAF bombers in "MiG Alley" in northwestern Korea.[18]

The new air threat was so unexpected because of a tendency to underestimate Soviet technological skills and deficiencies in American technical intelligence. The first shortcoming would not be overcome until *Sputnik* in 1957, and senators at the hearings after MacArthur's dismissal cited German scientists and British engines furnished to the Russians as possible explanations for the quick Soviet advance in aeronautical engineering. Vandenberg was concerned about the apparent feeling in the United States that the Russians "had masses of manpower and no brains," and military leaders scrambled to find out information on the new jet.[19]

This effort was complicated by FEAF's unpreparedness to gather technical air intelligence from captured enemy aircraft material. There were no FEAF collection teams in Korea until after the breakout from the Pusan perimeter, and they had to beg, borrow, and steal transportation support to get three North Korean propeller planes back to Japan. When Air Technical Intelligence investigators arrived in Korea from Air Materiel Command in October,

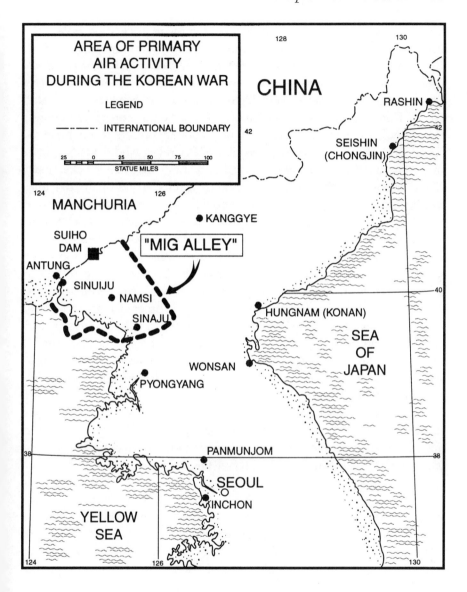

AREA OF PRIMARY
AIR ACTIVITY
DURING THE KOREAN WAR

LEGEND

– – – – – INTERNATIONAL BOUNDARY

25   0   25   50   75   100
STATUE MILES

CHINA

128   130

RASHIN

42

SEISHIN
(CHONGJIN)

124   126

MANCHURIA

KANGGYE

SUIHO
DAM

ANTUNG

"MIG ALLEY"

SINUIJU

NAMSI

SINAJU

HUNGNAM (KONAN)

SEA
OF
JAPAN

40

WONSAN

PYONGYANG

PANMUNJOM

38   38

SEOUL
INCHON

YELLOW
SEA

124   126   130

they had similar support problems. When they found a treasure trove of abandoned aircraft at Pyongyang, they managed to fill up three cargo planes with parts, but two had to be destroyed because they could not get airborne before the Chinese arrived.[20]

The man who saved FEAF's air intelligence program was one of the most amazing characters of the Korean War. When the North Korean invasion began, Chief Warrant Officer Donald Nichols was in charge of District 8,

Office of Special Investigations (OSI). During the next few days, he was the first to notify FEAF of the NKPA attack, maintained liaison with Republic of Korea (ROK) chiefs of staff for the American ambassador, designated air targets for the ambassador, and led a team of Koreans to Suwon airfield to destroy abandoned planes there. Before the war, he had traveled around North Korea in disguise, placed moles in the South Korean Communist Party, and established connections with important leaders throughout the ROK. His talents attracted the attention of Partridge, who made Nichols a major and put him in charge of Special Activities Unit Number One under Fifth Air Force headquarters in early 1951, with the responsibility to gather intelligence, perform sabotage, and aid downed UN airmen. In May the unit was designated Detachment 1 of the 6004th Air Intelligence Service Squadron under the operational control of the Fifth Air Force director of intelligence. By July, it became clear that the small organization had too many responsibilities, and Nichols was put in charge of the newly activated Detachment 2. Whereas the mission of the original unit had been limited to collecting air technical intelligence, his new command was ordered to collect positive intelligence "by any means necessary." By early 1952, Nichols controlled 665 American and Korean personnel in thirty-five subdetachments scattered throughout the Korean peninsula on both sides of the lines and was furnishing Fifth Air Force intelligence with between 600 and 900 information reports a month.[21]

Nichols was responsible for the first air technical intelligence on enemy jets in early 1951 when Partridge sent his Special Activities Unit fifty miles behind enemy lines by helicopter with air cover to examine the wreckage of a crashed MiG. Another combined USAF-Navy-ROK-British salvage effort in July 1951 recovered most of another MiG that had been downed off the west coast of North Korea. Army and Air Force technicians worked for two days dismantling the wreckage in shoals off the mouth of the Chongchon River, while aircraft from British and American carriers discouraged any interference. Late in the war, UN commander Gen. Mark Clark caused controversy by offering $100,000 to the first enemy pilot to desert with a MiG as part of project MOOLAH, but there was no indication that Clark's announcement had any impact on enemy air activity. When a disgusted North Korean pilot did fly his MiG-15 to Kimpo in September 1953, he claimed to have no knowledge of the money he had earned.[22]

These intelligence-gathering efforts and combat experience soon revealed that the enemy interceptor was well built and a "great machine." Its engine was more powerful than any the United States had in service, and the MiG-15 could climb faster and go higher than any USAF or Navy jet. At midrange and high altitudes, it even had a speed and turning advantage over the F-86, the best UN fighter. It was not as rugged as the Sabre, however, and had an inferior gunsight. It also had a limited combat radius of only about 160 nautical miles. It achieved its high performance by sacrificing many features that were standard on USAF aircraft, such as hydraulically boosted controls and emergency backup systems. And in the key areas of experience and aggressiveness, American pilots had a big edge. However, the immediate impact of the MiG was enough to deny FEAF effective aerial reconnaissance near the Yalu River at a critical time in the ground campaign, thus depriving decision makers of possible information about the exact nature of Communist reinforcements swarming into North Korea.[23]

Fears of a massive influx of Chinese ground troops motivated the State and Defense Departments to reexamine the employment of atomic weapons. State Department policy planners in November thought that the military benefits of their use were uncertain, and political fallout would be considerable. Members of the Army Staff G-3 section thought that "from the military point of view, the situation is more favorable for employment of atomic bombs than it was in July." They persuaded Collins to submit a memorandum to the JCS mentioning that "in the event of an all-out effort by the Chinese Communists, the use of atomic bombs against troops and materiel concentrations might be the decisive factor in enabling UN forces to hold a defensive position or to effect the early drive to the Manchurian border." He asked that a study be made to "determine the conditions under which the employment of atomic bombs would be indicated," the most suitable targets to be hit, and what additional policy and operational preparations were necessary "to insure our ability to use this bomb if and when we deem it appropriate." The JCS concurred and referred the memorandum to the Joint Strategic Survey Committee for the preparation of "comments and recommendations" on Collins's questions.[24]

Collins submitted his memorandum on 20 November. Four days later, a confident MacArthur surveyed the Yalu River line. He noted that hydroelectric facilities that had been overrun by his forces had been closed down for a month before being taken, and no Communist protests about losing power had been forthcoming. He concluded that any concern about hydroelectric facilities in North Korea was "a product of British-American speculation" and could not have been a major factor leading to Chinese aggression. He restated his plans to seize the whole border area and expected no further Soviet or Chinese reaction. Critics have accused MacArthur of having blind faith in his own infallibility or of ignoring the growing signs of Chinese intervention, but his optimism was largely a product of his faith in airpower. It had always come through for him in World War II. The Army chief of staff believed that MacArthur's "overreliance"

FEAF fighter bombers play a key role in repelling the North Korean invasion, reinforcing MacArthur's considerable faith in airpower. Here an F-80 strafes a small town sheltering enemy troops and vehicles. Some buildings and a vehicle on the road have been set afire. (USAF photograph from USMA Special Collections)

on his air forces was based solely on his successful destruction of immobile Japanese fixed installations on his island-hopping campaign in the Pacific—a much different target from the "highly mobile, flexible armies of the Chinese." But airpower had achieved much for MacArthur in Korea, as well.[25] It had slowed the initial Communist advance, stiffened his defense of the Pusan perimeter, helped smash the enemy in his counteroffensive, and wiped out most of North Korea's industry. Now his unleashing of its fury in November appeared to have deterred or crippled further Chinese intervention. In fact, the threat of UN air attacks against Chinese troops and cities had given Mao Zedong and his subordinates pause, and it appears that they did not commit to entering the war until the Soviets promised to provide many planes for the Communist Chinese Air Force and to participate extensively in air defense of the Chinese homeland.[26]

American airpower had helped carry MacArthur to the Yalu. But Chinese landpower was about to throw him back.

4

CHOOSING NEW TARGETS AND RESTORING THE BALANCE

But the thing that concerns me now is that as the result of the Korean war you hear upon the floor of the Senate and throughout the country that maybe the Air Force is not all that it is cracked up to be, because they have not been able to knock the enemy out of the Korean operation.

SEN. WILLIAM F. KNOWLAND[1]

The application of air power is not very well understood in this country by people in general, in my opinion. While I was and am today against bombing across the Yalu, it does not mean by any stretch of the imagination that I might not be for it tomorrow, a month from now, or 6 months from now. Air power, and especially the destruction of strategic air power, should go to the heart of the industrial centers to become reasonably efficient. Now the source of the materiel that is coming to the Chinese Communists and the North Koreans is from Russia. Therefore hitting across the Yalu, we could destroy or lay waste to all of Manchuria and the principal cities of China if we utilized the full power of the United States Air Force.

GEN. HOYT VANDENBERG[2]

At the first National Security Council (NSC) meeting after the extent of Chinese involvement became evident in late November, airpower again dominated the discussion. However, this time it was the threat of a Communist air attack that concerned decision makers. General Bradley briefed that the enemy had 300 aircraft in Manchuria, including 200 two-engined bombers with the range to strike crowded UN airfields. Retreating road convoys were also vulnerable. In reply to a question from the president, Vandenberg stated that the only effective defense against the new threat would be to either hit the enemy airfields or withdraw many of our own planes to Japan. Admiral Sherman discussed similar threats to the Navy and agreed that in the event of enemy air attack, we would have to not only pull back down the peninsula but also hit back. Shortly thereafter, Assistant Secretary of State Dean Rusk advised the ambassadors of those nations providing military aid to the UN effort that "if the Chinese concentrate air power in Manchurian air fields and use it in Korea, it will be necessary for us to bomb the bases in Manchuria." The JCS did not necessarily agree with this, however, because of fears that such action might bring in the Russians. In that eventuality, Collins saw no alternative but to consider the use of the A-bomb. One of Rusk's subordinates even proposed using nuclear weapons to destroy the power installations in North Korea as a "heavy blow" against the Communist economy if the situation became grave. This was seconded in a vehement recommendation for escalating the war, a memorandum by Col. Noel Parrish, the assistant secretary of the Air Staff, that argued that the United States should quit trying "to fight World War II over again." He also advocated conventional raids on Manchurian industry, the leaking of news that we had developed "secret atomic radiation booby traps" to poison strips of territory, and the instigation and support of "murderous subversion" in Russia and Eastern Europe.[3]

Collins and Cabell made an emergency trip to see MacArthur in the first week of December. CINCFE believed that if the all-out Chinese Communist attack continued, UN forces would have to withdraw from Korea if restrictions on air and naval action against China were not lifted and significant ground reinforcements were not received. However, if MacArthur were allowed to begin a naval blockade and aerial bombardment of Communist China, make maximum employment of Nationalist troops, and possibly use atomic bombs, he was confident that his forces "should continue to hold the best possible positions in Korea." Stratemeyer asked for three more fighter wings, as well as two medium bomber groups with atomic capability positioned on Guam or Okinawa, but Cabell did not think that any such augmentation was available. Although Collins concurred with MacArthur's conclusions, he promised no reinforcements and returned to Washington to discuss the military situation in the Far East with his colleagues on the JCS.[4]

They remained hesitant to further expand the war unless the enemy did so first. Eventually, contingency plans were cleared through the Department of Defense, the Department of State, and the president that were based on the premise that if the Communists mounted a major air offensive from Manchuria or the Shantung peninsula against UN forces, FEAF would immediately attack those air bases. Although final authority to put the plans into effect remained with the highest levels of government, in an emergency, when such approval would be difficult to get, the JCS was authorized to act on its best judgment. MacArthur was not fully informed of these contingency plans because of fears that he would overreact and perhaps take "action in advance of receiving a directive." In discussions involving the JCS and Secretary of Defense George Marshall in April 1951, they cited this specific incident as a principal justification for McArthur's dismissal.[5]

The Chinese onslaught in November did not change the official hesitance about the use of atomic weapons in the Far East, however. The Joint Strategic Survey Committee study resulting from Collins's November request reaffirmed that the primary use for the A-bomb should be "in the face of imminent disaster which cannot be averted by other means." But the Air Force assistant deputy chief of staff for atomic energy feared that enemy manpower reserves were so great that resorting to nuclear weapons would just provide the Russians with invaluable tactical and technical intelligence without preventing the destruction of the UN force. When General Vandenberg queried his commanders on their opinions, even LeMay thought that atomic employment was inadvisable, unless as part of a campaign against Red China. LeMay's opinions were seconded by O'Donnell, who thought that the weapon's "unwise use in the Far East against a tactical target" would accomplish little except possibly bringing the Russians into the conflict. The SAC commander was adamant, however, that if atomic bombs were to be dropped, his organization should direct the operations.[6]

The diplomatic implication of even suggesting their use was demonstrated when Truman mentioned the possibility at a press conference on 30 November. When the president remarked to the assembled press that the United States would take whatever steps were necessary to meet the military situation, someone inquired if that included the atomic bomb. Truman replied that it included every weapon we had. He continued, "There has always been active consideration of its use," though he qualified this by saying that he did not want to see that happen. "It is a terrible weapon, and it should not be used on innocent men, women, and children who have nothing whatever to do with this military aggression." Later the same day, a clarifying press release was issued emphasizing that only the president could authorize dropping the atom bomb and "no such authorization has been given." But the international damage had already been done. Following on the heels of earlier statements by the secretary of the Navy and the commandant of the Air War College that had intimated American readiness to conduct a preventive nuclear war, Truman's remarks, which could be interpreted to imply that MacArthur already had some authority to use atomic weapons in an emergency, increased the allies' anxiety that they were about to be drawn into World War III. Prime Minister Clement Attlee of Great Britain felt compelled to rush to Washington for consultations on behalf of the alarmed nations of Western Europe. Arab and Asian delegates in the UN were also concerned, and they repeated accusations that America seemed willing to use the bomb only against non-Europeans.[7]

Acheson did not look forward to talking with Attlee, whom he described as speaking with "all the passion of a woodchuck chewing a carrot" and whose thoughts seemed just "a long withdrawing melancholy sigh." The JCS concurred with the State Department position for those meetings that conceded no restrictions on American actions but emphasized the desire not to antagonize our allies or use the bomb. In private, Truman promised Attlee not to employ nuclear weapons without consulting Britain, but Acheson persuaded the president that such a policy would cause too much trouble with Congress, and the final communiqué from the leaders mentioned no such commitment. The meetings were enlivened on one occasion when early-warning radar in Canada picked up an unidentified aerial formation heading for Washington. Air defense forces were put on full alert, but the objects were probably geese and soon disappeared from radar screens. The furor over Truman's remarks soon dissipated, but international concern about the potential for mass destruction from American airpower continued to influence diplomatic initiatives. In a typical example, the prime minister of Canada expressed his reluctance to brand China an "aggressor" in the UN because he feared that it would lead to another "bombing of Shanghai" by sanctioning USAF retaliation against Chinese cities.[8]

The State Department remained sensitive about UN attitudes about nuclear weapons. After discussing the possibility of bombing the North Korean hydroelectric facilities with State Department representatives in January, Vandenberg asked LeMay to go with him on a short trip to Korea to evaluate the situation. Aware of his reputation and State Department concerns, LeMay asked Deputy Secretary of Defense Robert Lovett to check with Acheson to see if the secretary thought that LeMay's presence in the Far East "might have any bad effects." Key State Department advisers were unanimous in opposing the SAC commander's inclusion in the trip. Acheson told Vandenberg, "General LeMay had come to be something of a 'Mr. Atom Bomb,' and . . . we felt it would excite people unduly." Vandenberg left him behind.[9]

EVALUATING USAF PERFORMANCE

One reason LeMay wanted to go to Korea was to check the status of SAC B-29 groups. O'Donnell had just wired him that Bomber Command crews were exhausted and needed replacement. (See chapter 6 on personnel rotation policies.) O'Donnell was justifiably proud of his unit's accomplishments, noting in the introduction to the command history of its first four months that his aging B-29s had performed "unorthodox missions for which the aircraft was not designed nor the crews trained." He still thought that it was a mistake to divert SAC resources from their mission to deliver "a decisive atomic offensive deep at the heart of the enemy" to carry out "close or general support of ground forces in localized wars," but he extolled the professionalism of his "mature and responsible" crews that made the transition possible. When questioned later by Congress about his claims that his Bomber Command had been misused, he complained, "I think this is a rather bizarre war out there, and I think we can learn an awful lot of bad habits in it."[10]

O'Donnell was not the only one judging air operations in Korea. Back in August, Stratemeyer had requested that Professor Barton Leach be assigned to him "to collect, analyze, and record all data pertaining to operations of FEAF in the Korean War." While at Harvard Law School during World War II, Leach had encouraged and then administered a program to supply civilian "operations analysts" to supplement the staffs of senior Air Force commanders. Stratemeyer did not get Leach, who was retained by USAF Headquarters to supervise overall collection efforts, but a colonel from USAF Operations Analysis was sent to FEAF to begin gathering data. Although the Air Staff did not believe that another strategic bombing survey was necessary or possible in what was primarily a campaign of "tactical interdiction," it did want target damage information available for future studies. At about the same time, the public disputes over close air support convinced some USAF leaders that "a coalition of agencies are putting on pressure to further split up U.S. air power." As congressional hearings began on plans to expand the Air Force, Vandenberg and Secretary of the Air Force Finletter were especially suspicious of Carl Vinson, chairman of the House Armed Services Committee and a Navy-Marine sympathizer who favored giving ground commanders more control over tactical aviation. He had already announced that he planned to hold hearings to investigate the conduct of close air support. The Air Force leaders decided that they needed to gather supporting data on USAF performance in Korea, with special focus on tactical accomplishments. In September, the Air Staff notified Stratemeyer that it planned to form an evaluation group headed by "a civilian of some stature" with a "first class general officer as top military man and the actual operating executive." In October 1950, Vandenberg directed Maj. Gen. Glenn Barcus, one of the service's tactical experts, "to make an evaluation of the performance of the Far East Air Forces in the Korean war with particular emphasis on the tactical support of ground forces." In November, the secretary of the Air Force appointed Dr. Robert Stearns, president of the University of Colorado, to head the field evaluation. As an "impartial civilian not connected with the Air Force," he was supposed to recommend policy changes based on lessons learned and to be prepared to answer any congressional inquiries. The other services also began conducting their own investigations. The Army, which had just filed a formal protest with the JCS about USAF lack of interest in close air support, sent Brig. Gen. Gerald Higgins, director of its air support center. In the theater, the Far East Command Operations Research Office and Gen. Edward M. Almond's Tenth Corps conducted additional studies.[11]

The Air Force evaluations were by far the most comprehensive. Since Vinson had been quoted as saying that his inquiry might begin in early January, Stearns had to return with a preliminary report before then. He gave Air Force close air support generally high marks, especially emphasizing the superiority of jets in that role. He did concede that joint doctrine and communications had to be improved, and a better antipersonnel air weapon would be useful against masses of enemy manpower. He also noted shortcomings in night tactical air capability. He praised the B-29s for their strategic and tactical performance but noted in an ominous prediction for SAC that encounters with MiGs suggested that "unescorted formations of B-29s in daylight would suffer serious losses in penetrating a modern air defense system." The rest of the Barcus team returned to the United States by early February, and their voluminous report was even more detailed. It praised Air Force close air support and interdiction efforts and was very harsh in castigating those who denigrated them. It also repeated the shortcomings noted by Stearns.[12]

Leach's mission was to collate all the varied reports, including those from Higgins and the Far East Command Operations Research Office, and he told his bosses, "As to USAF performance in Korea it is now apparent that there is no significant dispute among military professionals." That was not completely true, as General Almond remained highly critical of USAF. He carried his complaints about the inadequacy of Air Force aircraft and commitment in ground support all the way to General Collins. Almond considered himself an expert on close air support and was especially incensed by Vandenberg's statements at a press conference in January that "the best way to support the Army is to knock out the mortar before it is made. . . . The least efficient way is to knock it out after it is already dug in." Almond interpreted Vandenberg's remarks as an Air Force rejection of the ground support role. Collins actually agreed with Vandenberg and explained to Almond that both Vandenberg and Kenney, new commander of the Air University, were emphasizing the necessity of concurrently gaining control of the air, isolating the battlefield, and furnishing direct support to ground forces. These were the same theater air missions promulgated by TAC supporters before the war. Almond was not satisfied, however, and would continue his dispute with the Air Force when he moved on to become commandant at the Army War College. He was particularly disturbed about the USAF preference for using multipurpose aircraft instead of developing a model strictly for CAS, a decision that might have made economic sense to the Air Force but implied to the Army that airmen would rather use those planes on other missions. Rather than have an aircraft and organization that could do an adequate job in a variety of roles, ground commanders preferred something dedicated to performing CAS for them exceedingly well, and they usually cited Marine air wings as an ideal example.[13]

Shortly after Almond forwarded his protest to Washington, the Far East Command Operations Research Office released a report on its own preliminary evaluation of close air support. Those data revealed why ground commanders like Almond preferred Marine methods. Whereas it took about forty-five minutes for an Air Force aircraft to respond to a division request through the Joint Operations Center that allocated assets, Marine forward air controllers estimated that they got bombs on target within ten minutes. Whereas USAF planes loitered over the target area for an average of thirty minutes, Marines spent about seventy-three. Marine divisions received an average of thirty-seven CAS sorties a day, versus thirteen for their Army counterparts. And while the average bombing distance from the front lines for USAF support missions was over three miles, for the Marines it was 1,600 yards, with half of the targets within 800 yards. The Barcus Report agreed with some of these observations, acknowledging the interest of ground force personnel in the ability of aircraft to remain "on station" for long periods, "bolstering the morale of friendly troops and lowering the morale of enemy troops." But the report defended USAF tactics, control procedures, volume of effort, and jets in their performance of CAS, while calling the comparison of Air Force and Marine performance in the press "invidious" and invalid.[14]

The report also took a detailed look at Bomber Command's operations. It evaluated B-29 performance in strategic, interdiction, night intruder, close support, and leaflet operations, emphasizing that "the specialized employment of medium bombers in the strategic role is a luxury we cannot afford." While also praising B-29 crews for their flexibility and success in destroying strategic targets and bridges, it was less convinced of the overall effectiveness of their attacks. It pointed out that most of North Korea's strategic sustenance came from outside its borders, interdiction operations were hard to assess, lack of tactics and training in night and close support operations hindered those missions, and airmen had no appreciation for the value of leaflet drops.[15]

THE PACE OF THE AIR WAR INCREASES

With the shift of the battle lines southward, Bomber Command found itself engaged mainly in interdiction operations, its fate for most of the rest of the war. The original Strategic Target Attack Plan had been based on limited intel-

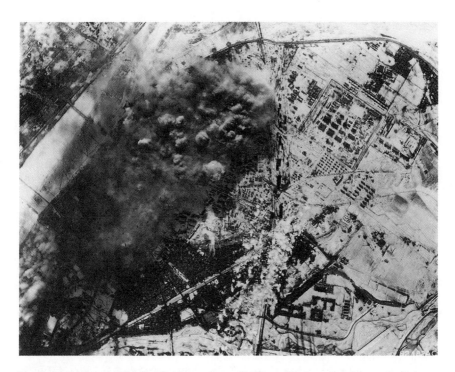

Bombs from Ninety-eighth Bombardment Group B-29s are silhouetted against smoke and snow as they fall on targets in Pyongyang during the first of two "maximum effort" incendiary attacks on that city in January 1951. The snow provided a white background to highlight the bomb images in the photograph, but it also limited the fire damage to the enemy capital. (RG 342 via NASM)

ligence of a closed North Korean society, however, and when additional objectives of strategic importance were discovered, FEAF went after them, conceding that "their destruction during the initial phase of the Korean war would probably have had a greater effect than did their later destruction." Among the highlights of Bomber Command missions during the UN withdrawal was a maximum effort authorized by MacArthur against Pyongyang. He believed that the authority granted him by the JCS for the destruction of cities and towns along the Yalu was now expanded under the current situation, and he planned to destroy the enemy capital, Wonsan, Hamhung, and the Suiho power facility. The attack on Pyongyang was conducted without any advance warning or publicity, and without informing the JCS. Although snow slowed the spread of fires, incendiary attacks on 3 and 5 January burned out 35 percent of the city. While General Vandenberg told the State Department in mid-February that "we have reached the point where there are not enough targets left in North Korea to keep the air force busy," the medium bombers still had plenty to do as UN forces attempted to stabilize their lines. Press releases during the month touted B-29 attacks on marshaling yards, supply centers, and barracks complexes. Crewmen sometimes reported raging flames from their attacks, and after "volcano like fires" swept one barracks area north of Pyongyang, a bombardier chortled, "There's a housing shortage in one part of Korea tonight." American leaders intended "to use air and naval action to make North Korea an example of what happens to an aggressor," and Bomber Command was leading the way.[16]

Requests by MacArthur to extend the air war to the hydroelectric plants were refused, however, even though he was prompted by the JCS to do so. During early November 1950, Far East Command staff had prepared a detailed report on the power facilities, based on occupation of many sites and data furnished by Japanese engineers who had run them. At the same time, the JCS had conjectured that Chinese intervention might be motivated by a desire to protect the hydroelectric complexes, and it had not objected to a draft French UN resolution guaranteeing the safety of the installations. With the Chinese fully committed in late December, the JCS queried MacArthur about the feasibility and desirability of destroying the dams and plants if Chinese forces crossed the thirty-eighth parallel. He replied that his medium bombers could do the job, but the decision to conduct such operations should be based on political rather than military considerations. A Joint Strategic Plans Committee study in January on whether to bomb the hydroelectric complexes received varied reactions from the services. The Navy generally favored the attacks, the Army feared the action would appear to be part of a U.S. "scorched earth" policy, and the Air Force was not sure it had the capability to harm the large dams and wanted to expand the target list to include the power complex in Manchuria. By the time MacArthur formally requested permission to strike the North Korean installations in late February, the ground situation had stabilized, and the issues within the JCS had still not been resolved. Assistant Secretary of State Rusk told Bradley that his department had no objections to the proposed attacks, but the JCS chairman said that the chiefs were "unenthusiastic" about any changes in their directives. They denied CINCFE's request and initiated a more extensive study of the issues involved. The JCS concluded in March that bombing the power installations would "not contribute materially to the Korean tactical situation," and attempts to predict its impact in the UN were "problematical." The JCS decided to delay such a course of action until the political or military situation had changed, foreseeing its optimum use "as one element of an overall program to bring pressure on Communist China."[17]

Rashin also remained off-limits to FEAF. On 15 February, MacArthur complained that the enemy was taking advantage of the port's immunity from air attack to build up reinforcements and supplies. He asked to take advantage of good weather to destroy docks, marshaling yards, and storage facilities by visual bombing. Maj. Gen. Maxwell Taylor, Collins's assistant chief of staff for operations, recommended that his boss get the JCS to lift restrictions at a 16 February meeting, but the chiefs expressed concern about the bombers being intercepted or hitting Russian vessels in the harbor. MacArthur replied that there were no indications that Soviet ships were using the port, and the only source for possible fighters to defend the city were Russian airfields near Vladivostok, "and such an overt act of war is not considered likely." Taylor again recommended that Collins get approval for the air attacks at the next JCS meeting on 19 February, but Secretary of Defense Marshall, Secretary of State Acheson, and the president all agreed that the limitations should not be removed at that time. The JCS informed MacArthur on 21 February that a "decision has been reached on higher governmental levels that restriction regarding Rashin must remain in effect for the present."[18]

Despite these continuing limitations, the overall pace of the air war picked up considerably after the Chinese intervention. From their full entry in late November until the beginning of Operation KILLER in the UN counteroffensive in late February, FEAF delivered about 40 percent of the bombs and two-thirds of the napalm it had dropped in the whole war. Most of the missions were flown away from MiG Alley, however, since the loss of the improved airfields around Seoul in late December meant that F-86s had to be based at Taegu or in Japan, too far away to escort bombers over northwestern Korea. By USAF estimates, 60,000 sorties during those ninety-two days damaged 266 bridges, hit 139 locomotives, destroyed 1,710 rail cars and 5,575 trucks, gutted 36 marshaling yards, sealed 91 tunnels, and inflicted 67,000 casualties on the enemy. Further Operations Research Office studies showed that the mixture of naphthenic and palmitic acids ignited by phosphorus was the most effective antipersonnel weapon for close air support, and it was also used extensively against vehicles and structures. Fighter-bomber pilots liked it because "when you've hit a village and have seen it go up in flames, you know that you've accomplished something." Many realized that although the rice-straw thatched roofs they were burning were supposed to be covering enemy troops, there was a good chance that there were innocent civilians there, too. Most would not generally use napalm on people they could see, except for troop concentrations, but one remarked that "you get conditioned, especially after you've hit what looks like a civilian and the A-frame on his back lights up like a Roman candle—a sure enough sign that he's been carrying ammunition."[19]

The original caption for this picture began, "This photograph tells better than words the effect of napalm tanks dropped by B-26s of the 452nd Light Bomb Wing on enemy barracks and supply buildings." The attack happened near Nae-ri in west-central Korea in late January 1951. The bomb landed behind the building and blew flames completely through it. The wood and thatch structures in Korean villages burned quickly. (RG 342 NA II)

Fighter-bomber pilots got no special recognition for troops killed or villages destroyed; they just wanted to survive their hundred missions and do what they could to win the war. They firmly believed intelligence reports that labeled targets as supply centers or troop concentration points, and they did their best to eliminate them. Although pilots tended to consider everyone in North Korea an enemy, even civilians, they were much more compassionate toward people in the South. But despite extensive warnings to stay away from enemy targets, many innocent South Koreans became victims of the painful horror of napalm as UN forces drove northward. A British reporter described the plight of a tram driver from Seoul who had fled the approach of Communist forces in early 1951 to stay with relatives in a remote village. One day in March, the Chinese army arrived and billeted among the people there. The next day, UN aircraft came and dropped napalm. Though some distance from the point of impact of the bombs, he was still drenched from head to foot with the burning fluid. His whole body was covered with a hard, black crust sprinkled with yellow pus, and he could not sit or lie down. The doctor of the British Twenty-ninth Brigade had seen twenty-five similar cases that week and managed to transport the man to an overwhelmed Civil Assistance Command. Eventually that organization arranged for evacuation schemes and civilian hospital care for such cases, and a civil assistance officer was attached to each division in Eighth Army.[20]

The new commander of that army was especially concerned about the damage his forces were causing in South Korea and did his best to limit it. After the death of Walton Walker in a jeep accident in December, Lt. Gen. Matthew Ridgway had taken command of Eighth Army, and his speedy rebuilding of its fighting spirit must be recorded as one of the greatest leadership accomplishments in military history. Shortly after taking over, he issued an order to his retreating ground forces that "the execution of demolitions and necessary military destruction in South Korea shall be such as to combine maximum hurt to the enemy with minimum harm to the civilian population." His sentiments were well known throughout his army. After a subordinate division commander complained to General Almond, then leading Tenth Corps, that the burning of enemy villages in his sector where no enemy was present went "against the grain of US soldiers," Almond felt obligated to inform Ridgway about his tactics. Almond explained that he was denying shelter to the enemy, especially using air and artillery support to destroy all structures, mostly deserted, "which are used or suspected of being used by enemy personnel," and therefore driving them out into the open during the bitter winter weather. He emphasized, "Major effort has been directed to the natural lines of approach and to those areas in which the meager population remaining appears sympathetic to and harbors the enemy." He sent Ridgway detailed maps of the targets he had destroyed along his front and in the enemy rear. Captured prisoners affirmed the success of Almond's tactics, revealing that the subzero temperatures had taken a heavy toll on their ranks. Almond also relied heavily on napalm strikes in his rear areas to burn down villages in "guerrilla infested areas." Ridgway did not order any changes to Tenth Corps' procedures, but at a subsequent commanders' call he highlighted the restraint shown by Chinese forces in Korean occupation and warned against "the wanton destruction of towns and villages, by gun-fire or bomb, unless there is good reason to believe them occupied" by the enemy.[21]

Although Ridgway was determined to limit damage to South Korea, he was also willing to do just about anything to safeguard the welfare of his soldiers. As soon as he took command of Eighth Army, he began bombarding Far East Command with requests for new weapons. Ridgway inquired about the possibility of employing poison gas in case an evacuation of the peninsula became necessary, but MacArthur informed him that "U.S. inhibitions on such use are complete and drastic," and even if that attitude changed, the UN would never permit the use of chemicals. Ridgway also was concerned about deterring a Soviet atomic attack on the vulnerable port of Pusan during a withdrawal. He advised that advance preparations for American use of nuclear weapons in the Far East should be completed, followed by a warning from the president to the Soviets that we were ready to strike with atomic bombs if provoked. Ridgway also prodded MacArthur to develop a white phosphorus bomb to air burst over massed enemy troops and encouraged FEAF to make a 1,000-pound napalm bomb to be dropped from B-29s. After replacing Mac-Arthur as CINCFE, Ridgway took up his battle for an airburst weapon with the JCS, which furnished him with some white phosphorus-filled chemical bombs for tests. Soon thereafter, FEAF also experimented with night airdrops of fifty-five-gallon drums of napalm from C-119 transports, an operation ironically named SNOWBALL. Ridgway's objective for these weapons was to "wipe out all life in tactical locality and save lives of our soldiers." He was worried that the enemy might someday employ napalm as well and had his staff investigate what could be used to provide soldiers a few seconds of protection if they were struck by it, allowing enough time to discard the item before it could burn through. The best suggestion he received was for troops to use their rain ponchos.[22]

As Ridgway drove his rejuvenated army north in March, big air battles flared up in MiG Alley in northwestern Korea, where Bomber Command B-29s escorted by Fifth Air Force fighters battled their way through enemy interceptors to take out bridges and supplies. The Yalu had been frozen over thick enough to support vehicular traffic, but with it beginning to thaw, the bridges between North Korea and Manchuria again became important targets. It was apparent that only the F-86 Sabre was an effective counter for the MiG-15, and the Fourth Fighter-Interceptor Group was now redeployed to forward fields around Seoul. Still, the round-trip from Kimpo to the Yalu was 430 miles, and at high speed the Sabres could spend only twenty minutes at most on patrol. Communist Chinese Air Force pilots had also begun flying combat missions with their Russian mentors in January, though they would not be ready to participate on a large scale until the fall. Once their MiG pilots got some combat experience from their sanctuaries in Manchuria, the Chinese even tried to refurbish bases in North Korea to extend their aircraft's limited range, challenge UN air superiority, and perhaps even influence the battlefield. Intelligence reports conjectured that the Communists might be preparing to use MiGs in a ground support role, and they did attempt a few costly raids with IL-10 ground attack planes. O'Donnell had not believed that the forward airfields were appropriate targets for B-29s, but he had been returned to

Of all UN aircraft, only the North American F-86 Sabre could match the Mikoyan and Gurevich MiG-15 in air-to-air combat. These two Sabres of the Fifty-first Fighter-Interceptor Wing are preparing to engage enemy jets over MiG Alley in mid-1952. To increase its maneuverability in the impending dogfight, the bottom plane is dropping wing tanks used to extend its range. The top one has already done the same. (RG 342 NA II)

command of the Fifteenth Air Force after the completion of a six-month tour. His rotation may have been accelerated by a press report that misquoted him as urging the immediate use of the atom bomb on Communist China. Although a personal investigation by Vandenberg exonerated O'Donnell, the incident caused the Air Force some embarrassment. O'Donnell's replacement, Brig. Gen. James Briggs, had developed effective plans to deal with the enemy airfields in North Korea. Bomber Command mounted an aggressive campaign against them beginning in mid-April and, despite considerable opposition, forced the Communists to abandon their construction efforts within three months. FEAF's ability to keep these forward airstrips neutralized severely limited the utility of Communist airpower and represented a major success in the air war for UN forces. Stratemeyer also tried to get LeMay to mount a bombing mission with B-36s from the United States, but LeMay declined because of logistic limitations, especially shortages of engines and spare parts.[23]

FEARS OF AN EXPANDED WAR

April also featured another flurry of activity concerning atomic weapons. There was much anxiety in the United States. Opinion polls showed that one-third of the American public favored a general war with Communist China, and a majority advocated air attacks on Manchuria. Signs of Chinese air and ground preparation for their spring fifth-phase offensive and a corresponding buildup of Soviet forces in the Far East alarmed the president enough for him to order nuclear weapons and more SAC bombers to Okinawa on 6 April. Vandenberg had begun requesting the transfer of atomic bombs from the Atomic Energy Commission to the Air Force in March, when it became apparent that Russian troops were massing in Manchuria and more than seventy submarines had assembled at Vladivostok and Sakhalin. Intelligence reports that month also revealed that Stalin had told Foreign Minister V. M. Molotov "to handle matters in Asia," and a reliable high-ranking Polish defector revealed that "Soviet Far East Command has been instructed that rendering of necessary assistance to insure success of offensive takes precedence over avoidance of third World War." Vandenberg and Bradley convinced Truman that the Chinese and Russians might be prepared to do anything to push the United States out of Korea, perhaps even to invade Japan. This would mean the beginning of global war, and the Air Force needed to be able to respond quickly. LeMay was informed of Truman's intentions on 5 April, and on the seventh he met with Vandenberg to finalize plans. They decided to deploy the Ninth Bomb Wing from Travis Air Force Base to Guam on a training mission and then to maneuver it to Okinawa "for a possible action against retardation targets." (Retardation targets were attacked to slow an enemy ground advance.) On the eleventh the JCS issued LeMay a directive to prepare plans "against targets listed and targets of opportunity in the Far East." After the bombers deployed, this time with the nuclear cores to complete nine bombs, LeMay sent his deputy, General Thomas Power, to the Far East to coordinate with the new CINCFE, General Ridgway, and direct any atomic operations. This was such a sensitive mission that when the Air Staff found out that a congressional committee was heading for Guam at the same time, they directed that Power "be missing" during their visit. Although the nuclear-capable SAC B-29s, and sometimes B-50s, never moved to Okinawa, the deployment to Guam continued until the end of the war. LeMay complained on numerous occasions that the need for frequent squadron rotation kept "one of our atomic wings in a constant state of disruption."[24]

This incident raised many issues about atomic operations in Korea for both SAC and the JCS. LeMay was concerned about retaining control of such missions and designated Power as "Deputy Commanding General, SAC X-RAY" with that responsibility. These arrangements were finalized in a 2 May meeting among Power, Stratemeyer, and Hickey, which also produced a memorandum on planning for SAC "atomic retardation operations" in the Far East. When Power returned to the United States, atomic responsibility in the theater passed to the chief of Bomber Command, which meant that he still took orders from FEAF for conventional operations but answered to SAC on nuclear issues. MacArthur had asked for his own atomic capability for the early stages of an expanded war on two occasions—in December for thirty-four bombs primarily for retardation targets, and in March to hit enemy airfields on "D-Day." Inspired by a series of alarming messages warning of possible Soviet reaction to the approaching completion of a peace treaty between Japan and the United States, Ridgway renewed the requests in May 1951, bolstered by his new agreements with SAC. Two Army staff studies complained that SAC considered only strategic use of the bomb and had no appreciation of tactical strike capabilities. Planning, intelligence, command relationships, and training in SAC and Far East Command were inadequate to support Ridgway's ground operations with nuclear weapons. When one of these studies was discussed by the JCS in August, it directed CINCFE to test atomic delivery procedures by conducting simulated strikes in Korea with the coordination of SAC and the commander in chief, Pacific (CINCPAC), since the Navy also had some carrier-based nuclear capability. At the same time, Ridgway was asking that just such support be available to him, in addition to the preparation of atomic artillery. The JCS action resulted in exercise HUDSON HARBOR, four practice missions conducted by SAC X-RAY (under the temporary command of O'Donnell, who was supposedly on "a normal overseas inspection trip") on tactical targets chosen by CINCFE. For security reasons, the operations were presented as conventional strikes in support of frontline troops and would have appeared that way to observers where the ordnance was delivered, but they were conducted as close to actual nuclear procedures as possible, including waiting three and a half hours to get simulated presidential permission to release the weapons for a first strike. HUDSON HARBOR demonstrated that the evaluation of potential tactical atomic targets was inadequate and the delay between selection and delivery was too long. In addition, CINCFE and SAC disagreed on the best way to pick objectives. Ridgway wanted to base choices on each unique battlefield situation, while LeMay favored standard "yardsticks." As far as the Air Staff was concerned, the exercise failed to establish that there were any suitable targets for atomic weapons in Korea.[25]

SAC also remained concerned about executing war plans in the Far East.

The 2 May meeting affirmed that SAC B-29s would revert to LeMay's command immediately if general war broke out, but it soon became apparent that adequate information on strategic targets in China and the Soviet Union was lacking. In Cabell's memoirs, the USAF director of intelligence claims that he and Stratemeyer decided early in the war to fly reconnaissance missions over Manchuria on their own, to gather necessary data while shielding their bosses from blame. This might explain the existence of Russian documents about the interrogation of an RB-45 crew shot down near Antung in December 1950, although other accounts claim that the aircraft was on a mission over North Korea. There is no other evidence that the FEAF commander actually carried out the covert flights. Leadership in Bomber Command was being rotated every four months, and Brig. Gen. Robert Terrill now took up the gauntlet of obtaining adequate reconnaissance. In response to an April request from Ridgway to monitor the enemy air buildup, the JCS gave CINCFE the power to authorize such operations over China at his own discretion, and Terrill planned them as part of his SAC X-RAY responsibilities. The first mission by an RB-45 on the night of 5 June to get radar scope data for Manchurian airfields was intercepted and fired upon by Chinese fighters, but the aircraft escaped unharmed. Wrangling permission for more strategic reconnaissance missions from Ridgway as armistice negotiations began was an arduous process, and by mid-August only three had been conducted. By that time, the JCS had also limited missions to areas south of thirty-two degrees north latitude to prevent disrupting the peace talks. Still, by 1 November, USAF Headquarters felt confident enough about its intelligence to prepare a comprehensive map of Chinese air bases for the secretary of defense. Target reconnaissance requiring overflights of Russian territory was not authorized unless general war began. One way to work around operational limitations on intelligence gathering was by furnishing assets to the Nationalist Chinese and encouraging their use, and much key enemy order-of-battle information came from that source.[26]

While reconnaissance over Soviet territory was prohibited, missions were still flown over international waters off the coast to gather electronic intelligence or take oblique photographs. Smart recollects at least two occasions when Soviet fighters ambushed and shot down RB-29s performing that role, once over the southern Kuriles and another time about forty miles off Vladivostok. Other information gatherers were sometimes intercepted as well. In November 1951, two Soviet fighters downed a P2V bomber on weather reconnaissance over the Sea of Japan. They admitted that they had fired on the plane in a protest note, and the American ambassador to the UN informed the secretary-general and the press about the incident, as well as that the aircraft was over international waters. The State Department chose not to protest further, deciding that since the aircraft was on a UN mission, the matter was for its consideration and not a direct U.S.-USSR affair. Besides, any claims probably would not be satisfied and would just provoke a Soviet reaction, "magnifying the incident and consequently leading to further exchanges from which the US national interest could not hope to profit." The incidents were never brought up at the UN, and both the Soviets and the Americans preferred to keep later similar occurrences to themselves. FEAF could not determine why the intercepts occurred, nor why the Soviets did not try such tactics more often once they had demonstrated how vulnerable the snoopers were to their fighters. FEAF took as many precautions as it could, and the electronic monitoring operations continued because of their military and political significance.[27]

The Soviet-American confrontations in international and Japanese airspace culminated in late 1952. When another B-29 was shot down without warning in northern Japanese sovereign airspace in October 1952, Far East Command responded by strengthening fighter defenses in that zone and ordering UN aircraft to engage Russian aircraft that entered it. The State Department and JCS approved the stricter measures, along with plans to give wide publicity to the details of any more Soviet overflights, including the possibility of shooting one of them down. The next month, seven MiGs from Vladivostok attacked a combat air patrol of improved F9F-5 Panthers from the carrier *Oriskany* of Task Force 77 over international waters, and at least one Soviet pilot had to eject from his aircraft before it crashed into the sea. Probably fewer than half the enemy jets made it back to base, though the Navy was disappointed because faulty plotting had foiled any chance for the UN to finally grab a Russian airman. That incident was not publicized, nor was it repeated. Perhaps the close call gave the Soviets second thoughts, since they presented the UN with no more opportunities to capture pilots with provocations over international waters or Japan.[28]

The threat of Soviet airpower caused great concern in the Far East and Washington and was considered "the gravest initial problem" for Far East Command in case of a general war. War games in mid-1951 demonstrated that air defense of UN air bases and intelligence of enemy movements were inadequate. A simulated Russian attack by 2,000 aircraft, which included a mass assault on airstrips and even the firebombing of Tokyo, was projected to knock out 75 percent of FEAF's planes and most runways. A counterattack was moderately successful, but the overall results of the exercise showed the necessity for better intelligence, early warning, air defense, and dispersion. Additional fighter forces were also needed for the defense of Japan. When Ridgway became CINCFE, he initially gave precedence to problems relating to the defense of that island nation from Soviet attack. He flew all over the

April 1951 was a tumultuous month for Lt. Gen. Matthew Ridgway as he assumed much greater responsibilities with his appointment as commander in chief, Far East and United Nations Command. Here he attends a briefing at Fifth Air Force headquarters for the visiting secretary of the Army, Frank Pace, shortly before the announcement of MacArthur's relief. From left to right in the front row are Maj. Gen. Earle Partridge, Pace, Ridgway, and Army Vice Chief of Staff Lt. Gen. John Hull. Truman actually tried to get Pace to notify MacArthur of his dismissal, but a breakdown in the communications power unit at Pusan prevented the president's message from getting through. (Signal Corps photograph from USMA Special Collections)

country in his B-17 and also walked key terrain. The vulnerability of Japan was obvious, and it reinforced his determination to "avoid any action which might tend to embroil our nation in a world war," as well as to keep "all the forces under my command in a state of combat-readiness, prepared to deal with what the enemy *could* do rather than with what we thought he *would* do."[29]

As Ridgway's forces in Korea drove north in a slow but inexorable advance that would finally be stopped by the opening of armistice negotiations in July, another sort of battle raged in the United States. President Truman's firing of General MacArthur had caused a storm of controversy, and from the beginning of May until mid-June, the Senate Committees on Armed Services and Foreign Relations held joint hearings to investigate MacArthur's relief and the military situation in the Far East. One of the dominant themes of the testimony was the failure of American airpower to stem the Communist tide, whether because too much reliance or too many limitations had been placed on it. Issues discussed in great detail included shortcomings of interdiction, tactical versus strategic airpower, the inviolability of Manchuria and Rashin, and the surprising capabilities of the MiG-15. MacArthur blamed much of the Communist success on restrictions on his use of airpower, but he admitted that too much was expected against determined ground troops, a position seconded by Bradley. As the hearings continued, more and more senators admitted that they did not understand the limitations of airpower. One even expressed concern that the Air Force's failure to knock the enemy out of the war, whether because of insufficient force or unforeseen restrictions, had created doubts at home and abroad about the service's competence, which might embolden the Soviets and dishearten our allies. When confronted with queries about his service's actual capabilities, Vandenberg lashed back that "the United States is operating a shoestring air force in view of its global responsibilities." He used evidence of growing Russian power to bolster his arguments for more air groups. He also agreed with assertions that "so-called long-range strategic operation of air power" had not really been tried because of restrictions against striking Russia. In a portent of the future, he emphasized that airpower was principally a destructive force, and to be really effective in Korea, "you would have to almost lay waste all of those facilities which would lend themselves toward hiding or storing and stockpiling equipment" in the North. And despite that, and even if Manchuria and China were targeted, the Communists could still slip in supplies over the Russian border at night. O'Donnell was more confident, arguing that if his initial plan for firebombing could have been executed, the war would have been over by now. He emphasized the successes of the Air Force with statistics, comparing the 123,000 tons of bombs dropped in the Korean War with the 160,000 expended by twenty groups of B-29s in the incendiary campaign against Japan. When asked what the results of such tonnage were in the current conflict, he replied, "I would say that the entire, almost the entire Korean peninsula is just a terrible mess. Everything is destroyed. There is nothing standing worthy of the name."[30]

The discussions about airpower, like the hearings themselves, were generally inconclusive on issues of past tactics and strategy, but they did reveal a great amount of shared uncertainty about the future. The next few months would bring a real crisis for airmen like Vandenberg and O'Donnell, trying to apply the destructive capability of their air force in a military situation made more delicate because of sensitive armistice negotiations and more dangerous because of aggressive enemy air activity.

5
TALKING AND DYING

In fact it is only by relying on indiscriminate and inhuman bombing and bombard-
ment by your Air and Naval Forces in violation of the international law that the
present positions of your ground forces are barely and temporarily maintained. Without
such cover and support of indiscriminate bombing and bombardment the ground forces
would long since have withdrawn to no one knows where.

NORTH KOREAN GEN. NAM IL[1]

From various quarters we are receiving expressions of "grave concern" over SAC's
ability to execute the war plan. You are well aware of the strenuous efforts we have had
to exert in order to generate a degree of confidence in strategic bombers. We cannot
afford to have this confidence dissipated on the basis of an operation conducted under
conditions rigged in favor of the enemy and utilizing tactics which are not in accor-
dance with our established principles.

GEN. CURTIS LEMAY[2]

After replacing MacArthur and stopping the Communist spring offensive,
Ridgway now faced the daunting task of conducting complicated negotiations
with a difficult enemy. His initial instructions to FEAF had emphasized
restraint and the prevention of World War III, but once armistice talks began
and battle lines stabilized, he realized that airpower was his best method of
keeping military pressure on the enemy. This was fine with Weyland, who
believed that an armistice was a mistake. In his view, "Our losses in Korea are
light, we are inflicting heavy and disproportionate losses on the Communist
system as a whole, we are discrediting Communist philosophy and aims, and
I believe we are effecting a schism between the USSR and Red China." The
war was also providing a core of combat-seasoned veterans for expanding
American military forces. Ridgway informed FEAF and naval air units on 13
July, "Desire action during this period of negotiations to exploit full capabilities of air power to reap maximum benefit of our ability to punish enemy
where ever he may be in Korea." On 21 July he informed the JCS that a key
part of his plan "for unrelenting pressure on Communist forces" was "an all
out air strike on Pyongyang" with 140 medium and light bombers and 230
fighters, to be executed on the first clear day after the twenty-fourth. This

operation would "take advantage of the accelerated buildup of supplies and personnel" in the area, "strike a devastating blow at the North Korean capital," and make up for the many recent sorties canceled by bad weather. Ridgway also planned to drop warning leaflets along the lines of those suggested in JCS directives the previous summer. The text read:

> Citizens of Pyongyang, Chinnampo, Kangye and Wonsan! Within a day or so United Nations bombers will attack one of your cities in which your Communist leaders have built war factories and concentrated military supplies to be used in killing other Koreans! UN planes will destroy all military installations, including railway marshaling yards, communications centers, war material factories, supply depots, barracks areas, airfields and military headquarters.
>
> The UN Air Force will do everything possible to protect innocent civilians from the war forced on Korea by the Communist traitors. But you must act quickly. Leave these cities. Many others have wisely left cities where the Communists have arms depots and war installations. Join them, and preserve your lives so that you can help build a strong, free Korea after the Communists have been driven out. The UN forces wish to avoid harming civilians.[3]

Ridgway's plan caused quite a stir in Washington. The JCS immediately ordered him to defer his attack until he received further instructions, because "the specific strike and scale thereof have such serious and far reaching political implications at this time." Ridgway replied that he appreciated the "potentialities" of his proposal and recognized that his views were "based primarily on conditions within a single theatre, and that the problem has world-wide aspects." Unlike MacArthur, or most theater commanders in any war, Ridgway was willing to admit that his area of operations was not the most important. However, he still believed that his assault on Pyongyang was necessary to reduce enemy offensive capabilities in case negotiations broke down. As Collins prepared to ramrod approval for the attack through the JCS, Ridgway submitted a revision to his plan omitting advance warnings, a change that the Army chief of staff had already decided was necessary to "avoid placing undue importance" on hitting the capital. Ridgway justified this alteration because his air force had already been bombing "military installations in urban areas" for over a year with warnings, and civilians would probably be insensitive to one more. He also was concerned that prior notice would prompt the enemy to remove war material from the target areas, and any weather delays would allow even more time for the establishment of strong defenses. He admitted that he had altered his plan after receiving a copy of a JCS memorandum to the secretary of defense seeking presidential approval to authorize CIN-CUNC to "increase military pressure on the enemy" in case negotiations broke down, including unrestricted air attacks throughout the Korean peninsula and even hot pursuit over the Manchurian border to take out Communist fighters and antiaircraft defenses that attacked UN aircraft. This last provision caused considerable debate in the State Department and NSC, but in the meantime, the JCS approved Ridgway's revised operation against Pyongyang. The chiefs told him that they had been concerned that warnings singling out the enemy capital might "in the eyes of the world" appear to be an attempt to break off the armistice talks, and they directed that no publicity be given to the "mass" nature of the raid. The JCS considered such tactics "effective utilization of airpower," however, and expected to see more of them.[4]

Ridgway's fears of bad weather proved well founded. When the all-out attack on Pyongyang was finally mounted on 30 July, the weather deteriorated so quickly that all light and medium bombers had to be diverted to secondary targets. Although the 620 fighter and fighter-bomber sorties caused some damage, smoke and cloud coverage made assessment difficult. The attack was considered "profitable but not decisive," and another full-scale effort against the capital was scheduled for 14 August. This time Bomber Command hit the target, but only because the two SAC wings were prepared to use radar assistance to aim their bombs. The new commander, Brig. Gen. Robert Terrill, told SAC headquarters, "We ran into the same visual bombing difficulties we contended with in World War II." When the B-29s took off at 1100, scouts reported only scattered low clouds over the target area, and the B-29s were told to bomb visually. After taking an hour to assemble, rendezvous with fighters, and reach the initial point for the bomb run, the formation found that clouds had thickened to eight-tenth's coverage. The first wing in, the 307th, decided to hold its bombs and switch over to a radar method, the same tactic used by the third wing over the target, the Ninty-eighth. They hit about 65 percent of their objective while taking some hits from enemy antiaircraft guns. The Nineteenth Wing bombed in accordance with its original instructions and wasted its load. Ridgway was disappointed in the results and instructed Weyland to wait for excellent weather for any more major raids. CINCFE believed that the degradation of the Pyongyang strike because of poor visibility "had two marked disadvantages—failure to achieve best military results and the regrettable inflicting of civilian casualties outside the target areas, due to dispersion." Although the results were mediocre, they did encourage Bomber Command to continue to pursue radar bombing methods, which soon become essential for its continued operation.[5]

Ridgway was encouraged by his success in getting permission to bomb Pyongyang, and he reopened the issue of Rashin. He cabled the JCS that his aerial reconnaissance had revealed "extensive stockpiling of materiel and supplies" at the port, and with its highway and rail complex funneling supplies to all areas in the South, it was "a principal focal point for intensifying the enemy supply build-up in the battle area." In reply to queries about his specific plans, Ridgway assured the JCS that because of the uncertain weather conditions for visual bombing, he would mount only one or two normal strikes against the marshaling yard, and he guaranteed that the border would not be violated. The Air Staff supported the request for many reasons. An attack would hamper the enemy supply buildup and might pressure their negotiators out of "dilatory tactics" at the armistice talks. It was in keeping with current JCS directives to conduct no military operations within twelve miles of USSR territory and would show the Communists that "all of their sanctuaries are not privileged." Rashin was also considered "the last major profitable strategic target in Korea." The Air Staff discounted diplomatic concerns about a secret North Korean–USSR treaty giving the Soviets a long-term lease on the port, noting that another port covered in the same agreement had been bombed repeatedly with no Soviet reaction. The JCS agreed with the Air Staff arguments and, after getting presidential approval, authorized Ridgway to attack Rashin. Since the port lay beyond the range of Fifth Air Force fighters, carrier jets provided cover for thirty-five B-29s that conducted the mission in good weather on 25 August. Bomber Command hit the target area with 97 percent of the more than 300 tons of bombs dropped, and no follow-up raids were necessary.[6]

Although Ridgway managed to garner support from the JCS for his attempts to increase military pressure on the Communists by ratcheting up the air war, those efforts did not bear fruit at the armistice talks. During August, Adm. Turner Joy, the chief UN negotiator, tried to justify moving the armistice line northward because the resulting cessation of UN interdiction and strategic bombing would allow the Communists new freedom of movement to build up forces to renew their offensive. Joy argued that only tactical air strikes had anything to do with maintaining the battle line; deeper air and naval operations were a separate advantage that the UN would have to give up in an armistice and were therefore worth trading for additional space. The chief Communist negotiator, North Korean Gen. Nam Il, would accept none of that logic. While decrying the "indiscriminate bombing and bombardment of . . . our peaceful civilians and cities and villages," he admitted that it had "the effectiveness of 100 percent atrocity" and was the primary reason that UN ground forces could maintain their positions. He complained in a diatribe rife with propaganda, "You claim barbarism to be bravery, brutality to be strength, and an indiscriminate bombing and bombardment as a military superiority." He denied that air and naval forces could be considered independently from ground forces and asserted that the positions attained on the battlefield were the result of all combat power combined. Whether he really believed his comments or was just spinning a web of propaganda was irrelevant to the Air Force. Airmen interpreted his speech as support for their own claims about their contributions to the UN effort. The Air Staff got permission from Ridgway to declassify Nam Il's statements and circulated excerpts widely. They especially liked, "It is owing to your strategic air effort of indiscriminate bombing of our area, rather than to your tactical air effort of direct support to the front line, that your ground forces are able to maintain barely and temporarily their present positions." That could be used to support their argument about the superiority of interdiction and strategic bombing over close air support. But if someone accused the Air Force of neglecting tactical missions supporting the ground forces, airmen could also quote Nam Il's often repeated assertion that "it is only by the support of your air and naval forces that your ground forces are barely, temporarily, and unstably maintaining their positions."[7]

PROBLEMS WITH INTERDICTION

There were ominous signs of trouble for American airpower. After his attempts to influence negotiations in the summer, Ridgway's air priorities remained focused on battlefield support, and even the Rashin and Pyongyang attacks were primarily for interdiction, especially with the limitations imposed by the JCS. Yet that was a difficult task in Korea in 1951. As Eduard Mark has pointed out in his study of American air interdiction, the enemy's consumption of supplies was very low during the armistice negotiations, he had a large supply of labor to maintain communications, FEAF had too few aircraft for its many tasks, and the USAF lacked the technology for effective interdiction at night. Ridgway had high hopes that his air forces could prevent the enemy from building up supplies for another offensive, but that proved impossible. As a result, he became somewhat disillusioned with the capabilities of airpower and increasingly suspicious of Air Force claims. He once told Partridge and Stratemeyer, "If all the enemy trucks you report as having destroyed during the past ten days or so were actually kills, then there would not be a truck left in all of Asia." In his postwar memoirs he gave the Air Force credit for saving UN forces from disaster and providing essential support for his ground operations, but he also warned against expecting "miracles of interdiction" in future conflicts.[8]

FEAF would try almost anything to make interdiction operations more effective, including scattering these tetrahedral tacks over North Korean roads. The original caption explains, "The barb is a hollow tetrahedron with air outlets at the center (shown by circles), thus making them as effective against self-sealing tires as other types. The four-pointed barb will always land with at least one barb up, so that any tire coming in contact with it will be punctured." The Third Bomb Wing dropped many of these during its night intruder missions in mid-1951. (RG 342 NA II)

Part of the problem with interpreting the results of interdiction lay with the lack of joint doctrine. There was no agreed-upon definition of the term, and that contributed to differing opinions concerning its success. Ground commanders considered continuing enemy offensives as a sign of the failure of interdiction. Even during lulls in the action, Ridgway complained about the increasing numbers of mortar and artillery rounds falling on his troops. Airmen admitted that their efforts were not decisive but argued that they achieved great success in harassing and limiting the Communist buildup. Mission reports cited statistics about bridges downed, vehicles destroyed, and rail lines cut to demonstrate operational effectiveness.[9]

FEAF, with considerable naval support, tried its best to meet Ridgway's high expectations. FEAF attempted three different plans during 1951 to try to interdict the communications of the Communist armies, but they were all doomed to failure. The first, dubbed Interdiction Plan No. 4 by FEAF, aimed to destroy the entire rail system of North Korea. It proved to be too ambitious. Initially Bomber Command had some success, closing twenty-seven of thirty-nine assigned marshaling yards and rendering unserviceable forty-eight of sixty targeted bridges. But the cost was heavy. When all three B-29 groups conducted a mass raid against the Yalu bridges at Sinuiju on 12 April, swarming MiGs from the Soviet 324th FAD shot down three Superfortresses and damaged seven. Heavy losses during April that reduced Bomber Command to only seventy-five operational aircraft, logistical limitations that cut down the B-29 sortie rate, and the distraction of neutralizing airfields in North Korea meant that Fifth Air Force fighter-bombers had to pick up most of the interdiction load. The rail system proved too resilient to be effectively paralyzed, and the Communist spring offensives revealed the inadequacies of the campaign. When the lines stabilized in June, FEAF initiated Operation STRANGLE, focusing primarily on the road network from railheads to the front. The Navy, Marines, and Fifth Air Force were all assigned separate sectors to

Once the Yalu River thawed out in the spring of 1951, the heavily defended crossings between Sinuiju and Antung became important targets again. This tight bomb pattern on the Korean approaches from Ninety-eighth Bombardment Group B-29s on 7 April straddled the key rail bridge, but it remained standing. When Bomber Command returned in force to try to finish the job five days later, Soviet MiGs caused such heavy losses that Stratemeyer decided that the bridges were too dangerous a target for the medium bombers to attack again. Afterward, the Communists also began to build eight new bypass bridges in the area. (RG 342 NA II)

bomb. Roads were cratered, tetrahedral tacks were dispersed to puncture tires, and delayed-action and butterfly bombs were dropped to discourage repairs. Results again were disappointing. Enemy repair crews exploded the harassing charges with rifle fire or accepted the casualties necessary to fill the craters. Sometimes they just bypassed blockages on secondary roads. And they exploited Air Force limitations at night by conducting most movements after dark. FEAF came to regret the name selected for the operation as "an unfortunate choice of words," because it created high expectations that could not be fulfilled. In August a new campaign was initiated, the Rail Interdiction Program, though press releases and many high-ranking Air Force officers continued to refer to the new operation as STRANGLE. This was a more systematic effort than previous ones. The Navy took responsibility for east-coast lines, Bomber Command hit key bridge complexes, and Fifth Air Force fighter-bombers, which were finally all based within Korea, cut lines all over North Korea. Soon enemy repairs could not keep up with the destruction, and some rail lines were even abandoned. Fifth Air Force planners did not believe that the Chinese could support their forces with their limited truck resources and began to think that they might force the Communist armies to withdraw from the thirty-eighth parallel.[10]

But enemy countermeasures soon turned the tide. The Communists built duplicate highway bridges across key waterways and cached whole bridge sections near important crossings so repairs could be completed quickly. Fifth Air Force intelligence officers estimated that as many as 500,000 soldiers and civilians were working to maintain enemy transportation routes. Increased antiaircraft defenses of key targets took a heavy toll of attacking aircraft and affected their accuracy. Operations were also hindered by the increasing aggressiveness of enemy MiGs, now equipped with drop tanks to extend their range. Air Force planners projected the MiGs' operating radius as 285 nautical miles from Antung, well down the peninsula. Chinese pilots, trained by accompanying Russian units, began to engage in large-scale air battles for the first time in the fall. The Soviets coordinated the Chinese efforts and always sent an equal number of planes for major engagements. By September 1951, the Communists had more than 500 MiGs in their order of battle, whereas FEAF had only about ninety F-86s in theater. The Sabres were limited by operating distances from their bases to only about fifteen to twenty minutes' combat time near the Yalu and could not effectively screen so many MiGs. The enemy interceptors soon forced the less capable F-80 and F-84 fighter-bombers to stay south of the Chongchon River and often pounced on them even there, forcing the UN jets to jettison their bombs and run for their lives. News reports about such incidents alarmed allied ambassadors, who feared that they would lead to possible retaliatory attacks on Manchurian bases, even though the State Department assured them that "enemy air strength had not yet reached highly dangerous proportions." FEAF did not agree. Weyland, who had replaced Stratemeyer after his heart attack in May, warned Vandenberg in September that UN air superiority was in jeopardy unless FEAF could get more Sabres, but the request was denied. Vandenberg's staff advised him that sending more F-86s to Korea would seriously weaken continental air defense, the Air Staff could not support the units in the Far East even if they could be spared, and air superiority could not be guaranteed in Korea unless attacks on supply sources outside the country were permitted.[11]

Communist MiG-15s were not FEAF's only problem in the fall of 1951. Night heckling raids by wood and fabric PO-2 biplanes were becoming quite a nuisance. The "Bed Check Charlies" were almost impossible to detect, even with radar, and one managed to damage F-86s at Kimpo with two small bombs on 23 September. The Air Staff was concerned that the enemy's ability to "operate with slow obsolete biplanes almost at will" showed a serious weakness in Far East Command air defenses. Despite improvements, shortages in anti-aircraft units, deficiencies in radars, and a general lackadaisical attitude about the threat would hinder effective countermeasures into 1952. Interservice disputes also erupted. Navy representatives in Washington alleged that they had been denied the opportunity to participate in operations against the MiGs, but Weyland explained to Vandenberg that Task Force 77 carriers were currently assigned to interdict specific zones of eastern and central Korea and had not asked for other responsibilities. Although he had never denied or restricted the Navy's opportunities, he was not sure that Navy jets could compete with the MiGs. Task Force 77 shared his concerns, and when he inquired about their participation in fighter sweeps and escort duties, the Navy requested time to evaluate its aircraft. When news of this leaked to columnist Drew Pearson, he announced that the Navy had refused to help against the MiGs, further irritating relations between the services. There was also more disgruntlement about tactical air operations for Eighth Army. Although General Almond had departed the theater, others took up his battle with the Air Force over close air support. Maj. Gen. Gerald Thomas of the First Marine Division became so incensed with perceived deficiencies in Fifth Air Force CAS that he declared that he wanted Marine aircraft or none at all and took his complaints up with Ridgway. The new commander of Eighth Army, Gen. James A. Van Fleet, shared many of Thomas's concerns. When Ridgway visited Korea with Collins in late October, Van Fleet tried to persuade them to give him Marine aircraft and asserted that ground forces should control everything within fifty miles of the battle zone. His arguments were muted, however, by the fact that all three generals agreed that close air support needed to be "reduced to the minimum" so priority for the limited air resources available could be given to the interdiction program that seemed so promising at the time.[12]

When JCS chairman Gen. Omar Bradley visited the Far East late in September, "the only dark spot" relating to the future was how to deal with the enemy air buildup, especially if armistice negotiations broke down. He discussed numerous options with Ridgway, including hot pursuit and preemptive attacks, proposals that made UN allies very nervous. Ridgway and Weyland thought that fighters pursuing across the Yalu might be flying into a trap, having to face not only the increased number of aircraft at Chinese bases but possibly Soviet Air Force units from nearby districts that might participate in defensive air operations. Ridgway thought that in case of a Communist air attack, the best that could be hoped for would be to drive enemy jets off forward airfields and out of range of the front lines. Bradley communicated their opposition to hot pursuit to the JCS and NSC, and it was eventually dropped as a proposed action in the event armistice talks failed. When Vandenberg queried Weyland later in October on FEAF reaction to possible preemptive attacks on the Antung airfield complex, Weyland again pleaded for additional Sabres, claiming that the enemy had a 525-to-75 edge in high-performance jet fighters. By then, Vandenberg had also received a letter from Maj. Gen. Frank Everest, now commanding the Fifth Air Force, which explained that because of spare parts shortages, the actual number of Sabres operational on any one day was no more than forty. This time Vandenberg promised to convert a wing of F-80s to the more capable aircraft.[13]

DEFEATING THE B-29s

That decision came too late for the Superfortresses of FEAF Bomber Command. The MiGs had left them alone from 9 July until 22 October to concentrate on UN jets, but on the day before Vandenberg agreed to send more F-86s to Weyland, that respite came to an end. FEAF intelligence discovered several new airfields under construction south of the Yalu River, ninety miles forward from the most advanced Communist air-base complex at Antung in Manchuria. Because of the threat these new airstrips posed to UN air superiority, they had to be destroyed, but Bomber Command, which had generally avoided the worst parts of MiG Alley since its heavy losses in April, was concerned about the 400 percent increase in MiG sightings in September. They did not know it, but the Communist air order of battle included the Soviet 303d and 324th FADs, as well as accompanying Communist Chinese Air

Force units. Bomber Command proposed to attack the targets at night with radar methods, but FEAF decided to give each field one daytime blow first because of the "greater effectiveness of visual, daylight, formation bombing." On 18 October nine B-29s hit Saamcham Airfield unopposed, but a similar raid against Taechon on 22 October was not so lucky. While the twenty-four escorting F-84s maneuvered against thirty MiGs some distance from the bombers, more enemy interceptors came out of the clouds above them. Three made passes through the formation and downed one B-29.[14]

This was just a prelude for the next day, the worst of the war for Bomber Command. FEAF provided all the support it could. Although the swept-wing F-86s were not used for close escort because it was too easy for trigger-happy bomber crewmen to mistake them for MiGs, the thirty-one available were sent out on a sweep to screen ahead of the bombers aiming for Namsi Airfield. The Sabres were boxed in by some of the 140 MiGs defending the target and kept out of the running dogfight that developed behind them. Nine more Superfortresses from the 307th Bombardment Wing, accompanied by forty-five Thunderjets and twelve Royal Australian Air Force (RAAF) Meteors, ran into a swarm of enemy interceptors. The Meteor was one of the first operational jets, and the British plane was badly outclassed by the Soviet fighters. Fifty MiGs circled the formation and attacked during the bomb run, overpowering the overmatched escorts while shooting down three bombers and seriously damaging five more. Most of the surviving B-29s had dead and wounded aboard, and two had to make emergency landings in Korea. The mission report excused the F-84s by observing that 150 F-86s would have been necessary to adequately escort the bombers.[15]

When Bomber Command diverted its effort to interdiction targets, the MiGs followed. Eight B-29s attacking the Sunchon bypass bridge the next day were struck systematically by more than sixty jets that pursued them for seventy miles to Wonsan after fighting through a screen of thirty-five Sabres. One bomber went down in the harbor, where seven of its eleven crewmen were rescued. Four more B-29s received major damage. Twelve F-84s and sixteen RAAF Meteors also did the best they could to protect the beleaguered Superfortresses. After a two-day pause "to evaluate the situation and interrupt the pattern of operations," missions resumed on 27 October. This time, eight B-29s escorted by sixteen Meteors and thirty-three Thunderjets with a further screen of thirty-two F-86s hit the Sinanju railroad bridge. Although 100-plus MiGs intercepted the formation, these pilots did not seem as aggressive or as well trained as those encountered earlier, and only one bomber received severe damage. Another tactic that helped the B-29s was that their flight plan was set

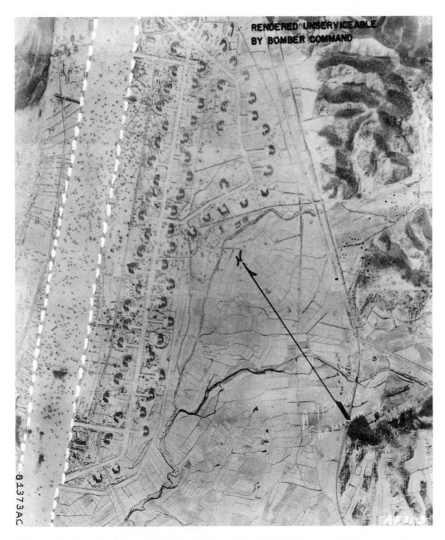

Although B-29s suffered heavy losses in daylight raids on North Korean airstrips in October 1952, the Superfortresses were able to keep the fields unserviceable with subsequent night attacks. The bomb craters on snow-covered Saamcham Airfield in December 1952 are a testament to the effectiveness of Bomber Command's efforts. Their success provided important benefits for United Nations Command by severely limiting the area of operations for Communist air forces. (RG 342 NA II)

up over the Yellow Sea to take advantage of an observation that the MiGs would not fight over water, presumably because the enemy did not want to have their pilots picked up by UN rescue teams. On the last daylight raid of the series, on Songchon railroad bypass bridge on 28 October, Superfortresses were not attacked at all.[16]

During the month, Bomber Command had five aircraft shot down by MiGs and four more damaged severely enough to require salvage, in addition to three lost in accidents. Fifty-five crewmen were killed or missing, and another twelve wounded. These casualties were catastrophic for an organization with fewer than ninety B-29s and crews, especially when most occurred during one week. At the end of the month, a meeting was held in Japan chaired by the new chief of Bomber Command, Brig. Gen. Joe Kelly, and the vice commander of the Fifth Air Force and attended by all the commanders of the bomber and escort units. They concluded that there was no way to stop the MiGs from getting to the bombers once the enemy interceptors attained a position above the B-29s, and that escorts that could not match the MiG's performance were not much use. In addition, fighter commanders complained that their jets were severely hampered by trying to stay with the much slower Superfortresses. The best way for friendly fighters to protect the bombers was to set up a screen to keep enemy jets a substantial distance away, but that was impossible for targets close to the Yalu and enemy sanctuaries. Although not explicitly stated in the minutes of the meeting, many airmen were suspicious that at least some of their opponents were Soviet pilots. Enemy tactics during the October air battles showed many World War II Russian characteristics, and the outstanding performance of certain individuals suggested "the expert showing the recruits how it is done." The enemy's reluctance to risk the capture of any pilots, and later intercepts of ground control transmissions that showed that as many as 90 percent of all Communist flights over Korea were using Russian call signs and controllers, only reinforced such perceptions. After the meeting, Generals Weyland and Kelly agreed to "employ no more B-29 formations on daylight missions under the present military circumstances." With no targets left to justify large B-29 formations that could protect themselves, and concerns about shortages of adequate escorts to counter aggressive attacks on smaller groups of medium bombers, commanders decided to exercise caution until tactics could be reevaluated. Never again would daytime waves of Superfortresses devastate North Korean targets. Newsreels that had once portrayed B-29s as symbols of American might now began to show the "rough go" they were getting from enemy defenses and to announce, "Faster bombers are in the making, but meanwhile our airmen make do."[17]

The events of late October had a wide range of repercussions in Washington. The Air Staff developed plans to sustain attacks against the most forward Communist air bases at Antung and to conduct operations against Red China by providing "sterilized" or unmarked mines to the Nationalist Air Force so that it could covertly mine four Chinese ports. The Senate Armed Services Committee requested "a clear statement of relative capabilities" of the F-86 and MiG-15 in aerial combat from the secretary of defense. The resulting report conceded the Soviet jet's edge in speed and climb but asserted that Sabre advantages in ordnance, control systems, and pilot aggressiveness more than offset those deficiencies. The JCS and USAF staff scrambled to find more F-86s to send to Korea, especially after the secretary of defense again expressed concern about the possibility of a Communist air attack if armistice talks broke down, and Ridgway asked for eight groups to reach parity with the enemy. Their efforts were severely hampered by the fact that North American Aviation factories were making only eleven new Sabres per month. The slump in fighter production was bad enough to inspire an investigation by Senator Lyndon Johnson's preparedness subcommittee, which called for the appointment of a full time "czar" in the Defense Department to establish realistic production targets and then ensure their attainment. After the JCS considered base crowding in the Far East and air defense requirements at home, they decided to reinforce the Far East by purchasing sixty F-86s from Canada. Along with previous augmentations and limited replacements from U.S. production, the FEAF would eventually have two full F-86 wings with a plentiful theater reserve, a total of over 150 aircraft. This was more than were committed to air defense of the United States, and twice as many as were assigned to cover bases in the United Kingdom.[18]

To raise the awareness of the American people about the Red air threat and promote support for an increased "air investment" in the war, Vandenberg held a press conference in mid-November after returning from a visit to the battle zone. He praised the results of Operation STRANGLE (an example of the confusion about the name of the interdiction campaign) and credited it with spurring the enemy air buildup that had created a "no man's air" in northwestern Korea. In a prelude to the scare from *Sputnik* a few years away, he cautioned a public surprised by the MiG-15 not to underestimate Russian technological prowess or determination. He described the October actions in detail and stated that the United States would have to reconsider "the entire issue of air strategy in Korea" if peace talks failed. Reporters interpreted this to mean that the air war might be extended over the Yalu, but Vandenberg refused to amplify his remarks. In his question-and-answer session afterward, the Air Force chief of staff revealed that recent tests of small atomic bombs in

Nevada had "given the Air Force a new tactical weapon which can be used against armies in the field." He qualified this by noting that there were still some technical details to work out on employment and there were no targets in Korea that required such ordnance, but he thought that the new weapons would be perfected and available by the time NATO air forces were built up in Western Europe. He also fended off questions about close air support by noting that both Ridgway and Van Fleet supported the current emphasis on interdiction, and he downplayed the extent of losses suffered by the B-29s in the October air battles.[19]

Bomber Command's daylight defeat caused considerable alarm at SAC headquarters, however. LeMay was concerned about the impact on the deterrent value of his force, as he received expressions of "grave concern" about SAC's ability to execute its war plans. He was incensed at a letter forwarded to the Air Proving Ground from one fighter pilot who hoped that "people there realize that any day the man behind the MIG directs it . . . the MIGs will knock down every B-29 that comes within 125–150 miles" of Manchurian airfields, whether the bombers were escorted or not. The security aspects of that revelation bothered Weyland as well and prompted him to instruct his subordinate commanders to emphasize "rigid self-discipline" in nonofficial correspondence to avoid "injudicious" or compromising information about "new equipment, developments, tactics, or techniques." LeMay explained to Kelly, "The fact that you have had a B-29 formation practically shot out of the air has serious implications, not only in the United States, but among our Allies and enemies as well." The Communists had their air defense problems simplified by the restricted target area and small bomber formations, but LeMay also complained that gunners had gotten careless during the summer lull and were using the wrong ammunition to destroy the MiGs. Problem solving was one of LeMay's greatest strengths, and he put his analytical skills to work on Bomber Command's situation. He suggested larger formations, ammunition studies, and modified firing computers, while promising to get Kelly new B-50 three-gun tail turrets and gunnery trainers better suited to prepare crewmen to deal with jet fighters. However, LeMay was not prepared to do everything to protect his B-29s. He did not want to reveal any details of war plan operations and would not allow Bomber Command to use chaff, electronic radar jamming techniques, cell tactics, or anything else that would give information to the enemy that "possibly will be used against us in the event of all out war."[20]

To survive in the new air environment, the B-29s concentrated on perfecting night bombing. In late 1950, LeMay had started to develop SHORAN (short-range navigation radar) capability for SAC in case they were called on to deliver atomic weapons to support troops in Korea, and he had prodded O'Donnell to investigate preparations for such operations in FEAF. Briggs realized early that normal radar scope bombing in times of poor visibility did not work well in Korea because of the lack of terrain contrast, and experiments with SHORAN there had finally begun in the spring of 1951. By the time of the October crisis, the medium bombers had some proficiency with it, as had been demonstrated during the August attack on Pyongyang. SHORAN is a high-precision position-finding navigation system. A transceiver on the aircraft sends signals to two ground beacons with known positions. By measuring the time required for the signal to make the round-trip, location can be determined by triangulation. The B-29 would travel along a set arc determined by the beacons until positioned over its target. With thorough training, accurate maps, and good reception, Bomber Command expected to bring its average SHORAN probable circular error (CEP) down to less than 500 feet—more than adequate for airfield destruction or bombing of supply points. However, accuracy declined to almost twice that figure during the last few months of 1951, as Bomber Command scrambled to install equipment in all its aircraft and to train all its crews in night bombing with SHORAN. Obviously, the tightly controlled flight path could make the aircraft vulnerable to enemy air defenses, and the B-29s had to resort to various electronic countermeasures to throw off enemy antiaircraft guns, searchlights, and interceptors. After losses began to mount, SAC and FEAF finally allowed the bombers to drop chaff beginning in August 1952, and that proved very effective. Although there were a few rough night raids, the Communists lacked a radar-equipped night fighter and never did employ a proficient night fighter force. The biggest dangers to the medium bombers during these operations were their own telltale contrails, and altitudes sometimes had to be adjusted or missions canceled to avoid them. During the first half of 1952, Bomber Command settled down to a routine of SHORAN operations against enemy airfields and bridges along key rail lines from Sinanju to Sinuiju and Kanggye and continued to improve its CEP as personnel became more familiar with the bombing system.[21]

The strain of almost two years of air war was taking its toll on the aging bombers and their crews, however. Because of a shortage of spare parts, the Air Force could supply FEAF with only enough support for an average of twelve B-29 sorties a day. During 1951, there were twenty-one major B-29 accidents involving engines or propellers, a repetition of a deficiency that had plagued the bombers in World War II. Ridgway became so concerned about the impact of B-29 crashes on the welfare and attitude of civilians around Tokyo that he asked Weyland to consider moving the 98th Bomb Group from Yokota to Okinawa. Crew morale was a worse problem. As enemy opposition increased, active-duty crews faced the possibility of multiple or extended combat tours, and more reservists were recalled to duty. The problems of manning an expanding force while fighting a frustrating limited war would become especially acute for the USAF in 1952.[22]

6
MANNING AND INSPIRING
THE FORCE

The jet age, around which all Air Force publicity is built, is so completely new to most individuals that its very newness is a source of apprehension to those who might otherwise be interested in aviation cadet duty. This apprehension is as old as is invention and progress. It affects those that have no wish to experiment or pioneer, but prefer to take up when the experimentation is over. Classify this as guinea pig fear.

COL. EMMETT B. CASSADY[1]

These people are guilty of using fear of flying as a technical device to shirk responsibilities for which they have been trained and which they have been directed to assume. By resorting to such subterfuge in an attempt to avoid duty not of their preference, they have demonstrated a deplorable lack of the fine moral fibre and character demanded of a commissioned officer.

GEN. CURTIS LEMAY[2]

I think that a large percentage of the self labeled jet hot-rocks back in the B-47 outfits in the Zone of the Interior with their crash helmets and silk scarves could take several lessons from these kids in the B-29 crews. . . . It's an interesting thing to note that most of these kids are Reserves, and darned good ones. I'm really impressed with the caliber of both the maintenance and flight personnel, and with the training system that has molded them into an efficient combat unit.

COL. P. D. FLEMING[3]

At the time the Korean War erupted, the new U.S. Air Force was authorized only 416,314 officers and men, and annual appropriations were sufficient to maintain only forty-two of forty-eight authorized air wings. The war changed that considerably. In November 1951 the Joint Chiefs of Staff agreed on a goal for an increased USAF of 1,210,000 military personnel and 143 wings by mid-1955, and at the end of the conflict the service mustered over 100 wings and almost 1 million officers and airmen.[4] Commitments expanded to match the growing forces, however, and the wartime strain on personnel and the replacement system was considerable. Initially, the length and degree of the deployment of American airpower to Korea had been unclear, but by 1951 it became evident that large reserve recalls would be necessary to relieve overworked active-duty crews in the Far East and elsewhere. These voluntary and involuntary recalls, along with the unfamiliar frustrations of limited war with limited resources, produced a series of incidents that led to a crisis of confidence concerning morale in the Air Force, even in the elite Strategic Air Command.

When the war began, the Air Staff rushed reinforcements to the Far East, most of them deployed on Temporary Duty status because of expectations that they would be needed for a relatively brief period. The first major additions were the SAC crews of the Twenty-second and Ninety-second Medium Bombardment Groups, but many more combat units were to follow. However, FEAF and USAF as a whole remained short of personnel in many technical specialties. The effects of the postwar drawdown and high wages in private industry left the service deficient in specialists in aircraft accessories, ordnance, communication, aviation engineering, and photographic interpretation. The most serious flight crew problems were in the Third Bombardment Group. Navigators and bombardiers for the B-26s had to fly three times the missions of other rated personnel until recalled reservists arrived for training in September. By then, FEAF had filled most of its shortages, at least for the short term, although some specialties such as photo interpreters would take more than a year to bring up to strength. However, the widening of the war brought on by Chinese Communist intervention forced Air Force leaders and planners to face the possibility of a long combat commitment in the Far East while the service was also undergoing significant expansion. Some sort of rotation system would have to be established for Korea while key personnel shortages throughout the Air Force were also being addressed.[5]

In early December 1950, Stratemeyer complained to Washington that many of his airmen had flown as many as 140 combat missions, and their morale was sinking because they saw "only one end—to be killed." He recommended mission limits, but Vandenberg refused to agree, fearing that the demands of the war might not allow such promises to be kept and that such an announcement would cause "adverse comment" from other services and the public, who might conclude that airmen were not doing their fair share. He conceded, however, that USAF "needed a leavening of Korean battle experience" and instructed Stratemeyer to establish a rotation program to return veterans as replacements arrived. The FEAF commander then applied his concept of mission limits to establish eligibility for return to the United States, with criteria of a hundred sorties for single-engine pilots, fifty sorties for crews of multiengined aircraft, one year in theater and 750 hours for troop carriers, and fifty missions for air-sea rescue and weather crews. Reports that Vandenberg received during 1951 indicated that the majority of returning airmen had flown fewer than the required missions. For a while, one exception to the rule applied to jet fighter aces, who were returned to the United States after their fifth victory. This policy was rescinded in February 1952 because FEAF could not afford to lose such capable and experienced leaders early, and the practice had the potential to cause dissension with other pilots required to complete a full combat tour.[6]

While USAF leaders were struggling to establish a rotation policy for Korea, a team from the Air University Human Resources Research Institute was conducting a survey of "human factors" at five FEAF bases. They found much uncertainty about war aims, indicating that more indoctrination was needed, especially for officers in the theater. Whereas the researchers had expected to find "an unwilling group of airmen being led by dedicated officers," instead they discovered the opposite, that "caution, indecision, and division of opinion was more characteristic of officers than of airmen." In a portent of problems to come, the team found that among all pilots, those who flew B-26s were the most dissatisfied with their jobs, "due perhaps to the presence of a large proportion of involuntary Reserves." These reservists also believed that they were being slighted on promotions. Light bomber personnel held unfavorable opinions of the importance of their units in the war, as did B-29 crews. Morale was not high at the five bases surveyed, but the researchers were encouraged that it was not lower, considering the disappointing military situation at the time.[7]

Despite optimistic reports to the chief of staff that aircrews were rotating without experiencing excessive combat exposure, problems foreseen by the study group in B-26 units, along with concerns about mission limits, did not go away with the new policies. In May 1951, Vandenberg received a full report on the relief of the 452d Bombardment Wing commander in Korea. The entire unit had been recalled to active duty from the reserves in August 1950—the first time in Air Force history that this had been done—and it had flown its first combat mission over Korea in October. While the other B-26 wing in Korea had been dedicated to night intruder operations, the 452d was given the more dangerous daylight missions. The relief of one of the Air Force's most respected B-26 veterans attracted much attention within the service, including a thorough examination by the inspector general (IG). Officially, the general concerned was relieved "because of his inability to cope with problems which fall to the lot of combat commanders" and because "his combat leadership was devoid of the exemplary conduct needed to keep his unit at the highest level of effectiveness attainable with resources at his disposal."

In a scene reminiscent of the movie *Twelve O'clock High,* he had complained loudly to visitors that his crews were so overtaxed that they "were getting glassy-eyed, had the shakes, and were yelling in their sleep." The IG reported that airmen had been led to believe that they would be rotated after fifty missions, and after reaching that number, three or four individuals stated that they did not intend to fly any more. When the commander was asked if he had explained that they could lose their ratings and commissions for such a refusal, he said that "they didn't give a damn." He stated that he did not pass down any personnel policies from higher headquarters "to his boys because they didn't believe them and he didn't believe them either." The IG found that the unit was so short of aircraft and combat crews that training had to be neglected in order to meet operational requirements. He conceded that the relieved commander had been "hampered by having people who were called quickly and against their wills," and that many of his airmen had already exceeded the fifty-mission limit while the flow of replacements promised little relief. A change in leadership, along with an improved replacement flow and a stabilized front, improved the unit's morale.[8]

The 452d Bomb Wing flew the Douglas B-26 Invader, USAF's primary light bomber during the early 1950s. Armed with rockets, bombs in an internal bay, and fourteen forward-firing machine guns, the aircraft packed quite a wallop. (RG 342 NA II)

Personnel strains in Korea were exacerbated by the impression of American leaders that the Communists might move on Europe next, necessitating a buildup of military strength there as well. LeMay remained concerned that diversions to Korea would reduce the ability of SAC to carry out its general war mission to attack the Soviet Union. These conflicting requirements complicated the computation of required tour lengths for SAC combat crews attached to FEAF. In January 1951, the commander of FEAF Bomber Command wired LeMay that his B-29 crews were exhausted and needed replacement. They now had between 400 and 600 hours of combat time, and operations were lagging "due to fatigue factors." With normal combat losses, emergency leaves, and hospitalization, and without a well-organized replacement system, the medium bomber groups could not even keep up their authorized strength of thirty crews. In February, SAC and FEAF settled on a goal of six-month combat tours involving the rotation of active-duty personnel between units in the Far East and the United States, designed to produce "an excellent distribution of our newly-acquired Korean experience." Crews were intended to serve only one six-month combat tour, which became a general standard throughout FEAF. The personnel demands would require the voluntary and involuntary recall of many reservists, normally for periods from seventeen to twenty-one months. Despite promises by Secretary Finletter that he would end involuntary recalls as soon as possible, during the first quarter of 1951, almost 20,000 reservists were involuntarily returned to active duty in the Air Force, the largest such call-up of the war. Half were officers.[9]

FEAR OF FLYING

Despite the February agreement, the six-month combat tour goal was hard to reach in 1951. By March, only twenty-five of thirty crews in each FEAF medium bomber group had been rotated, and eight of the replacement crews arrived incomplete. When Vandenberg visited the units in December, he found that their "major morale problem" was that many crews had been on station for more than eight months. He told the disgruntled airmen that relief was on the way and demanded that LeMay fulfill the six-month commitment. There were many reasons why the SAC commander was having trouble with replacements. Reserve recalls and training were going more slowly than anticipated. Many of those coming back on active duty had already seen extensive fighting in World War II. The deputy commander of SAC observed, "A lot of familiar faces are showing up in uniform." Some were not adequately trained for the jobs they were required to fill. A self-proclaimed B-29 "re-tread bombardier" from World War II was recalled to be a radar operator. He learned to operate the radar set on the night of his first combat mission from an officer who was going home; he was on his own for the rest of his tour. Insufficient training was not the only problem with the replacements. Of the first eleven crews provided by Continental Air Command for rotation, twenty-one airmen had to be replaced, usually because of age or physical disqualifications. Others requested grounding because of "fear of flying," the first signs of a problem that would reach crisis proportions in the Air Force by the end of the year.[10]

This was not a new psychological condition. RAF flight surgeons in World War I had diagnosed "aeroneurosis" that could be caused by training stress, accidents, or anxiety about combat. During World War II, Army Air Forces doctors classified pilots suffering from fear of flying separately from those with simple exhaustion. Eighth Air Force psychiatrists identified a transient "fear reaction" that usually disappeared quickly after grounding, as well as a more serious anxiety state about combat flying that developed over time and usually took months to overcome. Airmen who refused to fly without exhibiting any major physical symptoms could be accused of exhibiting a "lack of moral fibre," resulting in grounding and transfer, if not a court-martial. The problem had also appeared in the Twentieth Air Force. By June 1945, almost ninety B-29 crewmen had been removed from flying status for "anxiety reactions," and the commanding general ordered his subordinate commanders to work harder to eliminate flight refusals. During the Korean War, Dr. Lucio Gatto conducted a widely cited study of fear of flying (FOF) that identified two forms that were a bit different from the Eighth Air Force categories: a Basic Universal FOF that was a fear of injury from falling into the ground, which usually appeared in training, and an FOF Syndrome that had more complex causes and generally developed in pilots later in their careers.[11]

The chain of events that led to a phenomenal number of American airmen voluntarily giving up their wings began with the publication of Air Force Regulation (AFR) 35-16 in February 1950. One section directed commanding officers to suspend any individual "assigned or attached for flying who exhibits a fear of flying, a fear of flying certain types of aircraft, or lack of incentive for flying" and to have them examined by a Flying Evaluation Board. Another provision allowed personnel desiring suspension from flying status to submit a request through command channels to USAF Headquarters. This new regulation superseded wartime rules that allowed commanders to suspend officers who lacked incentive to fly under a provision entitled "Undesirable Traits of Character." The intent of the voluntary suspension was to permit rated officers facing personal problems to request a temporary suspension of flying status until they could correct their situation and return. The "fear of flying" provision was designed to allow commanders to dispose of officers who showed an incapacitating fear and to verify it with a psychiatric examination.[12]

This new policy caused no administrative difficulties in the relatively small and professional air service in the months before the Korean War. However, wartime personnel demands and Air Force expansion required a large recall of reserve officers who were not as motivated as active-duty professionals. By the end of 1951, about 800 officers in Air Training Command had taken advantage of the provisions of AFR 35-16 and given up their wings. There were two primary categories of rated officers who made up this group. The first were voluntarily recalled World War II veterans who had the impression that they would not be sent into combat again. The second were involuntarily recalled officers who had no desire to serve at all. The latter group had been selected from records that listed little more than their names, addresses, and specialties, with no hint of their family and business situations or personal motivations, or even details of their previous combat experience. Because of the chaotic state of their records, reservists often experienced problems with promotions or were placed in jobs for which they were unqualified.[13]

Cases were most plentiful in units training B-29 crewmen. It was easiest to find qualified veterans to serve in units with World War II aircraft, and the rapid expansion of SAC and the need to keep its worldwide striking force viable made recalls of Superfortress personnel a high priority. Crews who named their aircraft "The Reluctant Dragon" or "Purple Shaft" might have been expressing ambivalent attitudes about their deployment to the Far East. Combat conditions in Korea were especially harsh for the medium bombers. As described in the previous chapter, heavy losses to enemy MiG-15s in October 1951 caused the suspension of B-29 daylight missions over North Korea. By November 1951, SAC itself had grounded seventy-two observers and twenty-eight pilots for lack of incentive and fear of flying. LeMay refused to tolerate this loss of personnel and took a number of steps to counteract it. These included forcing unmotivated officers to resign, ensuring that only those truly desiring flying status were recalled to fill rated positions, and providing better training and indoctrination for reservists already on duty.[14]

Fear of flying spread through Air Training Command like an epidemic, and 134 more officers requesting grounding in January 1952 caused that organization to take stronger action, as well. An investigating committee found that "most of the individuals involved had made application to be suspended from a flying status as an administrative convenience in order to escape duty in Korea." Commanders were instructed to limit application of fear of flying provisions only to those who exhibited it rather than just professed it, and Flying Evaluation Boards were to base their decisions on acceptable evidence of actual behavior. Any shirking or disobedience of orders to fly by those whose requests were turned down would result in courts-martial or revocation of commissions. A trial at Keesler Air Force Base in February attracted service-wide interest as a test of the new policies. A navigator was convicted of malingering for feigning fear of flying to avoid transfer overseas and was sentenced to dismissal from the service and three months' confinement at hard labor.[15]

Reports from subordinate commands and publicity surrounding impending court-martials finally forced USAF Headquarters to get involved. In March 1952 the acting chief of the Aviation Medicine Division of the Office of the Air Force Surgeon General circulated among the Air Staff a staff study titled "Fear of Flying and Lack of Motivation to Learn to Fly." He cited a number of alarming trends that threatened the Air Force's ability to maintain the necessary quality and quantity of flight crews, beyond just problems with recallees. Among the disturbing findings were statistics that less than one-half of 1 percent of Air Force Reserve Officers' Training Corps (ROTC) graduates had applied for flight training, and that even after lowering qualification requirements, only 700 applications had been received for 1,600 pilot training openings in May. He suggested that the Air Force not only had to find better ways to motivate and train aircrews but also needed "an enthusiastic, sustained, and well-financed program to popularize flying throughout the entire country in order to re-establish a keenness for flying among the youth of the nation." Responses to the study supported its conclusions. Some blamed the lack of interest in flying on apprehension about jet aircraft and an unwillingness to experiment with the new technology. Only by appealing to a younger age group—those seventeen to twenty-one years old—would "exceptions to guinea pigitis" be found. Other suggestions included a television show to influence parental opinion and comic strips and movies to popularize the Air Force. This apparent drop in youth interest in aviation coincides with what historian Joseph Corn has portrayed as a period of decline in "the air-age education movement" in the late 1940s. The images of SAC bombers and the Cold War chilled enthusiasm for visions of global neighborliness and endless possibilities for progress that the airplane had generated in American education for decades. The number of articles on aviation in educational journals and courses incorporating aeronautical themes declined precipitously between the end of World War II and the early 1950s.[16]

While the staff study was circulating, the secretary of the Air Force and chief of staff took action to revise policies concerning fear of flying cases and standardize their handling in subordinate commands. In late March, the Air

At the height of the crisis over the "fear of flying" incidents, Vandenberg took time out to attend Founder's Day ceremonies at West Point on 16 March 1952. Pictured here walking by the superintendent's quarters (from left to right) are Vandenberg, Commander of the First Army Gen. Willis B. Crittenberger, USMA Superintendent Maj. Gen. F. A. Irving, and Army Chief of Staff Gen. J. Lawton Collins. West Point ties gave Vandenberg, class of 1923, and Collins, class of April 1917, a common background that facilitated their working together on the JCS. Although Vandenberg was younger, his exertions on behalf of the Air Force contributed to his rapidly declining health, and he died of cancer in April 1954. (USMA Special Collections)

Staff contacted major commanders to discuss their opinions about proposed changes. LeMay complained that the initial policy was too easy on "dead-beats" without moral courage who were just trying to avoid their responsibility. Trying that approach would result in "an Air Force that won't fight and composed of officers that won't fight." SAC evaluation boards were finding that officers appearing for review of their claims of fear of flying often had corroborating letters from others who had already managed to get their flight status revoked. LeMay wanted them all thrown out of the Air Force and feared that things were "snowballing on us." Secretary Finletter was concerned that current policy forced involuntary reservists to serve their seventeen months in another capacity while letting volunteers get out, and LeMay agreed that they should all be treated the same. He was particularly disgusted with airmen who brought their wives in front of the boards and said, "I am not afraid to fly— my wife is afraid for me to fly." LeMay did not want those kind of "deadbeats" either: "If he can't control his own family, how is he going to control men under him?"[17]

On 16 April, Vandenberg distributed the secretary's new policy to all commanders. Finletter put the responsibility for identifying the truly emotionally sick in the hands of medical officers and declared that any individual who was "professionally and physically qualified" yet still tried to avoid hazardous duty or combat should be separated from the service. Trial by court-martial was not precluded, but it was to be used only as a last resort for "clearly aggravated cases." Vandenberg added that it was imperative that commanders use "strong and understanding leadership" to control the problem and quickly move out affected individuals "before the contagion spreads throughout any unit or base in your command." There were exceptions to the policy for officers with over ten years' service that allowed some to be retained, but the vast majority of the cases involved junior officers with much less time in service.[18]

The secretary's policy statement came during a week in which Air Force "sit-down strikes" were getting considerable publicity. Finletter and Vandenberg had to field questions about them at hearings of the Senate Armed Services Committee on 16 and 17 April looking at military incentive pay and overseas allowances. In testifying about the need for flight pay, Vandenberg was asked the reason for recent "stay down" strikes of flying personnel. He explained that there were several factors involved: incentive pay was less than it used to be, the death rate was going up in combat, and "with involuntary recalls there came much pressure from families to keep the persons from flying." Vandenberg continued to emphasize the latter point in statements to the press. The tumult also attracted the attention of President Truman, and on 18 April the USAF deputy chief of staff for personnel provided the president's military aide with a summary of fourteen pending or completed courts-martial at U.S. air bases "for failure to participate in aerial flights." All were reservists who had been recalled, ten involuntarily. Later in the week, Vandenberg visited Randolph Field in Texas to check on the cases there. Six defendants who called themselves the "Randolph Reserves" had written to Congress and issued a statement accusing the Air Force of a number of transgressions. The public sympathy that this effort generated alarmed Finletter and helped inspire his new policies. After charges against two officers were dropped when medical and psychiatric examinations showed that they were incapable of handling flight assignments, the exasperated chief of staff denied to the press in San Antonio that the Air Force was adopting a "soft attitude" on refusals to fly. He expressed his regret that "a relative handful of recalcitrants" had hurt the good name of 62,000 rated officers prepared to "fly anywhere in the world that the national interest requires."[19]

Procedures outlined in the new policy actually were softer than those adopted by the Air Training Command (ATC) in February, and new instructions were issued to subordinate commands in late April. All officers seeking relief from flying duties were to be segregated at Scott Air Force Base, and any court-martial proceedings against them were to be dropped. The new policies did contribute to a rapid decline in the number of fear of flying cases, and the ATC crisis was over by late summer. More important in controlling the situation, however, was a halt in involuntary recalls of reserve officers and a provision that all volunteers had to be clearly told that they were being recalled for combat crew training and possible assignment to Korea.[20]

Concerns about crew morale and motivation did not abate in the field, however. Recognizing that fear of flying cases were related to problems with recalled reservists, a study done for the chief of staff based on February 1952 statistics revealed that less than 19 percent of the officers in the Air Force were regulars. The figure was less than 15 percent in FEAF. Between April and September 1952, that organization processed twenty-eight fear of flying cases under the new policy. Twenty-four of the airmen were Air Force Reserve; the rest were Air National Guard. Most had World War II combat experience, and sixteen had been recalled involuntarily. Evaluation boards concluded that "they were men of unstable and inadequate personalities" who often "failed to understand why there was a war in Korea, or they were held back by increased age and family responsibilities." Findings in these cases closely paralleled the experience in Air Training Command. Although the FEAF history optimistically reported that administrative supervision and superior leadership had the problem under control by the end of 1952, the report of the command surgeon for 1953 admitted that fear of flying was "more prevalent here in the Far East" than in the Air Force as a whole. Unlike the evaluation boards, he postulated that anxiety about combat hazards in addition to the dangers of normal flight caused most requests to avoid flying, and he reported much success with psychological therapy in such cases.[21]

FEAF fear of flying cases were not limited to multiengined bomber crews. Although the F-86 interceptor pilots got all the publicity and glory and did much to restore the interest of American youth in jets and flying, the fighter-

bomber pilots in less glamorous aircraft had more dangerous and less reward-
ing missions and suffered from far more fear of flying and other symptoms of
combat stress. Problems usually appeared after an average of eighteen missions. Sometimes periods of "enforced idleness" due to bad weather caused an
increase in fear of flying cases, as anxious pilots feared that they had lost their
combat edge. The psychiatric drug of choice for flight surgeons was alcohol.
All USAF combat units received mission whiskey during the war. Although it
was usually handed out by the fifth on a monthly basis, in the Eightieth
Fighter-Bomber squadron, flight surgeons started handing out shots of bour-
bon after each sortie to steady pilots' nerves. This practice did not last long,
however. When pilots were called on to conduct five or six missions in a day,
there was no one sober enough to fly by midafternoon. As with the bomber
crews, those fighter-bomber airmen who suffered from fear of flying were
usually reservists who had been recalled to active duty, and most had World
War II experience.[22]

Perhaps the most eloquent description of the fighter-bomber pilots' plight
was a song popular among Marine airmen providing close air support for UN
forces in early 1953. They especially hated attacks on heavily defended targets
such as Pyongyang—which they called "Ping Pong"—or those in MiG Alley.
The words fit the tune of "On Top of Old Smokey":

> On top of old Ping Pong,
> All covered with flak
> I lost my poor wingman
> He'll never come back.
>
> Though flying is pleasure
> And crashing is grief
> A quick-triggered Commie
> Is worse than a thief.
>
> A thief will just rob you
> And take all you save
> A quick-triggered Commie
> Will lead to the grave.
>
> Now come all ye pilots
> And listen to me
> Never fly over Sinanju
> Or old Kunari.

The moral of this story
Can plainly be seen
Stay east of San Diego
Be a stateside Marine.[23]

THE PROBLEMS ABATE

Although SAC had about 4 percent more regular officers than the Air Force average, the organization still reported 129 fear of flying cases by the end of March 1952. LeMay reviewed every case and was incensed at statements by commanders recommending that some individuals be retained in nonflying duties. He considered almost every case to be an attempt to avoid combat duty and instructed his commanders to take a hard line to make sure that fear of flying problems were "nipped in the bud at the unit level." Whether because of the new Air Force policies or LeMay's pressure, the number of such cases in SAC did decrease. The organization continued to receive voluntarily recalled pilots—over 700 in the first six months of 1953 alone—but USAF sometimes put restrictions on their use. When LeMay tried to rotate one fighter wing from Japan to relieve elements in combat, his request was refused because "this unit comprises many combat returnees and they have volunteered for the Air Defense of Japan, not Korean combat."[24]

The apparent improvement in the motivation of SAC bomber crews might also have resulted from a reduction in the frequency and risk of B-29 missions in Korea. After they had been driven from the daytime skies in October 1951, they operated primarily at night and had fewer targets to bomb. Still, there were signs that commanders in the theater were not completely pleased with the medium bombers' performance. In December 1952, the commander of FEAF Bomber Command, Brig. Gen. William Fisher, proposed a modification in the six-month rotation policy. He thought that a requirement to complete twenty-five combat missions in a five- to seven-month period would "provide an incentive for all crews to attain better performance" and reward the best crews with an early release. LeMay refused to change the current policy, fearing that any step-up in bomber operations would bring crews to their limit too quickly and strain a replacement system that was working smoothly with the six-month rotation. Fisher's proposal was motivated by a concern about excessive aircraft aborts and malfunctions, which Weyland suspected some crews were using as excuses to avoid tough targets. By establishing a fixed number of completed missions as the criterion for rotation instead of a set time period, crews would have more incentive to carry out night raids that

Fighter-bomber pilots suffered from more combat stress than the well-publicized jet aces. Concentrated and competent Communist air defenses made low-level attacks against important targets extremely dangerous. This F-80 is making a forced belly landing at its base in Korea because enemy gunners have shot away its landing gear. The top photo shows it bouncing in the air as it is settled down. Notice the large hole in the fuselage above the wing in the bottom photo. The pilot walked away unhurt. He really earned his mission whisky for that day. (USAF photograph from USMA Special Collections)

were becoming more dangerous as enemy searchlights and night interceptors got more competent and weather conditions deteriorated. By April 1953, abort rates over some difficult targets were "unusually high," and Fisher and Weyland decided to set an example to discourage a recurrence. Investigation of individual cases turned up one commander of a perfectly functioning airplane who had "turned off the target prior to bombs away because he had been illuminated by searchlights and the flak in the target area ahead was very heavy." Fisher reported to LeMay that "even his crew was disgusted, and it appears to be a clear cut case." A court-martial was initiated, but Weyland decided to let the airman resign. The FEAF commander noted that "the primary effect which I wanted has already been obtained through preferring charges." The performance of all Bomber Command crews improved because "their pride ha[d] been hurt," and there was a sharp decrease in the abort rate. Weyland also wanted to avoid any "publicity of cowardice in the face of the enemy" that a trial would bring.[25]

One of LeMay's staff officers who had been a fighter pilot reported to the Ninety-eighth Bomb Wing for duty late in the war, and he wrote back to SAC headquarters about his experiences learning to fly bombers. He was very impressed with the professionalism and competence of the B-29 crews he served with, especially since most of them were reservists. Crew discipline was outstanding, and he was especially amazed by their ability to take off and land "in rain and fog, at night." Enclosed with his letter was a set of baby pictures with humorous captions reflecting the attitudes of the men in his crew. An angry-looking face was labeled, "What—back up to the Yalu?" while a drooling and wide-eyed visage was matched with, "Nope, I don't think combat is affecting me." Under the last picture, which showed a baby with a stubborn look and a set chin, the copy read, "You're damned right they ain't keeping me 7 months." The letter was sent after the armistice had been signed, which probably made such things easier to laugh about. The officer had learned that "there seems to be a slightly different feeling in your stomach when driving along in a bomber and waiting for the other guy to hit you first as compared to having a fighter strapped under your parachute with which to go after him." He told his old bosses, "If your object in sending me over here was to gain this knowledge, you may consider said education acquired."[26]

The U.S. Air Force had also learned a great deal. A number of factors had contributed to the crisis of confidence concerning aircrew motivation during the Korean War. These included poor education of airmen about the reasons for fighting in Korea, sloppy and inconsiderate recall procedures for reservists, and uncertain rotation policies. Revised personnel practices considerably improved service morale and performance, but studies of fear of flying incidents had also highlighted the need to better inform the public about the Air Force mission. Although reducing the age limit, test score requirements, and required duty tour for aviation cadets alleviated the problem of filling pilot quotas, the Air Force leadership realized that it needed to devote more resources to public relations. In mid-July 1953, LeMay traveled to Paramount Studios to consult with Beirne Lay, who had coauthored the novel *Twelve O'clock High* and worked on the script for the movie version. USAF had close relations with Hollywood, and the Air Force Association's program to salute the nation's air arm at the Hollywood Bowl in 1951 was attended by more than thirty top film stars, along with 20,000 service personnel, guests, and conventioneers. Lay was writing the script for another movie that would star Jimmy Stewart, a former World War II bomber pilot himself. The result of the project was *Strategic Air Command*, which came out in 1955. Lay's proposed story line projected that "streaking jet bombers and the newest operational techniques of SAC" would be the "star of the piece," but the film's drama would come from "the groping ascent of a man to his full stature" as a dedicated pilot defending his country. Its message hearkens back to some of the recommendations that came out of the surgeon general's staff study on fear of flying. While glorifying the Air Force and SAC to the American people at large, it also has themes aimed at inspiring reservists. The thinly disguised LeMay character, General Hawkes, recalls Stewart's Tom Hamilton with the express purpose of setting an example for the command by getting him to stay on active duty when his required term of service is up. The reluctant hero is involuntarily taken from the glamorous life of professional baseball and soon meets other recalled reservists complaining about the need to leave the service quickly to attend to family and business responsibilities. But even though his baseball team needs him, he decides to extend beyond his required twenty-one-month tour because of patriotism and a love of flying, especially in the flashy new B-47 jets, thereby inspiring other reservists to do the same. Only when an injury disqualifies him from being a pilot does the hero consider returning to the ballpark. There is no fear of flying or dying here, just a sense of duty and the wonder of flight. The movie was an accurate reflection of the dedication and professionalism of LeMay's revitalized SAC, and it reinforced the USAF image as America's first line of defense.[27]

No one appreciated the pressures on recalled reservists more than the regular officers who served with them. James A. Van Fleet, Jr., USMA class of 1948 and son of the Eighth Army commander, volunteered to fly B-26s in Korea. As has been noted, the light bomber wings relied heavily on the reserves, and he realized the sacrifices they were making. He wrote in a letter to his mother in early 1952:

The time has come that your husband has my support in carrying out America's fight for the right of all men to live without fear. Do not pray for me, but for my crew, who are not professional men, but civilians whom the United States called upon to defend their homes in this moment of need. They have wives who wait for their return, families not yet started. I will do my best. It is my duty at any time.

In the heat of combat, the dividing line between "professional" and "reservist" disappeared quickly. They shared the same success, or the same failure. In this tragic case, the young pilot and his crew died together on their first mission.[28]

7
APPLYING AIR PRESSURE

In summary, finding lucrative targets in North Korea is not an easy task, but it is certainly not an insurmountable one. Finding targets for destruction is basically a problem of directing the available reconnaissance and intelligence effort toward that end. At present it is not so directed. It is believed that once the concept—destruction—is clearly stated and made known to all operations and intelligence agencies, targets can be found, developed, and successfully attacked. Thus, within present restrictions, the maximum pressure can be brought to bear on the Communist Forces.

COL. R. L. RANDOLPH AND LT. COL. B. I. MAYO[1]

I know of no ground commander who has taken part in the Korean war who is satisfied that he is getting the best close air support possible. . . . However, over a period of 18 months, we have conducted a reasonably effective campaign for the first time under a truly unified command—without serious involvement in opposing service policies. It would appear undesirable to become embroiled in them at this late date.

BRIG. GEN. EDWIN WRIGHT[2]

The unfortunate death of young Van Fleet came during a trying time for his father and all UN forces in Korea. As peace negotiations punctuated by heated arguments about armistice lines and prisoner repatriation dragged on, interservice disputes about close air support erupted again at Far East Command Headquarters. Continuing to pursue the issues he had broached with Collins in October, the Eighth Army commander penned a letter to Ridgway in December 1951 outlining his views and summing up a year and a half of Army complaints about the Air Force. While grateful for the air superiority and interdiction program provided by FEAF, he expressed "the reaction of all ground commanders from company to corps level when I state that close support in this theater has not been developed to the degree which ground commanders anticipated." Deficiencies included insufficient sorties available for CAS, airfields too far away from the front lines, delays caused by overcentralized control from the Joint Operations Center and insufficient control parties, and "the failure, since World War II, to develop special aircraft and armament capable of providing more effective close support to the ground forces." He proposed that three squadrons of Marine aircraft be put under his operational

110

control. These propeller-driven planes would be better able to operate from rough fields closer to the front and, despite Air Force claims, were still perceived by ground commanders as better suited for CAS than jet fighter-bombers.[3]

Weyland, who had provided so much support for Patton in World War II, had some sympathy for Van Fleet's position, and his new deputy for operations, Brig. Gen. Jacob Smart, spent considerable time visiting Army units to understand their point of view. He witnessed some infantrymen whom he thought were shooting at imaginary enemies, but on another occasion an artillery shell killed an officer only twenty yards away. He understood why the soldiers wanted any help they could get in rooting the enemy out of dug-in positions, even though he believed that it would be an inefficient use of air-power. He could sense the disappointment in the Air Force that troops felt after heavy air attacks, when the enemy returned to the trenches and rolled their guns back to the mouths of caves to resume firing. Smart was suspicious that the Chinese even set fires on purpose to attract tactical air strikes and provide a false sense of accomplishment, while in reality the effort was a waste of ordnance and diverted aircraft from more important targets. However, it was "understandable that frontline commanders who are concerned with immediate real and imagined threats would show little sympathy for applying available air forces to the destruction of enemy strengths that are remote in distance and time when viewed from their perspective."[4]

Although the airmen in FEAF believed that they understood the ground perspective, they still were not willing to decentralize tactical air support. While conceding the need for continued improvement in tactics and procedures in his reply to Van Fleet's letter, Weyland refused to give up any CAS responsibility. He emphasized that the Air Force had to have total control over all friendly air assets, and it would be inappropriate to depart from a recent agreement at the departmental level on Joint Action Armed Forces (JAAF) that had established such a policy. Ridgway gave both letters to Brig. Gen. Edwin Wright of his staff to review. Good interservice relations were a high priority with Ridgway, who had instituted a program as commander of Eighth Army that involved the interchange of senior noncommissioned officers and petty officers. The knowledge of the perils and hardships faced by the other services strengthened mutual respect and esprit de corps within the ranks. Ridgway expected the same from his officers and was generally very pleased with the cooperation he got from his Air Force and Navy counterparts. In this case, Wright thought that Weyland was being too inflexible but had strong support in his favor from the new JAAF regulations. Wright proposed that Ridgway avoid getting involved in any dispute over interservice policies that might endanger the reasonable effectiveness they had achieved "for the first time under a truly unified command." Instead, he should forward the letters to Collins to discuss with the JCS. Ridgway refused to do so, basically telling his staff to limit knowledge of the dispute to those already involved and to let Weyland and Van Fleet work out their differences.[5]

The dispute eventually simmered down, mainly because of a desire for interservice harmony and the precedent of the new JAAF, though vestiges remained. On the day the younger Van Fleet's B-26 went down, Ridgway and the commander of the Fifth Air Force, Maj. Gen. Frank Everest, met with the Eighth Army commander to discuss the search for the missing airman. After arranging for the handling of personal messages and notifications of next of kin, the discussion turned to enemy air capabilities. The threat of an enemy air buildup after an armistice reinforced Van Fleet's concern about the need to construct new airfields in South Korea, and Ridgway assigned the mission to Weyland "as a matter of urgency." All present also agreed that UN forces needed more aircraft, especially if a peace agreement permitted the enemy to rehabilitate facilities in North Korea and extend airpower southward. Ridgway had initially included a prohibition against any airfield construction in his terms for an armistice but had been ordered by Washington to drop that demand. Giving up that provision was "bitter medicine" to Ridgway, who feared the threat to South Korean security that would come from reestablished North Korean airpower.[6]

Young Van Fleet had died in a night intruder mission trying to hinder the enemy's efforts to sneak supplies up the front. As a staff officer in Tokyo, Smart wanted to ensure that his knowledge of combat conditions was as realistic as possible, so he also flew on one of the B-26 night operations. He called it "an eye opening experience. In the first place, our side of the line was lit up like Fifth Avenue in New York City while the other side was dark as pitch." All towns were blacked out, either on purpose or because of a lack of power, and the only visible lights were on the roads. As the enemy truck drivers became aware of the approach of Smart's airplane, all those lights went out too. A C-47 then dropped a flare, and the bombers behind it tried to pick out something to attack. The same tactic was used against bridges. Even with illumination, targets were hard to spot at night, and heavy enemy antiaircraft fire added to the problems pilots faced. The experience reinforced Smart's opinion about the ineffectiveness of interdiction "when there was little or no activity by enemy ground forces, and their need for additional resources was limited or nonexistent." Airpower could not keep transportation routes destroyed indefinitely, and the enemy had the choice "to fight or not fight as their ammunition and other resources permitted." Far East Command intelligence reports supported his conclusions, indicating that the Communists

This improved facility at Osan was one of the first projects constructed under the UN airfield building program initiated in April 1952. F9F Panther jets of the First Marine Air Wing were rotated up from their southern base at Pohang-dong to fly close air support and interdiction missions from the new airstrip. The fighter-bombers could carry much more ordnance once they were freed from the weight restrictions of catapult launches from carriers. (RG 342 NA II)

were adequately supplying over 900,000 men and had built up the capacity to launch an offensive at any time with fifty divisions.[7]

The Navy shared Smart's frustration with interdiction. By the middle of 1952, its aircraft had been involved in twelve different phases of interdiction, none of which was deemed very successful. From July to October 1950, the carriers had denied the enemy daylight use of roads with armed reconnaissance. In November, they had concentrated on Yalu River bridges. In December 1950 and January 1951, close air support was the top priority, although some interdiction missions were flown along the northeastern coast. In late January, bridge destruction along the east coast rail route became a secondary priority, and it became the main effort for the carriers in February. In March, Task Force 77 succeeded in significantly reducing traffic along its assigned railway, but the enemy shifted operations to the western rail net and resorted to "vastly increased numbers of trucks." The Communist spring offensives of April and May again forced the carrier aircraft to concentrate on close air support, but in June they joined Operation STRANGLE for four months. In

October, Task Force 77 abandoned STRANGLE to join the FEAF program of widespread rail cuts, but the enemy had dispersed enough repair crews to be able to fix 100 breaches in only twenty-four hours. To make these repair efforts more difficult, in January 1952, bombing efforts were concentrated on destroying 1,000- to 4,000-yard sections of track and roadbed, which usually took more than a week to fix. The campaign was supplemented with attacks on small boat traffic in February and with coordinated operations with surface ship gun strikes in April. Despite these efforts, the Navy considered the interdiction effort to be a failure, primarily because of the inability of aircraft to operate effectively at night and in bad weather. Because of such limitations, Task Force 77 aircraft could patrol enemy territory only about 35 percent of the time, and during part of that period only a few night "hecklers" were present. Marine airmen involved in the interdiction campaign trying to catch enemy trucks on bridges and roads at sunrise and sunset had a simpler explanation why their efforts were unsuccessful: "We hate to admit it, but the gooks are just too smart for us."[8]

DEVELOPING A NEW AIRPOWER STRATEGY

As the war and truce talks continued through 1952, the stalemate on the ground and ineffectiveness of air interdiction inspired Smart to look for a better way to apply the airpower that was finally being augmented by increased American production. He directed two members of his staff, Col. R. L. Randolph and Lt. Col. B. I. Mayo, "to devise ways and means of exerting maximum pressure on the Communist Forces in North Korea through optimum application of FEAF effort." Smart was frustrated by the lack of UN progress in ending the war, and his subordinates' mission was "truly a search for new ideas." Randolph and Mayo began with an examination of the course and results of the interdiction campaign, which had been focused on enemy railroads since August 1951. The objective remained to completely cut rail lines at selected points and force the enemy to use roads as the primary channel of supply. Planners then hoped that Fifth Air Force aircraft could cause enough attrition of enemy trucks so that frontline armies could not be supplied, thus subjecting them to "unbearable pressure, despite the lack of offensive ground action." It had not worked, despite over 15,000 rail cuts and at least partial destruction of 199 bridges. Enemy repair efforts, night movement, and MiG attacks had foiled FEAF efforts to close transportation routes. Randolph and Mayo also pointed out that the enemy's daily mortar shell requirement could be carried by only one truck or 100 coolies with A-frames, and it would be vir-

Brig. Gen. Jacob Smart in December 1952. As FEAF deputy for operations, he initiated the search for a better way to use its "destructive power as a political tool," which produced the new strategy of "air pressure." He enjoyed working for Weyland because they could "bounce ideas" off each other in an atmosphere in which innovation was encouraged. "There were free exchanges, which is so very important in conditions where the optimum course of action has to be discovered, weighed, amended, and accepted with prayers and the full realization that the adopted course could be wrong." (RG 342 NA II)

tually impossible for interdiction to stop all such traffic. In addition, FEAF losses had been heavy. The campaign had cost 243 aircraft destroyed and 290 heavily damaged, while only 131 replacements had been received. The two staff officers looked for a way to reapply American airpower to bring real pressure on the Communists to conclude an armistice.[9]

Their staff study was finished on 12 April 1952 and recommended that any air resources beyond those required to maintain air superiority "be employed toward accomplishing the maximum amount of selected destruction, thus making the Korean conflict as costly as possible to the enemy in terms of equipment, supplies, and personnel." Targets were prioritized based on the effect their destruction would have on the enemy, their vulnerability to available weapons, and the probable cost to FEAF of attacking them. Suggested objectives included hydroelectric plants (when they were cleared for attack by the JCS), locomotives and vehicles, stored supplies, and even buildings in cities and villages, especially in areas "active in support of enemy forces." Based on the study, Smart planned to de-emphasize interdiction to concentrate on the new target systems, aiming to "bring about defeat of the enemy as expeditiously as possible" rather than "allowing him to languish in comparative quiescence while we expand our efforts beating up supply routes." He knew that the well-dug-in enemy was under no real pressure on the front line and needed very few supplies to sustain operations during the stalemate. Smart also believed that attacks should be scheduled "against targets of military significance so situated that their destruction will have a deleterious effect upon the morale of the civilian population actively engaged in the logistic support of the enemy forces." He knew that the selection of proper targets to influence enemy decision makers would be difficult, not only for operational reasons, but also because of uncertainty about who those key decision makers were and how their minds worked.[10]

Ridgway's initial determination to influence negotiations with airpower had been tempered by his disappointment in the results of the interdiction campaign and early battles with the JCS about bombing Rashin and Pyongyang. He also appeared hesitant to risk anything that might cause the Communists to break off the peace talks. They had already used air attacks on the negotiating site as an excuse to do that twice—once with apparently faked evidence, and another time because of an actual UN bombing error. His successor in May 1952, Gen. Mark Clark, was not as skeptical about the efficacy of airpower nor as reluctant to confront the JCS, who were also increasingly frustrated by the seemingly interminable armistice discussions. Clark described his previous experience bargaining with the Communists as American high commissioner for Austria as "two years of head-knocking with the Russians to teach me what it is that Communists respect: FORCE." The new commander also may have had more realistic expectations about interdiction. Ridgway had commanded a division and corps in northwestern Europe in the final drive against the Germans in World War II and had seen the obvious effects of Allied airpower on enemy fuel and transportation in speeding final victory. Clark had commanded an army in Italy, where another Operation STRANGLE had caused the Germans great logistical difficulty and produced some battlefield success but had failed to bring swift victory in another deadly struggle in mountainous terrain. When Weyland and Smart approached their new boss about their air pressure strategy, they were pleasantly surprised to find a willing listener. Weyland dealt with Clark personally from then on, providing photographs and plans for all significant air operations, thus keeping the Far East Command staff "out of the target selection business" and strengthening Clark's belief in the importance of hitting targets in enemy rear areas.[11]

The FEAF Target Committee began discussing ways to initiate the new "destruction" campaign soon after the staff study was completed. In late April, Bomber Command's target priorities were redesignated as "airfields, railway systems, and supply and communication centers." In May, Fifth Air Force fighter-bombers conducted two major attacks on industrial targets—motor repair and hand grenade factories in North Korea. By early July, the committee agreed that a revised Target Attack Program had to be developed reflecting the new destruction priorities. Smart cautioned everyone that the modifications should be referred to as "not a major change in policy, but rather a shift in emphasis from delay and disruption operations to destruction." Use of this terminology was intended to prevent arousing "further Army desires for close air support," as well as controversial newspaper headlines.[12]

The FEAF directive outlining the policies of the new "Air Attack Program" was published in the second week of July. It was shaped by three major factors. The first was that the Communists had massed "considerable airpower" in the Far East that could be used offensively against UN forces at any time. The second was that the enemy's major source of supply was off-limits to air attack, while transportation routes from sanctuaries to the front lines for small enemy supply requirements were relatively short. The last key factor was that with a stabilized front, friendly ground forces needed only minimal close air support. First priority for FEAF air action remained air superiority, followed by "maximum selected destruction" and then direct support of ground forces. Specific targets within the second category were prioritized as follows:

1. Aircraft
2. Serviceable airfields
3. Electric power facilities

4. Radar equipment
5. Manufacturing facilities
6. Communication centers
7. Military headquarters
8. Rail repair facilities
9. Vehicle repair facilities
10. Locomotives
11. Supplies, ordnance, petroleum, lubricants
12. Rail cars
13. Vehicles
14. Military personnel
15. Rail bridges and tunnels
16. Marshaling yards
17. Road bridges

The new directive still required that sufficient attacks be maintained against the rail system to prevent it from being able to support "extensive sustained enemy ground operations."[13]

HITTING POWER PLANTS AND CITIES

The first major target for the escalated air campaign would be North Korean hydroelectric plants. In March, Ridgway had rebuffed a request to attack them from Fifth Air Force and FEAF. His reasons had been that intelligence did not justify destroying targets whose primary use was for the civilian economy, and their destruction would not hasten Communist agreement to UN armistice terms. He would sanction attacks only if negotiations were hopelessly deadlocked or were broken off. To prepare for April discussions with the JCS, USAF Headquarters queried FEAF about "the feasibility and desirability" of attacking the installations, also as a possible response to a breakdown or continued deadlock in armistice talks. In preparing a response, FEAF asked Bomber Command what it would take to destroy the targets. The rather gloomy reply discussed the problems of conducting night SHORAN bombing so far from the beacons and predicted that anywhere from nine to twenty-nine days would be needed to achieve 50 percent destruction of each facility. Fifth Air Force was more optimistic, and FEAF told USAF Headquarters that it could accomplish the mission in two or three days, relying heavily on fighter-bombers. A May message from the JCS, probably intended to goad Ridgway into action, reminded him that the most recent directives specifically prohibited attacking only Suiho Dam on the Yalu, and the other power facilities were outside restricted areas. This clarification was based on a very strict reading of a 10 July 1951 compilation of existing JCS directives to CIN-CUNC that refused authority to conduct air and naval action "against hydro-electric installations on the Yalu River" but mentioned no other plants or dams. On 11 June 1952, Weyland sent Clark a plan to bomb all complexes except Suiho. In the meantime, Vandenberg was shepherding removal of all restrictions on attacks against Yalu River hydroelectric installations through the JCS. Far East Command received notification in time to add Suiho to the target list, and Clark approved the attack for 23 or 24 June, when Navy carriers would be available to hit eastern objectives.[14]

The addition of Suiho presented a number of difficulties to FEAF planners beyond its location on the Yalu in MiG Alley. It was a massive structure, the fourth largest dam in the world, and beyond the capabilities of FEAF to destroy. Even the smaller dams turned out to present similar difficulties. Smart reviewed techniques used by RAF "dam-busters" in World War II but discovered that USAF could not emulate them. As a result, penstocks, transformers, and power distribution facilities were targeted at Suiho and the other hydroelectric sites, instead of the dams themselves. The difficulty of completely destroying those diverse objectives limited the long-term effects of the eventual attack to some extent. However, a successful strike against the Suiho complex was seen as critical to applying effective pressure on Communist decision makers. Whereas most of the other hydroelectric facilities were for home use, planners knew that much of Suiho's output went to China.[15]

The operation began on the afternoon of 23 June. The raid on Suiho bears special mention as a model of interservice cooperation. It began with thirty-five F9F Navy Panther jets suppressing enemy defenses, followed by thirty-five Skyraiders with 5,000-pound bomb loads. All had been launched from Task Force 77, which was operating for the first time with four fast carriers. Ten minutes later, 124 Fifth Air Force F-84s hit the target, and the whole operation was protected by 84 F-86s. Within four days, 546 Navy sorties along with 730 by Fifth Air Force fighter-bombers had destroyed 90 percent of North Korea's electric power potential. The attacks had many repercussions besides a reduction in the production of Manchurian industry. The impact on North Korea was apparent to American prisoners of war (POWs), who never got to see the end of any of the propaganda films they were exposed to that summer "because in no instance did the electric power hold out for the full showing." British Labour Party members denounced the bombings in Parliament as a provocation that could lead to World War III, and only Prime Minister Winston Churchill's announcement that he was appointing a British deputy for the UN Command in Korea mollified them. Secretary of

This photograph of the Fusan No. 1 hydroelectric plant in July 1952 shows the heavy damage caused by FEAF fighter-bomber attacks. The original caption proclaimed, "The recent strikes destroyed the generator and control house, severely damaged the entire transformer yard, and made the three panstocks unserviceable." (RG 342 NA II)

Defense Robert Lovett publicly endorsed the addition to Clark's staff, and he also provided the misleading explanation to the press that the JCS had given special permission for the raids on the hydroelectric plants based on "purely military" considerations. American newspapers were not fooled and speculated that the attacks that "plunged much of North Korea and a good part of Manchuria into darkness and industrial paralysis" were the start of a new "get tough" policy to break the stalemate over POW treatment at the peace talks. Some congressmen even questioned why the plants had not been bombed earlier. Both Churchill and Lovett denied that the attacks signified any change in UN policies.[16]

Perhaps most incensed about the action was Brig. Gen. Wiley Ganey, new chief of Bomber Command. Overzealous Fifth Air Force fighter-bombers had taken out targets reserved for his night attacks, and he suspected a deliberate effort within FEAF "to show up fighter bombers and tactical bombers as superior to strategic bombers against any kind of target." He feared that some elements of the Air Force "were playing solidly into the hands of the Navy and

Marines in the airpower struggle." Weyland told Ganey that he too was angry at the course of events, although B-29 losses on night missions in June were on the increase, and Weyland could not have been disappointed that the medium bombers were spared the risk of testing strong enemy defenses. However, he was not pleased with all the fighter-bombers' results and allowed Bomber Command to go after the Chosen Number 2 plant on 19 and 21 July. Although results were excellent, Ganey felt slighted again when the Navy, which had conducted what he called "parasite attacks" on 19 July, took all the credit in the press for damaging the plant.[17]

Ganey suspected that FEAF might have let Fifth Air Force hit Bomber Command's hydroelectric targets to support "FEAF's effort to obtain responsibility for delivering the tactical A-bomb." When Ganey attended a practice at FEAF headquarters for a briefing to be presented to USAF Vice Chief of Staff Gen. Nathan Twining, Weyland stopped Smart from discussing their proposal to General Vandenberg on the subject, leading Ganey to assume that Weyland did not want Bomber Command to know about it. A thorough USAF Headquarters staff study in May 1952 still concluded that the political drawbacks of employing atomic weapons in the Korean conflict, except to avert a disaster, outweighed any military advantages, but commanders in the theater believed differently. The continuing Communist air buildup increased UN commanders' awareness of the vulnerability of their crowded airfields and led Weyland in June to persuade Clark to request nuclear-capable F-84s to hit counterair targets, if required, especially airdromes in Manchuria. War-gaming of the Far East Command Emergency War Plan by Clark's Joint Strategic Plans and Operations Group in April 1952 envisioned that a determined Soviet effort against current UN forces featuring heavy air attacks could take all of Korea and half of Japan, even with American employment of atomic bombs. Inherent in Clark's request, which the JCS granted, was an assumption that SAC units, including the B-50s deployed on Guam, would be going after strategic targets if the war expanded, as well as a belief that the medium bombers were "poorly suited" to penetrate the enemy jet fighters and radar defenses protecting key air installations. Interrogations of Communist prisoners at the time revealed a fairly accurate assessment of American intentions concerning the use of atomic weapons. Both the Chinese and the North Koreans indoctrinated their troops that the United States would not use the bomb in Korea for a number of reasons, including a lack of targets, fear of Soviet retaliation, and humanitarian impulses. Most soldiers believed this, but they also expected that the atomic bomb would be used against them if UN forces suffered significant reversals on the battlefield.[18]

The operations against the hydroelectric plants highlighted a number of misunderstandings and misconceptions within the UN and U.S. command structure about the conduct of the air war. Although the JCS told Ridgway in May that he had possessed the authority to attack any part of the target system except Suiho since the previous July, that was not apparent from other JCS discussions in the spring of 1952. In late March, General Bradley asked for the State Department's opinion about air strikes against the complexes, and Deputy Undersecretary of State H. Freeman Matthews incorrectly stated that it "had never objected to the bombing of power plants." When Matthews asked a week later whether Ridgway was restricted from such action, Vandenberg replied that he did not know. The Air Force chief of staff then mentioned that he planned to query Far East Command about the feasibility of striking a number of targets and asked Matthews if he thought that hydroelectric plants should be added to the list. Matthews saw no reason why not, and Vandenberg included them in the inquiry that inspired FEAF's internal discussions in April. Although the JCS believed that it had fully cleared all obstacles before the June attacks, afterward, Secretary of State Acheson, on a visit to England at the time of the operation, apologized to members of the House of Parliament that he should have consulted them first, but a "snafu" had foiled his intentions to do so. He emphasized to his audience in London, however, that the hydroelectric plants were bombed purely on military grounds, because they "were supplying most of the energy which was used not only by airfields which were operating against us but by radar which was directing fighters against our planes." This issue came up concurrently at a Department of State-JCS meeting. Bradley mentioned how a newsman at Lovett's press conference had asked if the raids had been conducted to refute Senator Robert Taft's accusations that the UN had lost air superiority over North Korea. Bradley complained, "It is amazing how people read political implications into everything."[19]

Perhaps General Smart understood Clausewitz's dictum about the connection between war and politics better than anyone in Washington, for he was indeed aiming for some political impact from his stepped-up aerial operations. His bosses in the theater shared his hopes, though they all agreed that they would tell the press "there was no relationship between these attacks and the armistice talks." The next sign of increased air pressure was an all-out assault on Pyongyang, which the JCS cleared for attack in early July. Operation PRESSURE PUMP on 11 July involved 1,254 sorties from Fifth Air Force, Marine, Navy, Korean, Australian, South African, and British aircraft by day, and fifty-four SHORAN-directed B-29s at night. Psychological warfare leaflets warning civilians to leave the city were dropped before the strike as part of Psychological Operation BLAST, designed to demonstrate the omnipotence of UN airpower and to disrupt industrial activity in the city. Radio Pyongyang was knocked off the air for two days, but when it came back on it announced that the "brutal" attacks had destroyed 1,500 buildings and inflicted thousands of civilian casualties. Intelligence sources reported that one extra benefit from this attack was a direct hit by an errant B-29 on an air-raid shelter used by high-ranking officials that resulted in between 400 and 500 casualties. The effort was repeated on 29 August in an operation called "All United Nations Air Effort," which involved more than 1,400 sorties and had a special purpose: "to achieve psychological benefit from our ability to punish the enemy through airpower" during the Moscow Conference between the Chinese and Russians. Smart also scheduled additional attacks on targets in the far northwest of the peninsula to further "display the effect of our air power" to the attendees.[20]

The way these raids were perceived in different parts of the world reveals much about differing views on the efficacy of American airpower. The British press emphasized the multinational composition of the strike force and gave equal coverage to North Korean accusations of nonmilitary damage, while also noting the irony that antiaircraft guns surrounding the "undefended city" claimed to have downed ten UN aircraft. The *Times* observed, with some optimism and surprise, "the signs are that, in spite of the bombing, the enemy has become more eager for a ceasefire." An Asian delegate to the UN summed up the fears of his bloc: "It seems to me to be a dangerous business, this policy of mass air attacks while the truce talks are going on. Knowing the Chinese, I think it likely that they would regard the signing of an armistice under such military pressure as a loss of face." Chinese representatives in Delhi characterized the recent air attacks as "19th century gun boat tactics" and assured Indian diplomats that the operations would have no effect on Communist forces or negotiators. American press coverage played up the mass nature of the raids, along with the fires and explosions they caused among stockpiled Communist supplies. It also highlighted the heavy defenses of the "peaceful city" and pointed out that civilians had received ample warning about the bombing. Newsreels portrayed "a relentless attack on the city's rich military targets" by UN fighter-bombers of five nations, utilizing film footage provided by the Department of Defense. As with the hydroelectric complex attacks, American newspapers perceived the air activity as part of "a new initiative intended to demonstrate to the Communists that they have nothing to gain and much to lose by prolonging the present deadlock."[21]

Pyongyang was not the only North Korean city or town attacked during the air pressure campaign. An FEAF operational policy directive, dated 10 July 1952, outlined the new Air Attack Program to all subordinate units, and they moved swiftly to comply. Task Force 77 also participated. More than thirty joint "maximum effort air strikes" against key industrial objectives were conducted by Navy and FEAF aircraft in the latter half of 1952. Targets included supply, power, manufacturing, mining, oil, and rail centers. On 20 July, Fifth Air Force B-26s began night attacks on enemy communications centers using incendiary and demolition bombs as part of the implementation of Operations Plan 72-52, designed to destroy "supply concentration points, vehicle repair areas and military installations in towns where damaged buildings were being utilized." To increase the effect of the air attacks, beginning on 13 July, Psychological Operation STRIKE dropped warning leaflets on seventy-eight towns warning civilians to get away from military targets. Illustrations depicted

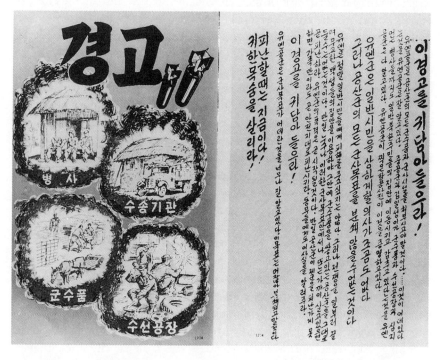

This leaflet is typical of the bombing warnings distributed over North Korea in August 1952. The text of the back page reads, "*Heed This Warning!* The UNC Air Force must destroy all communist military supplies and installations—and it knows where they are. It knows the Chinese Communists and Kim Il Sung have been hiding supplies, repair centers and troops inside your homes and shelters. Aerial photographs continually prove this. The UNC wants to protect Korean civilians, but *the UNC must destroy these military targets.* The UNC does not want to make you suffer, but the Communists—by prolonging the war and using your homes to build up their supplies—force immediate action. If you and your loved ones live in or near these targets, leave immediately. The bombing attacks will start soon. If the Communists will not let you leave, send your families to safety. Warn your friends to do the same. Heed this warning. The UNC knows where these targets are located; they will soon be destroyed. *Flee to safety now! Save your lives!*" (RG 342 NA II)

North Korean transportation routes and support facilities. The text announced that the UN Command knew where all military targets were but wanted to protect innocent civilians. They were advised to leave immediately with their families and friends and to stay away from the danger area for days because of delayed-action bombs. In addition to the 1.8 million "psywar" leaflets dropped by Fifth Air Force between 13 and 26 July, Radio Seoul broadcast a series of warnings before each night attack advising civilians in the specific target area to seek shelter. Newsreels called the bombing operation a "warn 'em, sock 'em campaign." A 5 August press release from General Barcus, now commander of Fifth Air Force, announcing the widespread attacks and explaining that the radio notices and leaflet campaign were a "concerted humanitarian effort at reducing civilian population casualties" still brought protests from the State Department. It feared that the warnings and bombing operations might be exploited by enemy propaganda and would harm the UN position in world opinion. Weyland, who believed that few useful targets remained in North Korean cities and towns anyway, relayed Washington's and General Clark's concerns about the release to the embarrassed Barcus, who said that he got the idea from Weyland's own public information officer.[22]

The press releases stopped and the mass STRIKE warnings were curtailed, although occasionally civilians were still given advance notice of some raids. But the bombing of North Korean towns and cities continued unabated. Superfortresses returned to the daytime skies in September 1952. LeMay, visiting the Far East to coordinate issues concerning the use of atomic forces in the theater, sent the mission off with a pep talk emphasizing the survivability of "a properly formed formation." However, the bulk of the B-29 missions remained at night, and they, too, joined in the bombing of communications centers. By early 1953, Bomber Command considered small cities and towns "the last currently vulnerable link in the supply and distribution system for the communist armies." Intelligence reported that they had been all taken over as supply and troop centers, and they were too heavily "flaked up" for daylight attacks by lighter bombers. Contrail problems and bright moonlight, which helped night interceptors, limited operations along the Yalu to one week a month, so the medium bombers spent most of their time hitting airfields and communications targets in the rest of North Korea.[23]

THE SEARCH FOR TARGETS CONTINUES

Clark was pleased with the strikes against the hydroelectric plants and Pyongyang and was anxious to continue the air pressure campaign. Weyland gave him a detailed briefing on FEAF target selection in late July and explained that they did not expect to find any targets in North Korea comparable in importance to the power facilities. The key military installations in most towns and cities had already been hit, and "incidental to the destruction of those military objectives," in Weyland's estimation, "the destruction of the towns and cities ranged from forty to ninety per cent." He said that he could wipe out the rest of the urban areas but was loath to do so because they were "primarily residential." Clark agreed that "he did not himself want to recommend the complete destruction of these towns." Weyland then covered the remaining target possibilities: Rashin, Sinuiju, Uiju, and some metallurgy plants and installations. Clark offered to check into remaining JCS restrictions about Rashin and also agreed to study a memorandum from Weyland that asked the JCS to give CINCFE authority to conduct preemptive strikes against Manchurian airfields "if it became evident that the Communists were about to launch a major attack against our installations." Weyland did not expect Clark to submit the request, nor the JCS to grant it, but Clark did authorize photographic reconnaissance missions by an RF-80 and two RF-86s over Manchurian airfields that were executed on 1 August.[24]

Weyland must have also provided a copy of his request to Vandenberg, because in early August, the Air Force chief of staff took up the issue with the JCS. He noted that the compilation of JCS directives furnished to CINCFE in July 1951 emphasized that only the JCS could authorize retaliatory strikes against the Chinese mainland or Manchuria, and the president had to approve any preemptive attacks. At that time, the Communist Chinese Air Force (CCAF) was estimated to have 1,000 aircraft, of which 400 were jet fighters. Vandenberg estimated that the CCAF now had 2,100 aircraft, including 1,300 jets, and CINCFE needed to be able to take action without the delays involved in getting clearance from Washington. Although the JCS remained reluctant to give Clark such expanded authority, it did have the Joint Strategic Plans Committee do a thorough study of Chinese targets to determine what the requirements would be to expand the war. Plans to destroy the capability of the CCAF envisioned an initial night attack on ten jet bases, followed by the bombing of twenty-six more bases and two repair facilities within eight days. The initial attack would require 1,000 tons of high-explosive bombs or ten atomic weapons, and the follow-ups would need much more—14,000 tons of high-explosive bombs or eighteen A-bombs. Five thousand tons of conventional weapons would be required each month to keep the CCAF crippled. After that, overland lines of communication could be interdicted with an initial attack of 9,500 tons of high explosives or fifteen atomic weapons and a reattack requirement of 10,000 tons of high explosives per month. Another

27,000 tons of high explosives could take out key power and production facilities. All these estimates assumed ideal bombing conditions; requirements would be about triple otherwise. To carry out the full attack plan, FEAF would need six medium bomber wings and five fighter-bomber wings, requiring considerable augmentation that would stretch USAF resources thin and leave many other areas vulnerable to the Soviets. The JCS preferred to let its current directives stand, while hoping that an armistice could be achieved with the forces then at FEAF disposal.[25]

Some members of the FEAF staff remained skeptical about the shift from interdiction to destruction, most notably Brig. Gen. Charles Banfill, Weyland's deputy for intelligence. In late August, he sent Smart a detailed memorandum outlining the reasons why "factors restricting the successful application of this program are of such a nature as to make results commensurate with the cost extremely doubtful." The enemy had moved most industrial facilities into a "safety zone" in the northeast that was heavily defended and out of range for Fifth Air Force fighter-bombers and SHORAN stations. Other smaller targets had been moved underground. The principal sources of supply and most important strategic targets, however, were outside Korea's borders. Banfill lamented, "We are somewhat in the position of trying to starve a beggar by raiding his pantry when we know he gets his meals from his rich relatives up the street." He was concerned that while FEAF aircraft searched for the few lucrative targets to destroy, unrestricted enemy transportation was allowing Communist forces to increase their artillery fire by a factor of ten and triple UN casualties. He concluded, "Although rail interdiction may not prove decisive, statistical evidence indicates that immediate resumption of the rail interdiction program is warranted."[26]

Smart sent back an equally detailed reply explaining his rationale for the new program. While conceding that "the majority of medium bombardment targets remaining throughout North Korea appear to be of marginal value," he argued that attacking them was still more useful than interdiction. Political and military restrictions combined with a static battle front made an effective program of interdiction "almost impossible of execution." Smart continued that the new policy had elicited "a more telling response from the enemy," as evidenced by "references to our 'savagery' by even the Communist armistice delegation." He interpreted the increase in enemy artillery fire as "a retributive reaction to our present pattern of air action, rather than the expenditure of a handy surplus accumulated since the curtailment of our interdiction program." If that was true, goading the enemy into action would increase supply requirements and generate some "truly remunerative air targets." He concluded, "I feel that the purpose of any air action is to bring about defeat of the enemy as expeditiously as possible, not merely to complicate his maintenance of a position in which demonstrably he not only can support but actually can replenish himself, despite our efforts to prevent his doing so." However, interdiction was just de-emphasized, not prohibited, while air pressure was applied "against an expanded target spectrum."[27]

Van Fleet also took advantage of the change in UN command to resurface his complaints about close air support. He proposed that most air effort be dedicated to the "forward battle area," that each of his corps get a Marine squadron in direct support, and that all air strikes be controlled by Army personnel. Weyland was indignant that Van Fleet had bypassed him and gone straight to Clark, and he lectured his boss on all the reasons why FEAF needed to control tactical air operations. Clark gave the proposal to his staff to study and eventually approved some "experiments" to improve air-ground operations. Van Fleet also asked for more B-29s in close support to hit 110 suitable targets in forward areas. Weyland did not believe that there were anywhere near that many lucrative tactical targets, and the operational record proved him right. Far East Command took no action on that request, as by that time, Weyland had convinced Clark that FEAF airpower was better applied contributing to *his* overall mission to bring the war to an end. In fact, Clark became so enamored with the possibilities of air pressure that he asked Weyland to get some SAC B-36s "on a rotational deal as a psychological threat."[28]

Weyland and Barcus "did lean over backward in meeting any and all legitimate requests from the ground forces," including devoting more B-29s to the main battle area, not just to prove their sincerity to Clark and Van Fleet but also because the airmen knew that Eighth Army really needed their support. This was brought home to Secretary Finletter during a visit to Seoul in October. During a private briefing that he and Weyland received from Van Fleet, the Eighth Army commander made "the candid revelation that the UN forces are in combat with a drastic shortage of artillery and ammunition." They had only 25 percent of the required 155mm rounds, and medium and light artillery was rationed at about 50 percent the normal rate of fire. This astounded the secretary. Weyland explained that despite periodic denials by the Army that any shortage existed, "every front-line division commander is aware of it." That was one of the primary reasons "for the Army's requests for exorbitant amounts of close air support—in order to substitute bombers on targets that would normally be fired upon by artillery." Clark barraged the Army Staff with requests for more artillery ammunition, arguing that shortages curtailed even limited offensive capabilities and "any appreciable decrease in our artillery fires has resulted in an increase in friendly casualties." He thought it ironic that he had to reduce his supply rate while enemy fires had tripled,

Far East commander Gen. Mark Clark (left) and Eighth Army commander Gen. James Van Fleet leave the briefing room at the forward command post of the Third Infantry Division in Korea. Both wrestled throughout 1952 with artillery shortages that limited UNC operations and contributed to Van Fleet's call for increased close air support. Clark did not allow such requests to detract from his air pressure campaign, however. (USMA Special Collections)

another sign of the ineffectiveness of aerial interdiction in static conditions. The Army Staff struggled with limited production capabilities at home and even shifted resources from Europe, taking "the grave risk of extremely low ammunition reserves for our European Forces and those of NATO Allies."[29]

Once in a while during 1952 FEAF did manage to find some lucrative industrial targets to hit. Mining facilities were attacked, and strikes were conducted against the remnants of North Korean industry that were mostly concentrated along the Soviet and Manchurian frontier. As Banfill had pointed out, many of these targets were out of range of Fifth Air Force jets. When Bomber Command conducted its last great daylight raid of the war against the Kowon marshaling yard in October, Banshees from Navy carriers had to serve as escorts. Usually, however, naval aircraft acted alone to hit such objectives. The largest carrier strike of the war occurred in September when 142 planes from three carriers destroyed the Aoji oil refinery and attacked other industrial targets at Munsan and Ch'ongjin. These were in an area less than five miles from Manchuria and less than eleven miles from the USSR, and the raids caught enemy fighters and flak defense completely by surprise. This time the British were notified a few days before the attacks, and they agreed that the objectives were "good military targets."[30]

In his messages to the JCS in late 1952, Clark continued to emphasize "firmness in negotiations to be supported militarily by continued heavy bombing attacks." The JCS agreed that "the principal factor favorable to the UNC in the present military situation on Korea is the air superiority which the UNC forces hold over North Korea." It deprived the Communists of the ability to support larger forces, enabled outnumbered UN ground forces to hold their positions, and constituted the most potent means to pressure the enemy into agreeing to acceptable armistice terms. At one time Bradley and Vandenberg even proposed to try to intimidate China with a mass B-29 raid aimed at Shanghai. The formation would come close enough to get picked up on radar and then "veer off about fifteen miles away and fly down the coast." The State Department discouraged it, however, fearing that such a "show of force might boomerang" with allies and world opinion. At the same time, agencies in Washington and the Far East continued to worry about the Communist air buildup that threatened UN air superiority. The Central Intelligence Agency (CIA) noted any increase in aircraft based in Manchuria and declared "Soviet participation in enemy air operations is so extensive that a *de facto* air war exists over North Korea between the UN and USSR." Ironically, by mid-1952, coordination between the CCAF and its Soviet mentors had almost completely broken down, but concerns that the Russians were really running the Communist air war became great enough in the Department of Defense that the secretaries of the Air Force and Army tried to persuade the State Department to allow more publicity about Soviet personnel fighting directly against American forces. Planning also continued for actions to be conducted in case negotiations broke down or the war escalated. Far East Command and the JCS considered air options, including attacks on the USSR, the use of atomic or chemical weapons, and the bombing of Chinese airdromes and communication centers.[31]

In the meantime, they also remained alert for any signs that the air pressure campaign might be working. In September, Clark transmitted an intelligence report to the JCS stating that bombing was breaking down civilian morale in North Korea. Cities and towns that had been subjected to UN air attacks were "bordering on panic." Civilians who had joined labor battalions because of job and food shortages or conscription were now deserting to return to their homes. They believed that the air attacks were really the prelude to a UN general offensive to end the war. The report also noted that the North Korean government was afraid that air attacks would motivate many civilians to join UN guerrillas. Information provided to the FEAF Target Committee added that the Communist government had to send special agents to help control the unrest in those cities hardest hit by UN air blows. Clark's optimistic assessment was seconded by the ambassador to Japan, but one "ancient report" was not enough to persuade the State Department or the JCS that an armistice was imminent. They continued to look for other signs that air pressure was producing results. Meetings between representatives of those agencies in September show a reversal of roles from two years earlier. Now military leaders were stressing the potential of airpower, while civilians expressed caution or skepticism. When Deputy Assistant Secretary of State U. Alexis Johnson stated that his department was "perturbed by the intelligence that Communist artillery and mortar have fired more rounds in the past month than ever before," despite the military pressure of stepped-up air raids, JCS representatives immediately defended the strategy. Cabell, now director of the Joint Staff, replied, "The more artillery they have the more targets we have." He explained that the campaign would take time to work, but the coming winter would increase the enemy's need for shelter and make targets easier to find. Twining added, "We are continuing to shoot down MiGs and if they weren't hurting they wouldn't send the MiGs down." Even the chief of naval operations offered support, citing the fact that a Marine Corsair had recently shot down a MiG as evidence that the Communists were running out of competent pilots. However, such optimism waned as the talks dragged on through the year, and the search continued for some way to apply more effective air pressure to produce an acceptable armistice.[32]

8

THE QUEST FOR BETTER
BOMBS AND BOMBING

Shoran, as you know, has a line of sight range, therefore, one of our major limita-
tions is the 210 mile range of the Shoran bombing equipment. There are lucrative tar-
gets beyond this limit. By bombing at altitudes above 25,000 feet some slight extension
can be had but at the expense of accuracy. Therefore, it is evident that to do our job we
need a longer range Shoran. I strongly recommend that the necessary research and
development be initiated to provide us with a system for accurate Shoran bombing at
ranges of 3,000 miles.

BRIG. GEN. WILEY D. GANEY[1]

There is no pay-off for a weapon which is erratic, temperamental and a logistical
burden unless its efficiency is very high relative to other munitions. While a very
unique characteristic could make it of interest for special purposes, BW-CW [biological
warfare and chemical warfare] can only incapacitate or kill and this is a characteristic
of most munitions. At present BW-CW appears to be no competitor to the atomic
weapon as a casualty producer and indeed is possibly but an even match for the newer
types of HE [high-explosive] frag bombs which are logistically simple and destroy mate-
rial along with personnel.

MAJ. GEN. HOWARD G. BUNKER[2]

Smart's air pressure strategy was the latest in a long series of efforts by American airmen to find the most efficient and effective method of employing their
airpower. The search was not just limited to tactics and techniques, it also
encompassed technology. And many of the new developments were motivated by the desire for accuracy that had shaped concepts of American airpower since the development of precision bombing doctrine at the Air Corps
Tactical School in the 1930s.[3]

The guided munitions that were so effective against Iraq in the Persian
Gulf War evolved from much simpler Azon bombs first used during World
War II. These "azimuth only" bombs could be guided by radio signals that
varied the pitch of their stabilizing fins to reduce deflection errors. The Sev-
enth Bomb Group used them to destroy forty bridges in the China-Burma-
India theater, though tests in Europe were less promising. Azon bombs were

limited in availability and reliability and were unpopular with pilots, who felt vulnerable while maintaining a straight and level course to guide them.[4]

When the Korean War erupted, FEAF quickly asked for some of the ordnance, now called Razon bombs, to help its bridge-busting efforts. An enterprising staff officer computed that the cost of flying hours and conventional munitions necessary to destroy one railway bridge in Seoul amounted to at least $781,000, and the guided munitions promised to be more efficient and economical. Technicians from the Air Material Command and Air Proving Ground accompanied the ordnance to prepare them for combat. However, difficulties outfitting the B-29s of the Nineteenth Bomb Group, combined with radio receivers that had deteriorated during storage, produced disappointing results. Of 228 bombs dropped during a test period in September 1950, only 110 could be satisfactorily controlled. Eventually, most of the problems were solved, and the last 150 bombs dropped had a control reliability of 96 percent. A total of 489 were used to destroy fifteen bridges. The project officer estimated that well-trained crews could knock out a bridge with a maximum of only four of the 1,000-pound bombs.[5]

The use of Razon was suspended in December 1950 in favor of the larger 12,000-pound Tarzon bombs. Like its predecessor, the new system required bombardiers to track the bomb by a burning flare on its tail and send steering signals by radio, but again, there was a whole series of bugs to work out. By March, everything seemed in order to use Tarzon in combat, and the weapon was employed unsuccessfully against key bridges at Sinuiju. However, operations the next month revealed that the bomb could not be jettisoned safely in an emergency, since the tail assembly had a tendency to break off and automatically arm the bomb. FEAF suspended Tarzon operations after twenty-eight had been used in combat; twelve had been controllable, and six had destroyed their targets. The project officer maintained that "one guided bomb is worth one thousand conventional bombs against line targets," but FEAF terminated the project anyway in late 1951. Weyland told the Air Staff in Washington that there were practically no appropriate Tarzon targets remaining, the effort of protecting the vulnerable delivery aircraft against flak and fighters was not worth the "small immediate tactical value realized from these missile drops," and the maintenance of Razon-Tarzon capability detracted too much from the Nineteenth Bomb Group's proficiency with visual and SHORAN bombing. In early 1953, FEAF briefly considered employing one of the Tarzon bombs that remained in theater against the transmitter for Radio Pyongyang, but it had no planes suitably modified to carry it. Despite the project's poor results, the Air Force managed to score some public relations points with it. Even after the FEAF project was terminated, the Air Force furnished film demonstrating the precision of the "secret" weapon to news-reels, which then speculated in accompanying narratives that the Reds had to be wondering why our bombing against them was so accurate.[6]

FEAF's disappointing experience with guided munitions did not discourage the Navy from trying its own experiments. Between 28 August and 2 September 1952, Guided Missile Unit (GMU) 90 launched six F6F-5K Hellcat drones from the decks of the carrier *Boxer* against targets in North Korea. The aircraft carried a one-ton bomb load and a television camera instead of a pilot. Once launched, it was guided by a mother ship that monitored the TV image and steered the drone via radio control. This was the same system tested by the AAF with "War-Weary" bombers in Project APHRODITE during World War II and proved to be just as unsuccessful for the Navy. One missile hit an undefended bridge, another had to be ditched because of faulty controls, and the others missed because of enemy jamming or human error. Although the commander of GMU 90 recommended that assault drones be put into operational use until more advanced missiles became available, his superiors did not agree. The television camera was too limited in its capabilities to pick up anything but high-contrast targets, and the expensive drones were very vulnerable to ground fire. In order to carry the drones on crowded flight decks, more valuable combat aircraft had to be left ashore. Evaluators did see some promise, however, in the system's reconnaissance potential. Two missions provided terrain pictures 100 miles from the *Boxer,* a foreshadowing of the capabilities demonstrated by the remotely piloted vehicles (RPVs) in use today. As with the Tarzon bombs, the Navy provided film clips of the drones for the newsreels. A segment entitled "Navy Launches Robot War" proclaimed the dawn of a new era in warfare, describing "guided missiles for the first time in combat, bringing the push button war of tomorrow into present day reality." The narrator even speculated that the robot bombers might "someday eliminate the human element from air war."[7]

The strangest air projectile tested was the HAIL missile. During World War I, the French had developed pencil-size steel darts called fléchettes that could be dropped on enemy infantry or cavalry from canisters carried under the fuselage of a plane. If released from an altitude of 1,500 feet, the needle-sharp missiles could gather enough momentum from gravity to go completely through the body of a horse. Several other nations also adopted the weapon, but it soon gave way to more sophisticated ordnance. The concept appeared again in Korea during the summer of 1951 with the HAIL project. These finned bullets were designed to be released from B-29 hoppers or a special fighter-bomber belly tank from 10,000 feet, and then develop enough penetrating force to pierce the steel helmets of ground troops. Eighty thousand of the antipersonnel weapons could be carried by one Superfortress, and with a ground dispersion of four missiles per square yard, theoretically, one bomb load could cover quite a wide area. The FEAF target analysis division believed that the weapon could be used for flak suppression or against enemy construction projects, but it was primarily seen as something to decimate large offensive concentrations. Bomber Command tried to get the missiles to use against enemy searchlights but could not get permission. The name of the missile was eventually changed to LAZY DOG to avoid hinting at its purpose, but that had no impact on its utility. Communist forces remained so dispersed or dug-in that its employment was never considered practical.[8]

Although high-explosive bombs, napalm, rockets, and machine gun bullets remained the primary ordnance for close support and transportation interdiction, by 1952, each service took a somewhat different approach in delivering them. Since Navy jets could not carry much bomb weight because of the limited capacity of the catapults that flung them off the carrier decks, they were given the role of flak suppression for the Corsairs and Skyraiders that were the primary strike aircraft. FEAF considered the F-84E its best fighter-bomber,

The F-84 Thunderjet was the primary FEAF fighter-bomber in Korea. This aircraft from the Forty-ninth Fighter-Bomber Wing is using jet-assisted takeoff to lift its maximum load of two 1,000-pound bombs from a Korean runway too short to allow a normal takeoff. (RG 342 NA II)

with a maximum bomb load of two 1,000-pound bombs and four five-inch rockets. Modified F-80Cs could carry over 4,000 pounds of ordnance in ideal conditions. However, Korean runways and temperatures were not ideal, and FEAF aircraft usually could not operate with their maximum loads.[9]

Although the naval propeller aircraft could carry more bombs, both services recognized that jets were more survivable. Neither could afford heavy losses of their valuable assets, and in mid-1952 they were prompted to change their tactics because of more accurate enemy ground fire. During the strikes against Pyongyang, Fifth Air Force fighter-bombers sustained significant damage on 27 of every 1,000 sorties. Operations analysts discovered that most hits were received at altitudes below 2,500 feet, and Barcus established a minimum altitude of 3,000 feet for fighter-bomber attacks. Vice Adm. J. J. "Jocko" Clark, commander of the Seventh Fleet, took similar action with his flyers of Task Force 77, ordering them to recover from dive-bombing attacks at the same height. This resulted in considerable degradation in bombing accuracy, since bombs had to be released at 5,000 feet or higher to allow pullout at the new minimum altitude. An intensive Fifth Air Force training program could only achieve a practice CEP of 225 feet from the increased elevation, and in combat, results were worse. In early 1953, operations analysts expected that only 16 percent of bombs from fighter-bombers would fall within a circle with a radius of 150 feet, and by the end of the war, less than 50 percent of their deliveries were coming within 500 feet of target center. Only 4 percent of bombs were hits on pinpoint targets. This was a considerable decline from the 11 percent direct hits achieved during 1952. The accuracy of attacks on line targets had also deteriorated, though not as much. The Navy, too, was concerned about a falloff in accuracy. Carrier pilots had been using glide-bombing tactics suited for rail interdiction, but with the shift to more heavily defended transportation and supply centers, air groups had to switch back to neglected dive bombing. The commander of Task Force 77 declared, "The Korean war is ultimately a dive bombing campaign. Dive bombing must be revived." As with the Fifth Air Force, he ordered more training to correct deficiencies. The Marines had continued to focus on dive bombing and close air support and had not enforced the altitude restrictions, which increased the risk to their aircraft but maintained their high esteem with the ground troops they supported.[10]

NIGHT BOMBING AND RADAR AIDS

Interdiction results against vehicles were also disappointing, reflecting the continuing difficulties involved in night bombing. Tests conducted against trucks demonstrated that bombs had to impact within fifty feet to cause damage, and operations analysts concluded that night intruders could expect to destroy only 1.8 vehicles for every 100 bombs dropped. Both the 3d and 452d (later redesignated the 17th) Bomb Wings had been dedicated to night operations in June 1951, but that had not improved effectiveness. Many of the B-26s received to replace lost aircraft were not properly modified for night combat operations, and by late 1952, FEAF's official position was that the Invaders were "completely inadequate to perform night intruder missions." Personnel problems also contributed to these deficiencies. Since there were no B-26 units in the United States to provide trained replacement crews, and training schools were limited in capacity and lacking facilities, new light bomber crews arrived in theater poorly prepared for combat. The Fifth Air Force staff estimated that only one in ten of the B-26 observers who dropped the bombs had been to bombardment school, and the others were just becoming proficient when they became due for rotation. With the implementation of Operations Plan 72-52, Barcus shifted most of the B-26 effort to attacks on key supply centers, and eventually most sorties were conducted during the day. To keep losses down, an altitude restriction of 4,000 feet was placed on all but the most experienced crews. Only one squadron from each wing remained dedicated to the night missions. By the end of 1952, using new "hunter-killer" or roadblock techniques, they were claiming almost four vehicles destroyed per sortie, but that was not enough to cause any difficulties for Communist forces on a stable front. The Navy experience was similar, and in mid-1952 it began to divert most air assets from interdiction to close air support and CHEROKEE strikes—attacks against enemy supplies and reserves behind the front. Although the Navy and Air Force continued to operate basically in separate zones, joint air operations improved considerably during 1952. Much of this was due to the cordial relations between Vice Admiral Clark and his FEAF counterparts. He came to see Barcus often, and the Fifth Air Force commander sometimes visited Clark aboard ship. Clark was very responsive to FEAF requests for support. FEAF was especially impressed when Clark steamed his whole fleet north to rescue the navigator who had survived from the RB-29 shot down near Vladivostok. Interservice relations were also improved by General Clark's establishment of a true joint staff for Far East Command on 1 January 1953, with much greater participation from the Navy and Air Force, although air operations continued to be planned independently by those services.[11]

The remaining B-26 night operations, as well as the main B-29 effort, still relied primarily on SHORAN to place bombs on deep objectives. For strikes after dark close to the front lines, another system was used. The Fifth Air

Force's 502d Tactical Air Control Group operated a number of AN/MPQ-2 radars along the front. This was an improved version of the SCR/584 gun-laying radar from World War II. The radar operators were often referred to as "cliff-dwellers" because they lived out of vans that were often situated on high ground to maximize their coverage. In early 1951, they discovered that they could do more than just direct aircraft to and from targets; they could also determine when bombs should be dropped. The ground operator would first pick the target to be attacked, lock onto the incoming bomber, and compute the bomb release point based on the plane's course, speed, and altitude. He would then talk the aircraft over the target and give the signal for bombs away. The system could be used in any time of reduced visibility. B-29s began bombing with the MPQ-2 in March 1951 and continued to use it for some close support missions throughout the war, although the need for such operations declined as the lines became more stabilized. Smart witnessed a number of such night missions, and forty 500-pound fragmentation bombs from one B-29 often produced a spectacular show much appreciated by ground troops. He was not convinced of the utility of such operations, however, and was suspicious of enemy decoy and deception efforts. Postwar assessments tended to support his opinion. They revealed that the operational CEP for single aircraft directed by the MPQ-2 was 1,300 feet, mainly because of inaccurate target coordinate locations. This was an "uneconomical expenditure of effort" for medium bombers. Close support blind bombing by ground radar guidance with B-26s was not much better. Even after considerable efforts to improve accuracy, the CEP was still over 800 feet.[12]

It should be noted that the expected CEP for visual and radar bombing during the Korean War had improved somewhat from World War II, though precision was still, as Carl Spaatz had noted in 1944, "in a relative not a literal sense." Bombs dropped from a four-ship B-29 diamond formation thoroughly covered a rectangle about 500 feet wide and 2,000 feet long. Errors were increased by poor maps, lack of adequate target photographs, fatigued crews that initially had to load their own bombs, and old World War II munitions. Some of the high-explosive bombs had been in storage so long that their filler had settled and disturbed the normal center of gravity. This could produce dispersion errors of up to sixty mils. Most of these problems had been solved by 1952, however, contributing to the improved precision of the medium bombers.[13]

SHORAN remained the most accurate method for B-29 nonvisual bombing. General war plans were predicated on the ability of SAC crews to pick up targets from 25,000 feet or higher with their aircraft's AN/APQ-13 radar, whose scope could show contrasting terrain, especially land and water. Korea's mountains made reception difficult, and few targets were on the coast

Radar navigator 1st Lt. Kenneth Broga of the Thirty-first Strategic Reconnaissance Squadron monitors his SHORAN radio tracking equipment aboard an RB-29 on a photographic mission over North Korea. The success of his aircraft's mission depends on his ability to keep it on the proper flight line. (RG 342 NA II)

or on wide rivers to provide clear scope definition. Results of such radar missions in the first half of 1951 were disappointing, and they were abandoned once SHORAN proved its worth. Even after an extensive training program in SAC, the average CEP for radar delivery was almost 2,000 feet in late 1951. Bomber Command's high-altitude precision bombing averaged a CEP under 600 feet in visual conditions, and with training and experience, SHORAN proficiency approached that figure. All these statistics considerably bettered JCS planning estimates for accuracy, which were 3,000 feet for all-weather radar delivery, 1,500 feet for visual horizontal bombing, and 900 feet for SHORAN or MPQ radar guidance. Despite the impressive CEP achieved with SHORAN by Bomber Command, the system had significant drawbacks. Triangulation worked best when the station arcs were ninety degrees apart; as that angle narrowed, position accuracy declined. Because of the earth's curvature, the maximum range of the signal from the ground stations was only a little over 200 miles. This not only limited the targets that could be bombed in the far reaches of Korea but also made SHORAN impractical to use against

Soviet targets, meaning that the Korean experience detracted from the preparedness of SAC crews for general war.[14]

Most important for the airmen of Bomber Command, to best triangulate on the stations, the optimal approach to the target was by tracking along one of the signal arcs. This meant that for far objectives near the Manchurian border, there was often only one good avenue of approach. The enemy soon figured this out and concentrated defenses accordingly. On 10 June 1952, Communist night defenses destroyed their first B-29s. Four Superfortresses from the Nineteenth Group attacked the Kwaksan railroad bridge complex in clear weather along the only suitable SHORAN approach. Searchlights locked on each one in succession, and twelve jet fighters under ground control hemmed in their prey. The first two B-29s were shot down, and the third was damaged so badly that it had to make an emergency landing at Kimpo. The last plane jammed the searchlights with electronic countermeasures and escaped. Bomber Command scrambled to increase the survivability of its aircraft. They painted the undersides of B-29s with shiny black lacquer to make the searchlights' tracking job more difficult, got more jamming equipment to cover all control radar frequencies, and developed flash suppressors for the aircraft gun turrets. They also used different SHORAN arcs, staggered attack times and altitudes, and took advantage of low clouds that blinded the searchlights. They also learned to avoid moonlit nights and weather conditions that produced telltale contrails. Friendly USAF F-94 and Navy F3D night fighters were used to provide cover and barrier patrols, and the bomber stream was compressed to lower overall risk. These countermeasures would not have worked if the Communists had deployed a radar-equipped night fighter, but they never did, and after 30 January 1953, no more B-29s were lost to enemy night defenses.[15]

PSYCHOLOGICAL WARFARE

A number of B-29 night missions each month involved dropping leaflets instead of high explosives. Bomber Command generally flew one such mission a day and disseminated a little over a third of the leaflets in the theater. By the end of 1951, Superfortresses had already delivered over 275 million of them—15 percent to bolster morale in friendly rear areas, 30 percent to warn enemy civilians, and 55 percent to discourage Communist troops. The Psychological Warfare Section of Far East Command listed thirty-eight basic themes in its leaflet propaganda plan, but these could generally be grouped into nine categories. The Johns Hopkins Operations Research Office defined them as:

1. Checkmate: Consider how hopeless your present tactical situation is.
2. Bulldozer: Consider how strong we are; you are bound to lose ultimately; we have material superiority.
3. Sweat and Toil: Think how bad you feel because of what you have to put up with (winter, digging foxholes, weariness, etc.).
4. Home and Mother: Think how bad and resentful you feel because you are homesick.
5. Iago: Think of all the reasons you have for distrusting your superiors, your allies, your war aims, the Communists; you are being saved.
6. Skinsaver: Think of the chance you still have to save your life.
7. Nightingale: Think how well we will treat you as a prisoner of war.
8. Signpost: Think how safe it will be for you to surrender, if only you do the following things in the following way.
9. Desdemona: Think how unselfish and honorable we and our war aims are; you can see (from our bomb warnings) that we do not want to hurt you.[16]

Leaflet drops did not always go as smoothly as planned. Cpl. Robert Petosky and PFC Ralph Balash try to dump their load out of a C-47 in February 1951 while the slipstream blows many of the leaflets back into the plane. By then, FEAF aircraft had already dropped millions of pamphlets over enemy territory. It was much easier to use special leaflet bombs than to disperse the load by hand. Since they did not explode like regular munitions, the enemy often reported them as duds or suspected that they were being used to deliver biological warfare agents. (RG 342 NA II)

One widely disseminated leaflet aimed at North Korean civilians in Operations BLAST and STRIKE shows how these themes were combined in the controversial bomb warnings dropped on cities. The eye-catching red image on the front shows UN bombs dropping unerringly on a munitions factory, a picture emphasizing the precision of air attacks and the military nature of their targets. On the back is text accompanied by drawings of security police confiscating the leaflets while civilians are being forced to work at gunpoint. The writing states, "Although it must destroy communist militarists and their installations, the United Nations Command seeks to keep civilians from harm." It tells the civilians to stay away from military targets and cautions that their leaders will "conceal the warnings and force you to keep working." It concludes, "Who, then, has your interests at heart? Heed this warning."[17]

Not only enemy civilians were targeted. The State Department designed leaflets to drop on South Korean refugees to prepare them for the destruction they would find upon returning home. They pointed out that the damage was

Sometimes psychological warfare leaflets were dropped in an attempt to prevent refugees from fleeing or returning to their homes at the wrong time, and thereby clogging roads necessary for military movements. These hordes of South Koreans are fleeing advancing Communist forces in early 1951. (Signal Corps photograph from USMA Special Collections)

necessary to rid Korea of the invading Communists, emphasized the sacrifices made by all UN nations, and promised that the UN would help rebuild the country. A RAND study that examined the reaction of friendly civilians in World War II and Korea to air attacks by their own forces concluded that friendly populations would accept and sometimes even welcome the air raids if it was clear that they served a military purpose and it was apparent that the air forces were concerned with "selectivity of target selection and accuracy in the destruction of the targets selected."[18]

Of course, the Communists portrayed all UN bombing as indiscriminate and immoral and conducted a successful propaganda campaign of their own on the world stage. USAF Headquarters was always looking for ways to avoid providing the enemy with new material to exploit. It even directed that the soft-nose .22-caliber ammunition provided in emergency packets for downed aircrews to hunt game be replaced by rounds with full metal jackets, because of fears that "subject ammunition would provide an adverse propaganda value."[19] One aspect of Communist propaganda that caused special concern to American leaders involved accusations of chemical and biological warfare. An examination of the record is very revealing not only about the sensitivity of the United States to such charges but also about its early efforts to develop air-delivered nonnuclear weapons of mass destruction.

Communist allegations about U.S. bacteriological warfare were nothing new, dating back at least to 1949. The first charges of biological warfare (BW) use in Korea were made in the summer of 1950. The UN countered some-what by telling the United Press about a "super-secret bacteriological labora-tory" that had operated in Pyongyang under a Russian woman scientist since 1947 and been overrun by advancing UN troops. Although only about 400 starved rats were found in the facility, a North Korean doctor revealed that over 5,000 had been inoculated there with deadly diseases and then sprayed with a chemical that encouraged the multiplication of fleas. The Russian supervisor disappeared, supposedly leaving with other fleeing Communist officials.[20]

The enemy propaganda campaign expanded in 1951. In February, North Korea claimed that retreating U.S. troops had spread smallpox there in December 1950, and its foreign minister filed a protest about UN BW with the General Assembly in May. During the summer, North Korean radio announced the undertaking of antiepidemic measures because of the BW attacks. The first charges about chemical warfare (CW) came that same year when the Chinese Communists reported that poison gas bombs had been dropped along the Han River front on 23 February. Napalm was also included in a wave of accusations about UN CW that reached a peak in

August. Later, General Clark was particularly exasperated by reports from Britain that the Ministry of Defense had ordered British and Commonwealth forces not to use napalm, but this was denied by a visiting Marshall Alexander and the commander of the Australian fighter squadron at Kimpo.[21]

This was all just a prelude to the most vehement, and effective, BW propaganda campaign that began in early 1952. On 22 February, the North Korean foreign minister announced that the United States was carrying on BW against his country. At the same time, the Chinese press and radio made repeated references to the fact that the United States had granted immunity to Lt. Gen. Shiro Ishii and his captured subordinates of notorious Unit 731, which had conducted BW experiments in China. The unfortunate decision to provide immunity in exchange for information derived from the Japanese program was of no benefit to the United States but did enhance the credibility of future BW allegations. On 6 March, Communist newspapers in China reported that 448 American aircraft had flown BW missions over Manchuria the preceding week. Two days later, the Department of State Monitoring Service and the Foreign Broadcasting Intelligence Survey picked up a radio broadcast by Chou En-lai, the Chinese foreign minister, decrying the BW campaign as an attempt to wreck the armistice talks and making it known "that members of the U.S. Air Force who invade Chinese territorial air and use biological weapons will be dealt with as war criminals." At the same time, the CIA received an unconfirmed report that the Communists were preparing fallacious documentation to justify punitive action against the next captured pilot. The Chinese and Soviet press followed by publishing pictures of insects and germ bombs supposedly dropped by American planes over North Korea.[22]

Chou En-lai's statement caused a furor in Washington. The JCS and State Department advised Ridgway to make a strong denial of the charges and to warn the Communists about their responsibility for the fair treatment of POWs. After preparing a statement, Ridgway decided not to deliver it, since he believed that he had already issued enough vigorous denials. In addition to this action, the State Department got the International Committee of the Red Cross (ICRC) to agree to conduct an investigation of the allegations and accepted a similar offer from the World Health Organization (WHO). While Soviet representatives in the UN repeated the accusations and emphasized that the United States had not ratified the 1925 Geneva protocols against biological and chemical warfare, they also vetoed U.S. resolutions that would have permitted the ICRC and WHO inspections. The Chinese refused independent offers from those organizations, claiming that they were only interested in securing military intelligence for the Americans. The Communists asserted that proper investigations were already being conducted by "friendly governments." Soviet newspapers also expanded their accusations to blame the United States for hoof-and-mouth disease in Canada and a plague of locusts in the Near East. The secretary of the Air Force told the secretary of defense that his service believed that the propaganda was designed either to discourage U.S. exploitation of the "great military potentialities of BW-CW weapons" or to set the stage so the Communists could use their own BW-CW capability in a "Pearl Harbor" surprise attack. Although the first assumption was more likely, the second was more dangerous, and Finletter had his surgeon general inventory supplies of vaccines and antibiotics. Far East Command shared USAF concerns and expanded its BW detection and prevention programs while requesting biological and chemical munitions for retaliation.[23]

The U.S. Psychological Strategy Board, with representatives from the JCS, CIA, and State and Defense Departments, considered the BW propaganda the keystone of a detailed "Soviet hate campaign against the United States" that had been going on since January 1951. For them, propaganda of this type was a "horror-weapon," directed "not only against the United States, but against the very structure of human civilization." They realized that it presented special problems for the future. The accusations "might acquire a kind of retrospective credibility" if circumstances ever required the actual American employment of biological or chemical agents. The BW campaign "provided the Soviet Union with a means of harnessing the forces of nature to their propaganda advantage," since they could now blame any epidemic or insect infestation anywhere on the United States. Also, American attempts to help fight such problems could backfire. Doctors sent to fight a disease could be accused of spreading it, and planes spraying insecticides could be blamed for plagues. But the board also saw an opportunity to "indict the rulers of the USSR before the bar of world opinion for one of the most serious crimes against humanity they have yet committed." In the process, the United States could gather on its side "the moral and cultural leaders of the whole world," including those "most easily duped by communist peace-propaganda." If properly handled, countering the "hate-America" campaign would provide a "chance to shoot down, once and for all, the Stockholm dove" and achieve "more adequate recognition" from friendly nations and international organizations for disinterested U.S. efforts "to utilize our technological resources for the relief of human want and suffering throughout the world."[24]

The Psychological Strategy Board was not the only agency considering active measures to counter the propaganda campaign. American actions in the UN were actually part of a carefully planned strategy developed by Assistant Secretary of State for UN Affairs John Hickerson to discredit the Communist

BW charges. He knew that Soviet representative Jacob Malik would assume the Security Council presidency in June 1952, when the first report of the UN Disarmament Commission was due to come before the council. Hickerson was also aware that Malik wanted to debate the question of bacteriological warfare and expected the Soviet delegate to take advantage of the disarmament report to repeat the charges of BW use in Korea. Hickerson prepared two draft resolutions to introduce when Malik brought up the issue. The first proposed the creation of an impartial commission of inquiry. Hickerson expected that to be vetoed by the Russians, so his second resolution condemned them for frustrating the investigation. He knew that the follow-up proposal would meet the same fate as its predecessor but believed that the vetoes would expose Communist insincerity to all but the most biased observers and provide much positive publicity for the American position. The State Department liked the plan, and when Malik repeated the accusations on 18 June and submitted a draft resolution calling for all states to ratify the 1925 Geneva Convention prohibiting BW, Deputy U.S. Representative to the UN Ernest Gross was ready to reply. He gave a lengthy explanation of American motives and innocence, condemned the Soviets for their own work on bacteriological warfare, and circulated a draft resolution to permit the ICRC to have free rein to conduct an impartial investigation of all the Communist accusations. The Security Council rejected Malik's resolution and his attempts to bring North Korea and Communist China into the debate, and instead focused on the American proposal. When a vote was scheduled, Malik cast the lone dissent, as expected. Gross then introduced the second resolution recognizing the ICRC and WHO offers to help, condemning the Soviets' veto, and concluding from their refusal to allow the impartial investigation that the Communist charges "must be presumed to be without substance and false." The Security Council vote on that resolution was nine to one to one, with Pakistan abstaining and the Soviet Union casting its fiftieth veto. Although the resolutions were defeated, the United States did gain in public relations. Press coverage emphasized the Soviet intransigence, and Gross was featured in newsreels condemning the "false and malicious" BW charges of the Red campaign.[25]

The Communist accusations of germ warfare were echoed in the Eastern European press and had some impact in Asia, especially in India and Pakistan. There the charges reinforced suspicions about American treatment of the "colored peoples of Asia" and the belief that the United States "by its actions and failure to act" was prolonging a war that might develop into World War III. It appears that major Communist leaders initially believed that China and North Korea really were the target of a bacteriological warfare campaign, although

Chinese leaders had little incentive to thoroughly investigate the accusations coming from field commanders while the propaganda campaign seemed to be garnering support at home and abroad. Documents recently obtained from Russian archives revealed, however, that midlevel Chinese and Russian operatives cooperating with the North Korean government had faked evidence. Their actions included creating false infestation maps, gathering cholera and plague bacilli from infected people in North Korea and China, injecting condemned prisoners with the diseases, and burying infected bodies that could be found to support the epidemic claims. The effort was used in mid-1952 to convince two carefully chosen groups of observers, the International Association of Democratic Lawyers and the International Scientific Commission for the Investigation of the Facts Concerning Bacteriological Warfare in Korea and China, that the United States was indeed using germ warfare. However, by April 1953, the post-Stalin government in Moscow found out about the fabrication of evidence and determined that the claims concerning the use of chemical and biological weapons by U.S. forces were false. Fearing that revelations of the deception could be embarrassing and cause "political damage," Soviet representatives "recommended" to China and North Korea that they curtail their campaign, and the accusations promptly ceased.[26]

The most significant effect of the germ warfare propaganda was on the North Korean and Chinese home fronts. The common people and soldiers took the BW charges very seriously and were motivated to fight harder and support public health programs. Allegations that American aircraft were releasing smallpox and typhus germs caused Chinese troops to panic. The situation was worsened by outbreaks of cholera, plague, and meningitis, which the men assumed had been caused by the enemy but were really just part of the normal spring epidemic season. In March, the Chinese government launched a "patriotic health and epidemic prevention campaign" and asked citizens to kill insects and clean cities and roads. Millions of civilians were vaccinated, as were over 90 percent of frontline troops. Some American POWs also got some of the "monster shots" and reported that "all of North Korea had fever and sore arms." The result of the sanitation and health drives was a significant decrease in infectious diseases that allowed Communist officials to declare victory over American BW technology while propaganda continued to keep the UN on the defensive in treaty negotiations. The campaign also inflamed the civilian population in North Korea so much that they went out of their way to hunt downed airmen, ensuring that they had virtually no chance of evading immediate capture. Attempts to "propagandize" American POWs about BW sometimes backfired. One group of enterprising noncommissioned officers gathered up a number of dead beetles and spiders around their prison camp and painted "U.S. Mark 7" on their backs. Reportedly, "this counter activity threw the Commies into a spin."[27]

Besides additional accusations of American use of gas bombs, a new ingredient was added to the "hate campaign" in early May 1952. Radio Peking and *Pravda* provided excerpts from the confessions of two American airmen, 1st Lts. John S. Quinn, a B-26 pilot, and Kenneth L. Enoch, his navigator, who admitted that they had been forced to drop "germ bombs" by the "warmongers of Wall Street" as part of an extensive BW effort against China and Korea. Eventually, as many as thirty-eight fliers would confess to participation in BW, but the American government was most concerned with eight of them who had been featured in Communist propaganda films and broadcasts. Besides Quinn and Enoch, these included four more Air Force officers, along with Col. Frank Schwable and Maj. Roy Bley of the Marines. The State Department denied their claims, asserting that the statements had been induced by torture and brainwashing, and the Air Force painstakingly investigated every aspect of the confessions. They found enough inconsistencies to believe that the officers had not caved in completely, although the discrepancies could not be released immediately to discredit the statements because of fears that the Communists would harm the officers or that the information might help the enemy refine interrogation techniques. In March 1953, the Air Force and Marine Corps furnished declassified information to the American UN delegation for use in "an aggressive countercharge" there.[28]

Quinn and Enoch were suspected of being the most serious collaborators. Another pilot accused them of flying off course on purpose to defect. There were reports that Quinn went around to POW compounds lecturing on the evils of USAF germ warfare. Noncommissioned officers in one camp who came into possession of two pistols and ten rounds of ammunition reserved one bullet to use on him if he ever showed up to talk there. He also conducted interviews with foreign correspondents. The first visual evidence of their collaboration was Enoch's appearance in a film confiscated on its way to South America in late 1952. By early the next year, a second, better-quality film had been seized by U.S. Customs from a woman returning from a "peace conference" abroad. This one featured confessions by Quinn, Enoch, and two fighter pilots, 1st Lt. Paul Kniss and 2d Lt. Floyd Neal. The USAF Psychological Operations Division dispatched a chaplain with a copy of the film to Los Angeles to view it with Quinn's wife. She noted that he looked haggard and aged, and she showed the chaplain letters revealing her husband's "ultrapatriotic spirit." She asked if he would be court-martialed upon his return, but the chaplain assured her that the Air Force planned only to rehabilitate those subjected to brainwashing.[29]

The Air Force had some public relations plans as well, to supplement the theme of "forced false confessions" being promulgated by the State Department through its Voice of America and International Press facilities. When an American lawyer who had been interned in Shanghai for sixteen months returned with stories that he had been drugged with "truth medicine" to extract damaging statements, "it raised immediate speculation" that the airmen's confessions had been obtained the same way. The Air Force prepared its own film, first called "Brainwashing" but then changed to "Confessions—The Communist Way," to counter the germ warfare charges, but the Department of Defense did not approve its release. As the possibility of an armistice grew, so did Air Force hopes that it could recover the airmen and have them recant their confessions, although until the last minute there were fears that the Communists would not return them for that very reason. Clark received special instructions to demand accountability for the Marine and Air Force officers involved in the BW confessions if they were not repatriated, since "recovery of a single individual would be of inestimable value for National propaganda purposes, and have a salutary effect upon conduct of American military personnel in contact with Communist forces in future hostilities." He was even authorized to initiate "clandestine and covert activities" to find them and get them back.[30]

However, none of that was necessary. Five of the airmen arrived back in San Francisco in September 1953, and after sorting out a number of conflicting directives about USAF POWs who had confessed to BW, a representative from the USAF Psychological Warfare Division gathered written statements and made film and tape recordings. All the returnees claimed that they had been coerced by mental and physical torture, including threats of death, and Quinn claimed to have been brainwashed so effectively as to have become one of the "living dead men, controlled human robots" who did the Communists' bidding. Copies of the statements were given to the American UN delegation, and some film footage was provided for newsreels. Their coverage juxtaposed clips from the "so-called confessions" in the Communist movies with Air Force footage of the repatriated POWs talking about torture and threats, to show how the "big lie technique spawned by Hitler was brought up to date by the Reds."[31]

At the United Nations in late October, the American delegation presented the sworn statements and mounted a spirited attack on the Commmunist abuse of POWs while denying all the BW accusations. The *New York Times* even published a statement from Col. Walker Mahurin. He explained that Chinese interrogators had begun to maltreat him in October 1952 to force him to confess to BW crimes. He spent over a month sitting at attention on a stool for fifteen hours a day, and once did that for thirty-eight hours straight. After months of death threats and solitary confinement, he finally agreed to cooperate in May 1953. After two months of creating stories based on the suggestions of his interrogators, he signed and wire-recorded an acceptable confession on 8 August. He was then told that the war had ended on 27 July and he would soon be repatriated. However, the Supreme Command still did not like his statement, and he had to repeat his performance on 2 September with a new confession written mostly by his captors before he was allowed to head south for freedom.[32]

ACTUAL BW-CW CAPABILITIES

As another part of the effort to refute the Communist charges, Weyland offered to let UN Ambassador Henry Cabot Lodge reveal that FEAF had no BW capability, but he emphasized the security implications of the release of that sensitive information.[33] Although there had been a determined national effort to develop such a capacity, by the end of the Korean War, little had been achieved. The CW situation was not much better. What capability the Air Force had to deliver chemicals had not changed much since World War II.

The action that provided the impetus for American BW-CW programs was actually instigated before the Korean War began. The Secretary of Defense's Ad Hoc Committee on Chemical, Biological, and Radiological Warfare, called the Stevenson Committee after its chairman, Earl P. Stevenson, delivered its final report on 30 June 1950, five days after the North Korean invasion. Similar studies by the Research and Development Board in 1948 and a previous ad hoc committee in 1949 had focused on BW and the need for increased defensive measures, but the Stevenson Committee had a broader mandate and advocated bolder action. It made eight major recommendations. On 27 October, the secretary of defense approved those recommendations directing that steps be taken to make the United States capable of employing toxic chemical agents, including new nerve gases, at the outbreak of war and to research and test the offensive and defensive aspects of BW. He did not approve the development of a radiological warfare program and deferred a decision on the most controversial recommendation: to abandon the national policy that chemical, biological, and radiological weapons would be used "in retaliation only." The committee believed that these categories had erroneously been classified as "weapons of mass destruction" that were somehow more immoral than other types, thus leading to the current policy. As a result, "the use of certain weapons is subject to the permission of our enemies," and the United States was denying itself the use of weapons "which take advantage of the nation's great technical and industrial potential." The Air Force was strongly in favor of the change, but the Navy disagreed. The JCS finally recommended the deferment of any decision because the United States was not ready to employ CW or BW at the time, changing the policy would require coordination with the United Kingdom to change its position as well, and the existing standards still allowed increasing preparedness without risking "unfavorable political ramifications." The Air Force tried to change the policy again in late 1951 but eventually accepted the Army and Navy position that no alteration should be considered until a definite BW-CW capacity had been built up.[34]

That would prove to be a difficult task. In 1951 the United States possessed only 15,000 tons of CW agents left over from World War II and 580 tons of nerve gases captured from the Germans. Negligible quantities of biological agents were available in laboratories. Although the responsibility for developing, producing, and storing agents belonged to the Army's Chemical Corps, the Air Force was the service most interested in their application. In February the JCS directed the attainment of "an overwhelming retaliatory capability in CW and BW," and in June USAF Vice Chief of Staff Nathan Twining ordered the Air Force "to attain a world-wide capability in these fields on a priority equal to that of the Atomic Energy Program." By the middle of the year the service had put in orders for BW and CW delivery systems, made considerable progress with anticrop agents, and established a Biological and Chemical Warfare Institute at the Air University. By the end of 1951, USAF had procured emergency funds to procure more chemical and biological air munitions, obtained a test range for them in Canada, and done much conceptual work on their application. Chemical weapons were seen as being primarily for tactical use, while the strategic potential of BW against crops and large numbers of people interested planners most.[35]

However, the program expanded slowly in 1952. Even modest service goals proved difficult to achieve. SAC planned to reach its directed one-wing CW-BW operational capability for that year by just writing a standard operating procedure and briefing some key people, but the only BW mission in war plans was to strike Soviet cereal crops with TX-1, the causative agent of wheat stem rust. That was the only BW weapon available, although there was hope that AB-1, *Brucella suis,* the cause of undulant fever, would be in production at Pine Bluff Arsenal, Arkansas, as a personnel incapacitating agent by the end of the year. SAC preferred a killing agent, however. LeMay remained unenthusiastic about BW, even to the point of refusing to assist with the production of BW-CW training films that might give away "operational concepts."

Although Air Force planners saw much promise for the future, delivery systems were old and in short supply, and atomic bombs still seemed more viable and efficient weapons to SAC than biological ones. LeMay's staff did see some potential for using nerve gas against retardation targets and air bases. Even TAC, which seemed more positive about using BW-CW, could not meet its requirement to develop a light bomber capability unless the 452d Bomb Wing was returned from Korea. A RAND report on the Air Force BW program was highly critical and inspired a vigorous rebuttal by the Air Force deputy chief of staff of operations for atomic energy, who had overall responsibility for the BW-CW program. Among other criticisms, the report agreed with SAC's preference for atomic weapons.[36]

A major concern generated by the RAND report in USAF Headquarters was that it might be used by the Army Chemical Corps to justify "a more leisurely approach to the solution of outstanding problems." The Air Force was becoming very dissatisfied with the cooperation it was getting from the Army. Personnel shortages remained, stored munitions were deteriorating, and agent production was behind schedule. In April 1952 an interservice symposium was conducted to better coordinate the BW program. One of the attendees was Lt. Gen. Jimmy Doolittle (retired), Vandenberg's special assistant for science and technology. Doolittle was a true hero of World War II and one of its most ethical commanders, and he tried to assuage the moral qualms of those present by remarking, "In my estimation, we have just one moral obligation—and that moral obligation is for us to develop at the earliest possible moment that agent which will kill enemy personnel most quickly and most cheaply." The joint momentum of the symposium carried over to the formation of a BW-CW Inter-Service Coordinating Committee (ISCC), established at the request of the Army in May. The Air Staff had high hopes that the ISCC would solve their problems with the Army, but they were disappointed. In November, Secretary Finletter sent Army Secretary Frank Pace, Jr., a memorandum highlighting key issues that remained unresolved. These included the real planned uses of BW-CW and where the Navy fit in. For Finletter, the most fundamental question to be answered was, "What is our philosophy about the use of these weapons—from the moral point of view and from the military point of view?" He wondered whether to accept the recommendation of the Stevenson Report to abandon the principle of retaliation only. He mused, "It seems to me that we have to answer this question before we get into the military uses."[37]

By that time, the issue of retaliation had also reared its head in Far East Command. Spurred by the enemy propaganda campaign and queries from the Department of the Army about requirements to attain the ability to employ CW, Clark requested that he be given some retaliatory capability against enemy CW or BW. He also thought that the presence of U.S. chemical warfare munitions in the theater might deter the Soviets from employing theirs and planned to increase deterrence with a news campaign emphasizing UN chemical-biological-radiological defenses. Somehow the Department of the Army inquiries led Clark to believe that the JCS had "good available capabilities" in BW and CW, but when he briefed that to a visiting Doolittle, Vandenberg's BW consultant responded that "there were no practical capabilities in the field at this time." Weyland added that FEAF had no ability to deliver chemicals, and any backup capability in the United States was "rather limited." Far East Command was prepared to store and deliver CW artillery shells and land mines and even to maintain bulk chemicals, but FEAF lacked trained personnel and air delivery systems. The Air Staff scrambled to provide FEAF with the service support to stock CW munitions, along with plans to employ them, and it took the lead with the JCS in modifying retaliatory and stockpiling policies. FEAF also had the added burden of a USAF requirement to train one light bomber wing and one fighter-bomber wing to deliver CW ordnance by the end of 1953.[38]

By October 1952, the JCS had decided to allow the storage of CW in Far East Command, and 3,600 tons of World War II mustard gas were to be allocated to FEAF from Army stocks to dispense from spray tanks. In addition, bombs filled with phosgene and cyanogen chloride gas were to be provided. The enemy in Korea was considered very vulnerable to such a mix of munitions. Intelligence estimates placed approximately 45,000 assorted gas masks in the possession of frontline enemy troops. Captured U.S. and Japanese masks were supplemented by Chinese and Soviet models that were mostly old and poorly fitted. No more than 5 percent of enemy soldiers had masks that gave much protection against cyanogen chloride, and even those that did would quickly have their charcoal contaminated. Planners recommended the initial use of that gas to force unmasking, and then follow-up attacks with the other agents to increase casualties. In June 1953, a conference on FEAF CW plans decided to abandon the use of mustard gas from the spray tanks in favor of bombs with the other two agents. Against the primitive Communist CW defenses, any of the old delivery systems looked good. No BW capacity was anticipated in the theater prior to 1955. However, no CW stocks had been shipped to the Far East yet, either. The shipment of such a special cargo across the United States would be hard to hide, and Clark had informed the JCS, "It must be assumed that presence of chemical munitions in this theater will become known due to the use of Japanese indigenous labor in storage depots, by the presence and use of protective equipment, and by possible talk by military personnel." The JCS was unwilling to risk having such movement discovered while truce talks were under way. With the retaliation policy still in effect, and a growing sense that atomic weapons would be the proper response if the enemy escalated the war at that late date, there seemed no point in stocking the agents in the Far East at that time.[39]

When the war ended, American CW-BW stocks were not much more than when it began. Program progress had been so limited and use seemed so remote that the USAF assistant for atomic energy under the deputy chief of staff for operations recommended that all procurement of agents and munitions be terminated except for testing. The Air Force possessed about 35,500 tons of phosgene and cyanogen chloride, along with 400 tons of German nerve gas. The Chemical Corps owned 20,000 tons of mustard gas. American factories were making 4,700 tons of mustard, 750 tons of phosgene, and 750 tons of cyanogen chloride each month. Some production of nerve gas was just beginning but was still months away from significant output. Available BW agents consisted of only 2,500 units of anticrop rust. In addition, the Air Force had 5,000 tons of anticrop chemicals. Delivery systems included bombs and spray tanks, along with 24,000 BW antipersonnel and 63,000 CW nerve gas clusters waiting for fill. One of the new delivery means under development by General Mills Inc. was a balloon bomb similar to those launched against the United States by Japan in World War II. It was considered an especially effective way to dispense anticrop agents over Russia. By the time it reached field-testing in 1954, neither the balloons nor any other CW-BW system was needed in Korea. Air pressure with conventional munitions appeared to have finally brought about an armistice.[40]

9
THE FINAL ACTS

I concur in concept that max pressure, within capability of means and which can be justified by results, should be applied and maintained against the Communists. The capability for such pressure, without unacceptable cost, lies in the air arm. Effort has been and is being made to employ that capability so as to impose maximum punishment on the enemy. I feel that results have been satisfactory.

GEN. MARK CLARK, AUGUST 1952[1]

The more probable reason for failure thus far to achieve an armistice is that the UNC has not exerted sufficient military pressure to require the enemy to accept an Armistice on our terms. In the conduct of operations since the beginning of hostilities, the UNC has observed restrictions against the use of atomic weapons, crossing the Manchurian border, the use of Chinese Nationalist forces, and the imposition of a naval blockade against China. The UNC is confronted with numerically superior enemy forces, who occupy excellent, well-organized defensive positions in depth and who continue to provide themselves with adequate logistic support. Under these conditions it is evident that only by positive aggressive action with augmented forces and relaxed restrictions can an Armistice on UNC terms or a military victory be achieved.

OPLAN CINCUNC 8-52, OCTOBER 1952[2]

The possible application of air and naval forces without a ground offensive raises new problems of political and military strategy. These are new problems in the sense that responsible political and military policy makers have only begun to grapple with them. Forward thinking Air Force officers have been dealing for some time with the concept of applying airpower as the primary offensive action for obtaining acceptable objectives without launching land offensives to capture and control. Unfortunately, the US policy makers have been unable to express limited war objectives compatible with air force capabilities, primarily we think, because they have never thought in terms of other than ground warfare.

FEAF STAFF STUDY, 1953[3]

As the air war escalated into 1953, so did planning about the possible use of nuclear weapons. Many factors fueled this trend, including Clark's own offensive proposals. His ambitious Oplan 8-52 was designed to achieve a military victory or armistice on UN terms if current deadlocked negotiations were abandoned. The offensive would begin with air and naval attacks to destroy enemy air and logistic capability in Manchuria and China. Ground operations would be conducted in three phases of approximately twenty days each. The first would be a double envelopment to seize control of the Pyongyang complex. That would be followed by an amphibious assault on Wonsan designed to destroy enemy forces in the east and uncover their lines of communication. Phase three entailed the destruction of enemy ground forces while driving

Naval and marine aircraft flew about 275,000 of the more than 1 million air sorties conducted by UN air forces. The hydroelectric plant attacks had been followed by many coordinated maximum-effort air strikes, and by early 1953, joint air operations between Task Force 77 and FEAF were much improved. But the carriers felt increasingly threatened by the Communist air buildup. Even with alert combat air patrols, naval commanders believed they could not effectively defend against attacks by MiG-15s or IL-28s. (U.S. Navy photograph from USMA Special Collections)

remnants north of a line across the narrow waist of Korea. Although a key assumption of Clark's plan was that atomic bombs would not be employed, he realized that his scheduled attacks on enemy airfields in Manchuria and northern China and on "targets of opportunity" would be much more effective with the special weapons.[4]

The necessity to completely neutralize the enemy air threat from Manchuria increased when intelligence reported IL-28 twin-engined jet bombers stationed there. These were considered "the highest priority aircraft in the Soviet Air Force," and the decision to send such advanced technology to Manchuria while bomber units in the USSR retained more conventional planes seemed ominous. The IL-28 was estimated to have a top speed of 460 knots and to be able to carry a 4,400-pound bomb load with a range of 690 nautical miles. They could reach Japan from Manchuria, and even hit Okinawa from mainland China. They also increased the defensive problems for Navy carriers, which might not be able to intercept bombing or torpedo attacks by the jets. In January 1953, FEAF still had only 176 F-86s to oppose almost 700 MiGs in northeastern Manchuria, and the Air Staff feared a surprise attack on the few UN jet bases in Korea by IL-28s supported by strafing MiG-15s. One of the first concerns that new President Dwight Eisenhower brought up to the National Security Council was the need for better dispersion of UN aircraft in Korea. Air bases at Kimpo, Suwon, Taegu, and Kunsan all contained two or more wings, and FEAF had little space or engineering capability to build new fields or expand existing facilities. The Sabres were concentrated at Kimpo, only twenty-five minutes' flying time from the Yalu for an IL-28. In February, Clark again asked for permission to conduct preemptive strikes against CCAF bases in Manchuria, but the JCS remained reluctant to grant it because of the political fallout. The NSC had already cleared such action, but only if armistice negotiations had clearly failed and if authorized by the president.[5]

Besides frustration with progress at the peace talks and concerns about the Communist air buildup, the impetus to consider employing nuclear weapons was also accelerated by a sense that the new president might be more likely to support such action than his predecessor. Soon after the 1952 elections, Clark included a discussion of contingencies for the use of atomic weapons in a briefing on his war plans prepared for the president-elect's visit to Korea. A similar briefing had been conducted for the JCS, and Clark indicated to his staff that General Bradley had already approved the employment of atomic bombs if the offensive had to be resumed. When Clark asked if anyone on his staff had reservations about that course of action, he was surprised when Weyland expressed his disagreement. The FEAF commander found himself in a situation similar to that of Carl Spaatz in 1944. Then, the commander of U.S.

Strategic Air Forces in Europe had found himself being committed to a massive air attack on Berlin that he believed unsound and unethical but that his theater commander, Dwight Eisenhower, thought worthwhile if it could end the fighting. Weyland downplayed his moral concerns but had plenty of practical reasons why he thought that atomic bombs should not be used in Korea or China. He questioned whether enemy airfields deep in Manchuria could be neutralized even with nuclear weapons, since they were beyond fighter-bomber and SHORAN range. Large Chinese urban areas would be the best targets for atomic attacks, but the Russians would then downplay the effectiveness of the raids while exploiting their propaganda value, and they could also learn a lot about what the weapons could do. Clark was taken aback by Weyland's objections. The CINCFE emphasized that the decision to use atomic bombs would be up to the president and the JCS, and he was concerned that Weyland would "jump up and disagree with him" during any discussions with Eisenhower about their employment. Weyland confirmed that he "would loyally follow any decisions" arrived at by his superiors, but he felt that it was his "duty to express [his] views on air matters whether or not they might be completely in agreement with General Clark."[6]

Weyland's reservations had no impact on the course of events. When Clark submitted Oplan 8-52 to the JCS, he requested that they develop plans for his use of nuclear weapons. In December the Joint Strategic Plans Committee, with considerable help from the USAF director of intelligence, prepared a detailed analysis of how many bombs would be necessary to destroy enemy air bases, bridges, rail yards, munitions storage depots, and major troop concentrations. Discussions generated heated debate and conflicting opinions within the JCS for months, as they considered multiple options in case the armistice negotiations collapsed or seemed hopelessly deadlocked. Although most services came around to support Clark's plan in general, the Air Force disagreed. It thought that 8-52 required too much force augmentation and would need an unrealistic number of atomic bombs, between 342 and 482. Its competing plan was based on building up the ROK Army and increasing pressure on the Communist Chinese in stages, without a fixed geographical objective. This would allow for more control from Washington and less risk to allied support.[7]

However, when the JCS forwarded its recommendations to the secretary of defense on 19 May, they were much more in keeping with Clark's desires than the Air Force's. The JCS proposed air and naval operations against China and Manchuria, an offensive to seize a position at the narrow Korean waist, and the tactical and strategic use of atomic bombs. Air attacks over the Yalu would generally be limited to northern China and Manchuria. Longer-term objectives were destroying Communist military power in Korea while reducing their capability for further aggression, increasing the possibility of an armistice on UN terms, and creating conditions favorable for ROK forces to assume more responsibility for military operations. When the plan to expand the war was discussed at the NSC on 20 May, Eisenhower was concerned about the vulnerability of UN forces to Chinese aircraft and the possibility of Soviet air attacks "on the almost defenseless population centers of Japan." All participants agreed that the chance of Soviet intervention would be lessened considerably if the proposed operation could be carried out quickly. The president remained worried about the Soviet response to the plan, but he and the NSC recognized that the JCS plan was "most likely to achieve the objective we sought" if the war had to be expanded. Interestingly, planners and leaders seemed to assume that the Chinese would be defeated fairly easily by the operation, despite the fact that by mid-1953, Gen. Peng Dehuai had assembled 1.35 million troops in Korea and was preparing a major offensive of his own. Apparently unaware of the size of the force opposing them, or else supremely confident in the capabilities of their augmented forces and atomic weapons, the NSC directed the State Department to prepare an evaluation of the foreign policy implications of the new course of action and cleared the JCS to develop more detailed instructions for it, though on a strict "need-to-know" basis to maintain maximum security. As a result of that decision, the JCS directed Clark to prepare a plan with LeMay and CINCPAC to use atomic weapons if negotiations broke down. An Atomic Annex Coordination Conference was scheduled for 6 July 1953 in Honolulu, under protest from LeMay, who had not yet seen the JCS plan but thought that any nuclear operations by Far East Command should be undertaken only after the successful completion of a SAC offensive against China. But the signing of the armistice would cut the effort short.[8]

The last phase of the air pressure campaign may have contributed to finally ending the war. Clark and his subordinates continued to grapple with how best to execute this new concept of "employing air forces as the single strategic offensive in a war" by searching for new targets. The JCS supported their efforts and, except for delaying an attack on a major supply complex at Yangsi because of a nearby prisoner exchange, approved all of Clark's target requests, including more attacks on hydroelectric plants. The JCS did, however, prohibit any public statements announcing the intent of such operations to pressure the Communists into an agreement, fearing that if Communist prestige became "seriously engaged" they would find it difficult to accept any armistice. High-level statements had to treat the air attacks as routine operations "based upon solely military grounds." Ironically, as the raids were directed more and more at achieving a political settlement, the less this could be admitted in public as justification for them.[9]

Destroying the last major target system in North Korea would be hard to justify to world opinion as "solely military." Again, the escalation involved dams, although a different type from those that produced hydroelectric power or the Hwachon Dam, which had its floodgates blown open by Task Force 77 torpedoes in May 1951 to keep the Communists from manipulating Han River water to slow the UN advance. In March 1953, the FEAF Formal Target Committee began to study the irrigation system for 422,000 acres of rice in the main agricultural complexes of South Pyongan and Hwanghae. The deployment of North Korean security units to protect key reservoirs from guerrillas during the growing season indicated the importance of those targets to Banfill. His staff estimated that denying the enemy the rice crop from the area would cause a food shortage, tie up transportation routes with the necessity of importing rice from China, and require the diversion of troops for security and repair efforts. Clark advised the JCS that in case of a prolonged recess in the peace talks, he planned to breach twenty dams to inundate the two areas and destroy an estimated one-quarter million tons of rice, "thereby curtailing the enemy's ability to live off the land and aggravating a reported Chinese rice shortage and logistic problem."[10]

That was not the only proposal to escalate the air war. Weyland held back a Bomber Command attack that "would effectively [have] obliterated what remains of the city of Pyongyang" for possible later use, as another means to ratchet up pressure if necessary. He also appears to have doubted the military utility of the attack, just as he was "skeptical of the feasibility and desirability" of the attacks on the rice irrigation system. However, his planners convinced him to authorize attacks on three dams near important railways to wash the lines away as part of the interdiction program, even though among themselves they considered that rationale a "mode of deception" to keep the enemy from learning the true objective of destroying the rice crop. Fifth Air Force fighter-bombers hit the Toksan and Chasan Dams in mid-May, one of the most vulnerable times for newly planted rice, followed by Bomber Command's night SHORAN missions against Kuwonga Dam. Clark informed Washington that these missions had been "as effective as weeks of rail interdiction."[11]

The JCS quickly approved the bombing of two more dams by fighter-bombers to inundate jet airfields at Namsi and Taechon. The draft armistice agreement provided that the number of combat aircraft allowed within Korea for each side could not exceed the number in place on the effective date of the armistice, and Clark worried that the Communists intended to sneak high-performance aircraft into North Korea just prior to that day, possibly taking

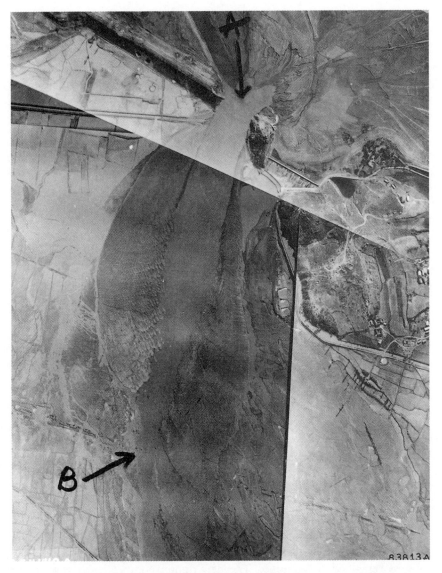

This composite post-strike photograph shows the effectiveness of the attack by Fifth Air Force F-84s on the Toksan Dam on 13 May 1953. "A" marks the breach in the dam, and "B" shows the inundated Communist supply route. Although the press release that accompanied this picture misleadingly reported that the dam held "electric-power producing water," it accurately stated that the "rushing waters washed out rail and road bridges and destroyed over 6,000 feet of the road bed" of the enemy railway, along with an antiaircraft gun position and a small airfield nearby. (RG 342 NA II)

advantage of marginal weather during the rainy season. His intelligence had noted an increased pace of airfield construction and "frantic repair efforts" after raids. Smart suspected that the airfields were just decoys to distract UN bombers from more valuable targets, but Bomber Command hammered them by SHORAN at night while fighter-bombers hit them by day. Clark knew that further dam attacks risked a negative reaction from allies and might affect the armistice negotiations, but he and Weyland believed that the missions had to be conducted to eliminate the airfields.[12]

Contrary to Clark's expectations, the dam attacks attracted very little notice in the world press. American newspapers were preoccupied with the exploits of the jet aces, and each MiG that was downed received more coverage than any bombing raid. The biggest war story in May was whether Capt. Joseph McConnell or Capt. Manuel Fernandez would hold the record for air-to-air victories. FEAF press releases dutifully reported attacks by F-84s on the earthen dams and mentioned that the Kuwonga Dam hit by B-29s was close to key rail and road bridges. North Korea decried "barbarous raids on peaceful agricultural installations" or attacks on water reservoirs that were not military objectives, but no one seemed to notice. Perhaps like the boy who cried "Wolf," the Communist complaints about UN air atrocities were not being taken seriously anymore. Or maybe because no mention was made about targeting rice crops, reservoirs did not seem to merit any consideration in the press as a particularly promising or questionable objective.[13]

In accordance with Far East Command and JCS desires, the dam attacks were also not highlighted in UN communiqués. Instead, the primary focus remained on the F-86s, whether in dogfights against enemy MiGs or delivering ordnance as a newly configured fighter-bomber. Sabres engaged in close air support beginning in February 1953. New F-86Fs with speed brakes could dive at a steeper angle than the F-84s, but operations analysts found their bombing no more accurate than that of the slower jets. Fifth Air Force considered the Sabre the most suitable fighter-bomber for the theater, mainly because its speed gave it an ability to survive enemy defenses superior to that of any other USAF fighter. Typically, the main Air Force criterion for effectiveness remained survivability. The new fighter-bomber had less loitering ability and a shorter range than other jets, and it had deficiencies in sights and wing station configurations for ordnance that still had not been corrected by the end of the war.[14]

FEAF press releases did not mention naval air operations. Instead, activities of Navy and Marine pilots were covered in the combat summaries provided by Far East Naval Forces. Although relations between General Clark's and Admiral Clark's airmen remained cordial, they each continued to fight their own separate air wars. By June 1953, however, the Navy was coordinating on joint target selection with Fifth Air Force, now commanded by Lt. Gen. Samuel E. Anderson. He was impressed enough with the Navy's cooperation to request its representation on the FEAF Formal Target Committee. Weyland indicated that he could not order the Navy to participate because the carrier aircraft were not under his operational control, but he told Anderson to invite the Navy to send a representative from the Joint Operations Center to attend future meetings. The armistice was signed a few days later, so the offer was never extended. Ironically, as service cooperation increased in Korea, the Air Staff in Washington was gathering combat data emphasizing the superiority of land-based over carrier-based aircraft to counter Navy attempts to increase the budget priority for aircraft carriers. Using numbers of sorties and tonnages of bombs dropped in Korea, USAF operations analysts argued that their jets and propeller-driven planes were far more cost effective than their naval counterparts.[15]

Those last few FEAF Formal Target Committee meetings were dominated by discussion about how best to exploit the possibilities of the dam attacks. New proposals included the use of delayed-action bombs to deter repair efforts and the dropping of leaflets that blamed the continuing air attacks, and the loss of water for irrigation, on the Chinese Communists. Weyland was adamant that the dam attacks were for interdiction purposes and vetoed a proposal by Smart for a psychological warfare campaign warning farmers and populations below all the dams in North Korea of their imminent destruction. While Weyland and Clark justified the dam attacks as interdiction raids, neither their planners nor the Communists perceived them that way. The Toksan and Chasan attacks did flood two key rail lines and many roads, but they also inundated nearby villages and rice fields. The flash flood from Toksan "scooped clean" twenty-seven miles of river valley, and both raids sent water into the streets of Pyongyang. Bomber Command delayed its attack long enough that the North Koreans were able to develop countermeasures, and by lowering the level of water in the reservoir, they were able to avoid the catastrophic results of the first two raids. This tactic also worked for the last two dams. The Communists put more than 4,000 laborers to work repairing the Toksan Dam and emplaced antiaircraft defenses around it. Weyland was amazed at the speed of their recovery operations. Only thirteen days after the strike, they had completed a temporary dam and all rail repairs. When Clark queried him as to what targets were left to exert more pressure for an armistice, the all-out blow on Pyongyang was all that came to mind. Clark had Weyland prepare a message for the JCS to get approval for the raid, but it was never sent.[16]

Right to the end, there was uncertainty about Communist intentions to sign the armistice agreement. Late in July, while the Chinese were mounting savage ground attacks that newspapers described as "a propaganda gesture in a dying war," Secretary of Defense Charles E. Wilson was holding a meeting between civilian and uniformed defense leaders at Quantico, Virginia. President Eisenhower attended the final day of the conference on 25 July, where he heard classified presentations from all the services. Two days earlier at an NSC meeting, he had expressed his concern that the "armistice might be a dangerous hoax," and he wanted to make sure that Clark kept strong forces deployed even after a peace agreement was signed. Council attendees agreed that "our atomic capabilities must be used against the Chinese Communists if the armistice is violated." The focus of the Quantico session was supposedly on future preparedness and deterrence, but Korea must have been discussed to some degree. LeMay was also in attendance, and in the middle of the conference he called SAC headquarters and put his command on standby to execute "an emergency plan for atomic air operations in the Far East." Whether he had been directed to do so or had just been alarmed by something revealed at Quantico is unclear, but his order was probably related to the decisions reached at the 23 July NSC meeting and would have prepared his command to respond rapidly with maximum force against Communist treachery. The action was a further indication of the lingering suspicion about Communist motivations, which would continue long after the armistice agreement was signed.[17]

The resort by the UN to such extreme measures as the dam attacks might have alarmed the enemy enough to influence their negotiating position to some degree. Although there is no evidence that warnings from the Eisenhower administration that the United States was prepared to lift restrictions on nuclear weapons ever reached leaders in the Soviet Union or China, and his own remarks at the 23 July NSC meeting imply that he did not think that the Communist agreement was a product of those threats, there were plenty of obvious signs that U.S. patience was wearing thin and the war might expand if it continued. Even if notice about the increased possibility of the use of atomic bombs was never transmitted through diplomatic channels, rumors about Eisenhower's threat to "raise the ante unless a cease fire was negotiated" were rampant throughout Korea and would have been picked up by the Communists from spies or POWs. There were also many other factors besides military pressure involved in the Communist decision to sign the armistice. The death of Stalin and continuing instability within the Kremlin, combined with riots in Czechoslovakia and East Germany, gave the Soviet Union plenty of incentive to disengage from Korea and shocked China as well. Late gains on the ground against ROK troops allowed the Communists to save face while making concessions for the armistice. Further delays might also allow South

Korea's unpredictable Syngman Rhee to further disrupt peace efforts and lead to more heavy casualties from artillery fire and bombing.[18]

Another indication that the UN might be preparing to expand the war was the increasing aggressiveness of American Sabres. This included widespread violations of the prohibition against "hot pursuit" over the Yalu River. The JCS became alarmed in March by press reports that this had become "common practice," but Clark assured them that his "current directives require full compliance with JCS policy and directives," and Weyland reported that "pilots conscientiously break off engagements at the Yalu, even though doing so enables MiGs damaged in combat to escape." That may have been the impression in Tokyo, but Fifth Air Force pilots in Korea sometimes inferred from their briefings that hot pursuit was allowed, or at least "winked at," and they took advantage of the leeway. Paperwork was then altered to cover up the incursions, including at least one in which UN planes destroyed Soviet MiGs at a base thirty miles inside China. Relaxing restrictions on the Sabres contributed to their smashing successes in air battles in 1953 and appears to have

A gun-camera photo of a MiG-15 about to fall prey to an F-86 in March 1953. As the exploits of American aces garnered more headlines, the quality of enemy airmen appeared to decline, and Communist pilots seemed increasingly reluctant to cross the Yalu, the temptation grew for the Sabres to hunt in Chinese airspace. Violations of the UN policy against "hot pursuit" were widespread in the spring of 1953. (RG 342 NA II)

caught their Communist adversaries by surprise. From January to April, sixteen MiGs were claimed for every F-86 downed—double the rate achieved in the previous part of the war. Between 8 and 31 May, the F-86s reported destroying fifty-six MiGs while losing only one of their own jets; the next month they claimed to have shot down seventy-seven more, probably destroyed another eleven, and damaged forty-one, without any friendly losses in air-to-air combat.[19]

During July, the tally was thirty-two MiGs reported destroyed at the cost of only two Sabres. A closer look at a mission on 20 July, which resulted in the only friendly losses that month, reveals how meaningless the restrictions about flying over the Yalu had become and just how dangerous life was for MiG pilots in their supposed sanctuaries. The official history explained that the two Sabres were "ganged" by aggressive MiGs near the mouth of the Yalu, and the official notification of their loss stated that they were "on an airfield reconnaissance mission along the Yalu River" and went down in North Korea. In reality, at least one of the aircraft went down in China. It was flown by Marine Maj. Thomas Sellers, an exchange pilot who was on his forty-third combat mission with the Fifth Air Force after already completing 100 with his own service. He was the leader of a four-man flight assigned the job of counting the MiGs north of the Yalu in Manchuria. Such missions were eagerly sought, for everyone understood that in order to really see what was on an airstrip, observing aircraft had to be directly over it. Despite the warnings about going across the river that were repeated in every briefing, the plane count missions "gave a legal excuse to cross the river where hunting was much better." Major Sellers's flight first examined the field at Takushan, thirty miles west of the mouth of the Yalu, and then turned back toward the river to check the next airstrip. He saw fourteen MiGs taking off from it and called on the other aircraft to follow him in on an attack. Only his wingman heard the call, and they quickly became embroiled in a melee. Major Sellers shot down two enemy jets before he was hit by cannon fire and crashed near the airfield. He was awarded a Silver Star for his actions, though the citation claims that he died in North Korea saving friendly fighter-bombers from enemy MiGs. Although such incursions over the Yalu might have been hidden from leaders in Tokyo and Washington, the Chinese witnessed them firsthand and probably assumed that the increasing boldness of the Sabres had been sanctioned by UN authorities. Indeed, this might have been the most obvious indication to Communist negotiators about the fraying of American patience and the possible military costs of extending the war.[20]

It sometimes took considerable collaboration from a normal flight of four aircraft to conceal the illicit excursions into China from air controllers. Some pilots developed a code-word system that they would use when they were out of voice control range of ground stations and were only being tracked on radar by the Identification Friend or Foe (IFF) signal, or "squawk," of the flight leader. Upon receipt of the proper code word, the leader who was going over the Yalu would "choke his parrot" and turn off his IFF, while one of the aircraft staying south of the river would activate his. While the flight leader and his wingman went off to stalk MiGs, the other two aircraft, including the one squawking IFF, would stay over North Korea and wait to link up with the returning hunters, who would be gone only a few minutes. The flight would then return together, and the ground controllers would be none the wiser.[21]

Sellers's letters to his wife reveal much about the thrill of flying the Sabres and the temptations that lured them over the Yalu. He was amazed at how much the F-86 outperformed the F9F he had flown for Marine close air support, though he found the fighter sweeps "tame" compared with the flak and air engagements he had experienced in the slower jets. Soon after arriving at the Fourth Fighter-Interceptor Group in May, he promised his wife, "I'll not take any unnecessary chances—such as going north of the Yalu and jumping MiGs in their traffic patterns such as some of the boys have done." He soon became convinced, however, that downing a couple enemy jets would guarantee him a commission in the regular Marine Corps after the war, and enemy pilots had become very reluctant to enter air engagements over North Korea. By late June, he admitted to his wife, "I'm determined to get a MiG as are most of the boys around here and it seems there is only one positive way of doing it and that is to go north of the Yalu." They all realized that anyone shot down "would be in the salt mines the rest of his life," but when aces like Maj. James Jabara wandered sixty miles inside China to down two more MiGs, every pilot in the group took notice. Although some lower-level commanders sometimes appeared to sanction the incursions, Fifth Air Force did not. Three days before his fatal mission, Sellers wrote to his wife, "You can stop worrying about our going across the fence into Manchuria—the 5th Air Force has put a stop to it threatening to court martial the next man to shoot down a MiG trying to land at his own field."[22]

Overall, the Communists had suffered a terrific beating from airpower. UN forces claimed a total of 838 MiGs destroyed, with 149 more probably lost and 936 damaged. As the experience with the Soviets early in the conflict showed, these numbers are probably highly inflated. Late in the war, Sabre pilots also got credit for kills if their gun cameras showed just seven regular or three incendiary hits on a MiG. The official logic was that the enemy jets "didn't torch off" in the thin air at high altitudes but would go down later. However, the Communist airmen in 1953 were not as competent as the Russians who had flown in the early air battles, and even the Soviet units that served in Man-churia after mid-1952 were less thoroughly trained and suffered high casualty rates as a result. Of 409 UN jets destroyed, only 110 were shot down in air-to-air combat. Although the Russians and CCAF could quibble over their loss ratio to the Sabres, the Chinese especially had to concede that they had not been able to challenge UN air superiority, and losses in men and material to bombing were considerable. Over the course of the war, FEAF had wreaked terrible destruction all across North Korea. Bomb damage assessment at the armistice revealed that eighteen of twenty-two major cities had been at least half obliterated. The tally sheet of percentage destroyed read as follows:

Anju—15

Chinnampo—80

Chongjin—65

Chongju—60

Haeju—75

Hamhung—80

Hungnam—85

Hwangju—97

Kanggye—60

Kunu-ri—100

Kyomipo—80

Musan—5

Najin (Rashin)—5

Pyongyang—75

Sariwon—95

Sinanju—100

Sinuiju—50

Songjin—50

Sunan—90

Sunchon—60

Unggi—5

Wonsan—80[23]

Raids on towns and villages had also been effective. According to a hastily compiled Bomber Command report in August 1953, of the more than 17,000 tons of bombs it had delivered during the war, almost 10,000 had been

Gen. William Dean, who spent most of the war as a POW in North Korea, reported that the remnants of towns that remained standing were "unoccupied shells," and the people lived in temporary villages hidden away from bombers. This supply center in the environs of Pyongyang was obliterated by B-29s in early 1953 and fits a British reporter's description of the ruins of a typical Korean village devastated by war as "a low, wide mound of violet ashes." (RG 342 via NASM)

dropped on 110 supply areas. In contrast, only about 2,000 tons had been expended destroying every possible strategic industrial target, the same amount used in the highly successful effort to neutralize North Korean airfields. Some of the most revealing observations about the effects of UN bombing came from Gen. William Dean, a POW in North Korea during most of the war. By 1952, most of the towns he saw were just "rubble or snowy open spaces," and what few houses remained "bulged with sacks and boxes of military supplies or food." Villagers had been moved to new temporary homes hidden in canyons. Air Force histories often cite his memoir as evidence of the effectiveness of enemy countermeasures and to justify the campaign against the towns, but he also noted that just about every North Korean he met had had some relative killed in a bombing raid.[24]

Clark and the JCS feared that the Communists would take advantage of the armistice to build up their strength to renew the fight, and LeMay received considerable pressure to deploy new B-47s to the Far East or fly over a B-36 as a show of force. After the armistice, USAF bombers continued to fly every day up and down the coasts of North Korea over international waters, as a constant reminder to the Communists of the threat of American airpower. In late August, one 19th Bomb Wing B-29 wandered over Vladivostok in bad weather, and was so heavily damaged by a Soviet fighter that the crew had to bail out over Japan. Newspaper stories of the crash did not mention the violation of Russian airspace, nor did the Soviets. FEAF Bomber Command was not inactivated and its units returned to SAC control until the summer of 1954, the same year the last B-29 was retired from service. LeMay and his command, along with their focus on nuclear deterrence and strategic missions, would dominate the Air Force in the years after the Korean War. The service was generally pleased with its performance and believed that its air pressure had been primarily responsible for producing the armistice. Perceived success provides little incentive for improvement, and because of this confidence and SAC's focus on general war, most of the lessons about airpower in limited wars were lost or deemed irrelevant. They would have to be relearned again, at high cost, in the skies over Vietnam.[25]

10
LEGACIES AND CONCLUSIONS

Our around-the-clock air operations brought to all North Korea the full impact of war. The material destruction wrought, the panic and civil disorder created, and the mounting casualties in civilian and military populations alike became the most compelling factors in enemy accession to an armistice.

GEN. OTTO P. WEYLAND[1]

The Korean War has been a very complex one. It has been a laboratory study of limited military action in the support of a very difficult political situation. Furthermore it has provided the air forces in particular with an opportunity to develop concepts of employment beyond the World War II concepts of tactical and strategic operations. . . . It is most important for us to understand that the last two years of the war were fought to secure favorable terms under which to cease hostilities. With this kind of objective the door is open for completely new patterns of air employment. The war to date has represented a short step in the direction of using air power as a persuasive force to attain limited objectives.

GEN. OTTO P. WEYLAND[2]

I haven't talked to anybody about Vietnam, but I did talk to this RAND type who was making a study of careers so he could pass it down to Vietnam. He said, "Vietnam was a Korea all over again, just going through the same birth pains."

GEN. EARLE PARTRIDGE[3]

The U.S. Air Force looked back at its first war with a great sense of pride and accomplishment. Despite limited resources and many restrictions, the "shoestring" service believed that it had been "the decisive force in Korea," the one primarily responsible for most of the UN success. This attitude was supported by many articles and historical studies praising FEAF's accomplishments in Air Force journals. Weyland himself contributed a number of capstone pieces summing up the record of his command and trying to capture lessons applicable to future conflicts. His article in the first *Air University Quarterly Review* after the armistice set the tone for future service interpretations of the war. He defended the USAF approach to close air support and claimed that it had destroyed over 150,000 enemy troops and 750 tanks in the first year alone. He admitted that the interdiction campaign did not completely prevent the Communist forces from conducting limited attacks or an obstinate defense, but "it was an

171

unqualified success in achieving its stated purpose, which was to deny the enemy the capability to launch and sustain a general offensive." It also was an important component of the punishing air attacks that were the primary UN offensive strategy the last two years of the war; despite determined enemy efforts to challenge UN air superiority, it was, in his view, what finally compelled the Communists to accept the armistice. He ended his essay with the insightful comment that the war had revealed the need to abandon strict divisions between tactical and strategic air operations, and a plea for the development of new ways to use airpower to achieve limited objectives in a new kind of war.[4]

He repeated many of these same arguments in an article he wrote for the *Air Intelligence Digest* that discussed the impact of jets on the war. He particularly praised the Sabres, fighter-bombers, and reconnaissance aircraft utilizing the new technology and stated that "the outstanding air-combat lesson of the Korean war was learned during the first few days of the conflict—namely that superior performance is the first and essential requirement of aircraft in modern war." He did not mention accuracy but argued that the cost of delivering ordnance by jet was only half that of propeller aircraft, primarily because of vulnerability to ground fire. "For every UNC jet fighter-bomber lost to ground fire, approximately two UNC propeller aircraft were lost." In Weyland's view, the biggest advantage that jets would provide in future wars would be increased flexibility to deliver atomic bombs with less dependence on weather, time of day, or "Nature's vagaries." He parlayed the success of his fighter-bombers in Korea and the promise of tactical nuclear weapons into an expanded role for Tactical Air Command when he took it over in 1954. However, there was a cost to this transformation. Focusing primarily on nuclear strikes in support of NATO was a sure way to garner budget support and force structure in the national security environment of the mid-1950s, but it skewed the focus of USAF tactical airpower away from limited and conventional wars. Weyland and his TAC successors struck a Faustian bargain with the atomic Mephistopheles, transforming the organization into a "junior SAC" concentrating on the delivery of small nuclear weapons. The F-105 Thunderchief, which replaced the F-84 and would bear the brunt of tactical air support in the early years of Vietnam, was designed to deliver a nuclear bomb after a high-speed, low-altitude approach. It was unsuitable both for air combat and for true close air support.[5]

Although Weyland was always careful not to criticize other services in print, he was not so restrained in communications with other Air Force officers, especially in response to accusations that air operations in Korea had been "indecisive." In early 1954 he provided a long defense against such charges to Partridge, now commanding the USAF Air Research and Development Command. Weyland argued that "the Air Force missions were consummated more decisively than were the land force missions," and any failure to "win the war" was a result of political decisions and restraints placed on all commanders. FEAF had maintained air superiority, provided effective close air support, prevented large-scale enemy offensives with interdiction, and compelled the enemy to sign the armistice with "around-the-clock air operations." In his view, the same source who claimed that airpower in Korea was indecisive "would have a hard time selling the idea that Sitting Bull did not achieve decisive results at the Little Big Horn merely because he did not annihilate the entire Seventh Cavalry."[6]

The Air Force itself was also very sensitive to any downplaying of its role in Korea. In 1955 the FEAF assistant deputy for operations, Col. James T. Stewart, was reassigned to Air Force Headquarters in a research and development planning and programming capacity. While there, the USAF Public Information Office (PIO) selected him to edit a book that would demonstrate the service's important contributions in Korea. The title, *Airpower, the Decisive Force in Korea*, conveyed the message the Air Force wanted to send. The PIO had already accumulated most of the material, consisting primarily of articles from the *Air University Quarterly Review*, and Colonel Stewart did some editing and worked with the civilian publisher that had agreed to print the finished product. His volume opens with Weyland's article summing up FEAF's air campaign and contains detailed studies of key bombing operations with some primary accounts that bolster the theme that "without question, the decisive force in the Korean War was airpower." At the same time Stewart was pursuing that project, Robert Futrell at the Air University was culling through his three classified historical studies of the war to produce his superb *The United States Air Force in Korea 1950-1953*. Futrell completed his work late in 1958 after Stewart's book had already been published. A detailed narrative of the air war, it also follows the themes of successful and decisive airpower that Weyland espoused and attributes the new postwar defense policies of President Eisenhower to the fact that "the years of the Korean war marked acceptance of the predominance of airpower among America's armed-force capabilities." Futrell maintained this position when he revised the book in 1983 as well.[7]

The U.S. Air Force definitely got the largest share of "New Look" defense budgets, although the emphasis remained on SAC and not preparations for another Korea. For a time, it appeared that Weyland's call for new thinking about airpower in limited wars might bring change. A 1954 Air War College thesis entitled "Air Power in Limited Military Action," by Maj. Richard Klocko, received wide circulation among the Air Staff and helped break down service resistance to Weyland's development of "Composite Air Strike Forces"

Gen. Otto P. Weyland received his well-deserved promotion to four stars in July 1952 and assumed command of Tactical Air Command in April 1954. He used the knowledge and leverage gained by the success of his tactical air forces in Korea to reshape a strengthened TAC, including the formation of Composite Air Strike Forces to deal quickly with limited wars. Weyland successfully deployed the new units for crises in the Middle East and Far East. However, he also began to focus on using his fighter-bombers to deliver nuclear weapons in support of NATO contingencies for a general war. The emphasis of "New Look" budgets, along with the predilections of his successors and the Air Force, would soon make that the dominant mission for TAC. (RG 342 NA II)

within TAC that could be deployed quickly to deal with "brush-fire" wars. But spurred by the "New Look" and the growing Soviet threat to NATO, the Air Force, and TAC with it, soon returned to its focus on general nuclear war.[8]

There was no real incentive to do otherwise. Perceived success in Korea reinforced the Air Force position that preparing for global war meant being ready for conflicts of lesser magnitude. *Air University Quarterly Review,* the USAF professional journal, published only two significant articles relating air-power to insurgencies in Southeast Asia during the entire decade of the 1950s. Nuclear strategies and strategists dominated U.S. military thinking and force structure, and strategic bombing of the enemy homeland remained the raison d'être of the U.S. Air Force. Even when RAND studies in the late 1950s for the Pacific Air Forces and Air University highlighted important differences between general and limited war, Air Force leadership failed to acknowledge them. The same studies also warned that American air forces were "predominately strategic forces deployed with intent to optimize the strategic assault on the source of Communist power," and even tactical air forces were "deployed primarily to support these strategic forces." USAF established training programs for the new threat of insurgent warfare in the early 1960s only after prodding by the Kennedy administration. Dennis Drew, an authority on airpower and a former Air Force doctrine writer, notes that USAF basic doctrine during the 1950s "seemed to assume that the struggles in Southeast Asia did not exist and, for the most part, that the Korean War had not happened." Service manuals stressed the strategic bombing mission throughout the 1950s, and although limited conflicts were occasionally mentioned, policy remained, "The best preparation for limited war is proper preparation for general war." The new USAF basic doctrinal manual that appeared in August 1964 devoted two pages to the subject of counterinsurgency, but thirteen were devoted to nuclear and conventional air operations in support of general war. Service emphasis "remained where it had been since the advent of nuclear weapons and the creation of the independent Air Force."[9]

The appointment of LeMay as vice chief of staff in 1957, and chief of staff four years later, reinforced the USAF emphasis on strategic nuclear bombing. By 1964, three-fourths of the highest-ranking officers on the Air Staff came from SAC. LeMay had completed that organization's transformation into the world's most powerful striking force and had even supported the making of two more movies to extol its virtues, *Bombers B-52* and *Gathering of Eagles.* Ironically, however, the most lasting image of his legacy comes from another film, *Dr. Strangelove: Or How I Learned to Stop Worrying and Love the Bomb.* LeMay has often been mistakenly identified with the character of Gen. Jack D.

Ripper, the commander who launches his bombers without orders to start World War III and counter the evils of fluoridation. LeMay decided early in his career that he lacked the political skills to be diplomatic with superiors and decided always to be blunt and straightforward with his opinions, "whether you liked it or not." He also appears to have enjoyed shocking people at times with some of his more inflammatory statements. But he would not start a war on his own. But like Gen. Buck Turgidson in the movie—the character that most resembles LeMay—he was going to make sure that if general war did begin, the United States would achieve the best possible result. Ripper's characterization was based more on Power, who succeeded LeMay as commander of SAC and remained in that capacity for seven years. He was an even more extreme advocate of SAC's mission than his predecessor. Power achieved notoriety in 1958 when he wrote a book on nuclear strategy called *Design for Survival*, but the secretary of defense would not approve its publication. In the book, Power decried disarmament and advocated a posture of overwhelming military superiority for the United States. He became famous in conservative circles as the author of the "banned book" and was the only military witness to testify against the nuclear test ban treaty before the Senate in 1963.[10]

In fairness to the Air Force, it was not the only service to focus on nuclear war at the expense of more limited conflicts. The Navy and Marine Corps had carried more than their fair share of the air burden in Korea. Possessing far fewer aircraft than FEAF, they had flown 41 percent of U.S. air sorties in the war, including 40 percent of interdiction missions and more than 50 percent of all close air support. They lost 1,248 aircraft, though only 564 were downed by enemy action, mostly during ground attack missions. The Navy learned much about the use of aircraft carriers in extended operations for force projection and realized the need for more capable jets and catapults. But the service focus also remained on general nuclear war. Postwar carriers were designed with new flight decks and support equipment compatible with nuclear bombers, and by 1954, all deployed carriers had nuclear weapons capable of hitting Soviet targets. Then the Navy's emphasis moved to perfecting ballistic missiles that could be fired from submerged nuclear submarines, resulting in the appearance of the first Polaris missile in 1960.[11]

Even the Army succumbed to the nuclear frenzy in the 1950s, with its focus on developing a Pentomic division to fight dispersed on the atomic battlefield utilizing 280mm cannons and the Davy Crockett mortar to deliver its own nuclear fire support. Soldiers returning from Korea to the Infantry School at Fort Benning in the summer of 1953 found themselves immediately involved in rewriting Army doctrinal manuals to incorporate the firepower of new tactical atomic weapons. However, the service remained dissatisfied with the close air support system that had been used in Korea. Almond continued to emphasize doctrinal disputes between the services at the Army War College, even preparing a student text detailing all the conceptual differences between the Army and the Air Force. Its purpose was "to enable a better understanding of the issues which hamper effective joint action in service planning at the present time." Efforts after the war to develop a mutually agreed upon air-ground system culminated in Exercise SAGEBRUSH in 1955. This joint test proved that the procedures outlined in the 1950 Joint Training Directive for Ground Operations, which had been used to shape Korean air-ground control, were "too cumbersome and time consuming" and needed revision. Unfortunately, the services could not agree on what those changes should be, although Army Chief of Staff Matthew Ridgway announced that the current Joint Training Directive had been recognized as deficient by everyone and would no longer bind the Army. The new Joint Air-Ground Operations Manual that came out in 1957 did not satisfy either service and described two different systems in separate chapters, the "Army Air-Ground System" and the "Tactical Air Control System" favored by the Air Force. Many Army officials also remained critical of the use of jet aircraft in ground support. They believed that such aircraft flew too high and too fast to find any targets except large ones for interdiction. They also believed that jets with heavy loads were too unwieldy to hit close air support targets accurately with the right ordnance, and thus risked causing friendly casualties. Ground troops who were subjected to bombing mistakes lost confidence in air support and quit asking for it. Although Army critics conceded that they had only anecdotal evidence to support their impressions, data collected by Fifth Air Force operations analysts showed that there had been a degradation in USAF tactical bombing accuracy against both pinpoint and line targets as the war went on. They did not attribute that decline to the replacement of F-51s by jets, however; instead, they concluded that it resulted from "restrictions upon the bomb release altitudes, the scarcity of good pinpoint targets, and the general character of a static war." Most impetus for the Army's development of helicopters came out of a desire to improve battlefield transportation, but some also resulted from hopes that this organic Army aviation could provide reliable close air support without having to rely on the Air Force.[12]

KOREA AND VIETNAM

None of the services were really ready for the situation they confronted in Vietnam, but again, civilian leaders based their early wartime decision making on high expectations for airpower. As Mark Clodfelter and Earl Tilford have chronicled, the Air Force had the wrong doctrine, equipment, and training to deal with limited war in Southeast Asia. Even America's expanded tactical airpower was not prepared for the new challenges. As Caroline Ziemke so eloquently stated, "Like Dorian Grey, TAC had sold its soul in exchange for vitality, and in Vietnam, the world got a look at its aged and decrepit conventional structure." Perhaps the Air Force could have successfully executed its initial proposal in 1964 for a classic strategic bombing campaign against ninety-four targets in North Vietnam that would have destroyed "its capacity to continue as an industrially viable state," but that contingency did not take into account the nature of the insurgency in the South or the concerns of President Johnson and his advisers about widening the war. While military leaders modeled their recommendations on strategy they believed had been successful in World War II, their civilian bosses hearkened back to the actions that had incited Chinese intervention in Korea. As the gradual escalation of ROLLING THUNDER (or "Rolling Blunder," as airmen refer to it today) continued, USAF had to relearn how to fight a joint limited war. The new campaign revealed again the difficulties with aerial interdiction of primitive and manpower-intensive supply systems and that USAF had still not developed effective night capabilities. For J. Lawton Collins, Vietnam reaffirmed a lesson learned in Korea: that "no amount of aerial bombing can prevent completely the forward movement of supplies, particularly in regions where ample manpower is available." The old interservice disputes about command and control and close air support quickly resurfaced, with additional friction over the role of helicopters. A RAND observer just back from Vietnam told Partridge that they were "reinventing the control system" all over again. Analysts of the early years of the air war in Vietnam noted that "not only were past mistakes repeated, but new challenges resulted in new mistakes." Command and control of tactical air operations was so bad it "would have led to disaster if U.S. forces had faced a capable air opponent." Ironically, the Barcus Report had come to the same conclusion about "coordination control" of joint airpower in Korea. Although the command of air elements in Vietnam was even more fragmented than in Korea, ROLLING THUNDER was primarily the responsibility of CINCPAC. It is interesting to speculate how the air campaign would have been conducted if it had begun a year earlier, when Gen. Jacob Smart was commander of the Pacific Air Forces under CINCPAC. Perhaps his Korean experience would have made a difference.[13]

Ironically, memories of the Korean air campaign had already helped keep the United States out of Indochina once. Ridgway became chief of staff of the Army in 1954 and remained disillusioned about the capabilities of airpower in limited war. In his book on the Korean conflict, he took a far different position from that of the Air Force, noting that the Army and Marines accounted for 97 percent of battle casualties and asserting, "it was the performance of the ground forces that determined the success or failure of the United Nations effort, which in turn determined the course of United States and United Nations policy." When he heard that the Eisenhower administration was considering testing the "New Look" with air intervention alone to save the beleaguered French garrison at Dienbienphu, he feared the United States had already forgotten the "bitter lesson" from Korea "that air and naval power alone cannot win a war and that inadequate ground forces cannot win one either." He was determined to avoid "making that same tragic error" in Indochina.[14]

Planning for Operation VAUTOUR (VULTURE) began in earnest in mid-April 1954 and had much in common with strategic bombing operations in Korea. The FEAF commander was now Gen. Earle Partridge, and on a routine liaison visit to Vietnam, he was informed by the French that the aerial operation to save Dienbienphu "had been cleared through diplomatic channels." Though he had heard nothing about it, Partridge notified the chief of FEAF Bomber Command, Brig. Gen. Joseph Caldera, to prepare a contingency plan. Bomber Command still had its wartime contingent of B-29s for a mass strike, but Caldera foresaw many problems with the operation when he flew to Vietnam to confer with the French. Among them were the fact that there were "no true B-29 targets" in the area, and bad monsoon weather necessitated the use of SHORAN guidance, which the French did not have.[15]

However, by that time, opposition to VAUTOUR had rendered such planning moot. Ridgway led the effort against it in the JCS, galvanized by the fact that the chairman, Adm. Arthur Radford, supported the mission. The Army chief of staff made his position very clear at a gathering at Radford's home for the visiting French chief of the armed forces staff, Gen. Paul Ely, on 20 March. When Radford asked if Ely just needed more airpower for success in Indochina, Ridgway challenged the assertion before the Frenchman could even reply, noting, "The experience of Korea, where we had complete domination of the air and a far more powerful air force, afforded no basis for thinking that some additional air power was going to bring decisive results on the ground." Ridgway had his staff conduct detailed studies on the difficulties involved with intervention in Indochina; presented briefings on their findings to the secretary of defense and President Eisenhower; and rallied the other service chiefs, including the Air Force's Gen. Nathan Twining, to support his position and isolate Radford. Key congressmen in early April also showed little confidence in the air option, warning, "Once the flag is committed, the use of land forces would surely follow," and demanding that Great Britain and other allies participate as well in a collective intervention. Democratic Senator Richard B. Russell of Georgia led the congressional opposition to VAU-TOUR. As chairman of the Armed Services Committee he had chaired the MacArthur hearings in 1951 and certainly remembered the acrimonious debates about the inflated expectations of airpower. When Great Britain refused to be drawn into "Radford's war against China," that ended any chance for VAUTOUR. Although American and French talks on intervention continued after the fall of Dienbienphu, no serious plans resulted. There is still some disagreement over whether Eisenhower really intended to intervene in Indochina, but the memories of the Korean air war were fresh enough in 1954 to inspire a vocal opposition that either reinforced the president's inclination to avoid direct military involvement in Vietnam or changed his mind by demonstrating just how perilous and divisive even a limited aerial intervention would be. Ridgway wrote of his role:

> When the day comes for me to face my Maker and account for my actions, the thing I would be most humbly proud of was the fact that I fought against, and perhaps contributed to preventing, the carrying out of some harebrained tactical schemes which would have cost the lives of thousands of men. To that list of tragic incidents that fortunately never happened I would add the Indo-China intervention.[16]

Unfortunately, Ridgway's independence and outspoken ways as Army chief of staff contributed to his early retirement in 1955, and he was not in a position of responsibility when problems in Indochina again tempted American intervention. Concerning Vietnam in the 1960s, Smart "was convinced that the terrible conditions that prevailed in Southeast Asia were not amenable to solution by the employment of military force," especially the destructive power of air strikes. Other veteran airmen from Korea disagreed. In March 1965, Power was the featured guest on NBC's *Meet the Press*. He had just retired after thirty-seven years of service, the last seven as "custodian of 90 percent of the free world's explosive firepower" at SAC. His book had been brought up-to-date and was finally about to be published. In it, Power recommended that the United States subject North Vietnam to the same type of air strategy used against Japan that MacArthur had refused to allow in Korea. Warnings would be issued that designated targets would be bombed if the aggression in the South did not cease. Power was convinced that after enough objectives had been destroyed, "within a few days and with minimum force, the conflict in South Vietnam would have been ended in our favor." Targets would be chosen for the "psychological impact of hurting their economy rather than trying to kill their citizens," but Power also admitted that it might take atomic weapons to finally coerce North Vietnamese compliance. He asserted that a few atomic bombs dropped on China would have ended the conflict in Korea, and because of overwhelming American strength, there was little risk of a nuclear war from similar attacks on North Vietnam. For Power, the incendiary bombs and warning leaflets he had dropped on Japan provided the inspiration for his ideal model for winning wars with airpower. As with the dam raids in 1953 just before the armistice, the LINEBACKER II B-52 attacks on North Vietnam shortly before the signing of the Paris Peace Accords appeared to justify the utility of unrestricted air attacks in a limited war to those who advocated them. Just as he felt in the early days in Korea, LeMay believed that concentrated bombing of North Vietnamese cities could have won that war "in any two-week period you want to mention."[17]

INSIGHTS FOR THE FUTURE

Although the longer air war in Southeast Asia reinforced insights from Korea about the difficulty of achieving decisive results with airpower in a limited war, the earlier "bizarre" conflict has some special characteristics even more relevant to the American strategic situation today. The impressive USAF performance in DESERT STORM again raised the expectations of what airpower can accomplish; at the same time, budget cuts have reduced the strength of the service to its lowest level since before the Korean War. However, it is hard to imagine any enemy being stupid enough to present us with another such opportunity to exert our high-technology firepower in open-maneuver warfare. With constrained resources and myriad operational possibilities, survivability of aircraft often becomes the dominant criterion for matching weapons platforms and missions, and the Air Force still prefers multirole planes that can be used for a variety of tasks. Fighter-bombers in Korea carried far fewer bombs and were not as accurate as medium bombers, but their survivability was superior in attacking heavily defended strategic targets, and they could also be used for close air support and interdiction, and sometimes even as interceptors. Jets did not have the loitering capability of slower propeller-driven aircraft that could wait around for on-call assignments, but again, superior speed on preplanned strikes lessened exposure to ground fire. Choosing survivability and acceptable performance in a variety of roles over maximum effectiveness in close air support might not please ground commanders, however, and that contributed to some of the interservice rancor

Jet fighter-bombers like this F-84 Thunderjet, shown striking an enemy position with napalm in early 1953, proved their versatility and worth in Korea. However, interservice differences about their proper use in close air support remained unresolved after the war. The F-84 was also the first fighter-bomber to be outfitted to deliver the new smaller atomic weapons, a capability that eventually diverted TAC's mission and aircraft development away from a focus on limited wars. Those deficiencies would have serious repercussions on the effectiveness of airpower in Vietnam. (Sergent Grover B. Smith Combat Photographs, USMA Special Collections)

over tactical air missions in Korea. This difference of opinion has not gone away. The USAF would rather buy multirole F-16s than less flexible A-10s, but the Army loves the ground support capabilities of the ungainly looking "Warthog" and has confidence that it will not be diverted to other types of missions far from the immediate battle zone.

The SAC experience in Korea shows the possible drawbacks of trying to use aircraft in too many different roles. The conclusion of the Barcus Report—that strategic nuclear bombers unable to perform conventional missions are "a luxury we cannot afford"—is especially relevant in these times of tight defense budgets, but there are risks in such employment. As the war went on, Far East Command came to believe that B-29s were poorly suited for theater missions against enemy installations protected by jet fighters and radar-directed defenses. As the second Weyland quote at the beginning of this chapter implies, and as the Korean War demonstrated, with the blurring of lines between tactical and strategic airpower, smaller fighter-bombers with conventional munitions can often deliver the decisive blows. And the failure of a nuclear-capable strategic bomber, even in an unfamiliar role, could threaten its deterrent credibility and the services' confidence in its capabilities. Another possible drawback to a focus on multiple missions is that orienting airmen for new roles could reduce their proficiency in more important ones. An IG report on Bomber Command in May 1953 noted that the SAC crews had perfected the night SHORAN missions they had to execute in Korea, but their ability to perform the visual or radar bombing required by the Emergency War Plan was nonexistent or uncertain. Or a commander might not want to use standard operating procedures, for fear of giving away free intelligence on more important missions or general war plans.[18]

Interservice differences over the control of theater aircraft remain as well. The use of a joint forces air component commander (JFACC) in DESERT STORM seemed to solve most problems with joint air operations, but much of the success of the allied air forces was due to their sheer numbers and redundancy. The Navy and Marines point out that the JFACC's staff was almost all Air Force and argue that the last "C" stands for "coordinator," so they should still maintain most control over their own air assets. One of the key lessons of any American joint operation, and especially in recent air wars, is that doctrine is not as important as personalities in maximizing performance. If the commanders of the different service components have the mutual confidence and respect to work together, their units will find some way to do so.

During the Korean conflict, inflated expectations of the capabilities of airpower influenced key choices by American decision makers in Washington and the Far East. Initially, many diplomats and politicians believed that airpower alone could turn the tide of the war, but by 1951, they were wondering how they could have been misled. Many ground commanders seemed to think "that if the Air Force didn't achieve a miracle it was no damn good." These leaders did not appreciate the limited utility of aerial destruction to achieve some ends or the limited striking power that FEAF really possessed.[19] Strate-meyer and Weyland actually did a fine job with the resources and restrictions they faced, fighting an unfamiliar enemy in an unfamiliar type of war, though it was not as perfect as their service believed. Their experience demonstrates the difficulty in limited conflicts of selecting airpower targets vulnerable and important enough so that threatening their destruction will have the desired political impact on enemy decision makers. However, the way the armistice was achieved allowed the Air Force to claim victory and avoid the deep intro-spection that might have reaped dividends, and saved lives, in Vietnam.

Even great success can sometimes have its drawbacks. In Korea, the United States had to face for the first time the legacy of its overwhelming air victory in World War II and the visions of decimated German and Japanese cities. In 1952, Rear Adm. W. S. Parsons, who had armed the first atomic bomb as a member of the crew of the *Enola Gay,* was acting as technical adviser for a movie on the life of its pilot, Paul Tibbets. He complained to the USAF Public Relations Film Branch that the script portrayed the key people who developed and delivered the bomb as being "all mixed up emotionally." He asserted that in reality they had all been focused on "fighting and winning," with no doubts about what they were doing, and admitted that "that is the terrible thing about war." The MGM scriptwriters replied that they had to portray "moral conflict" about dropping the bomb, because "we dare not portray in an American film today, an American airman killing eighty thousand Asiatics in a flash, and expressing no feelings of conscience about this, without seriously playing into the propaganda hands of the Kremlin." International reaction to American bombing in Korea demonstrated that the world still associated the application of airpower against an enemy homeland with images of Tokyo and Hiroshima. Even the much more precise air campaign in the Gulf War could not escape comparison to those World War II examples, especially in Asia and the Third World.[20] The same destructive power that makes airpower an effective deterrent by intimidating potential aggressors, or an effective military tool by punishing them for transgressions, can also make its use unpalatable to nations suspicious of American power or sensitive to civilian suffering. The military and political utility of the application of air-power must always be balanced against its diplomatic repercussions and the way its results will be perceived by world opinion. And as the disagreements over warning North Korean towns and cities demonstrate, what military leaders view as humane might not be interpreted the same way by diplomats or the press.

The Korean conflict has been called the "Forgotten War," but it has relevance today beyond the fact that North Korea is still a potential enemy. The airpower strategy produced by a combination of political, military, and resource constraints between 1950 and 1953 deserves study by leaders today struggling with similar dilemmas about the best use of the Air Force's destructive power in an uncertain world.

NOTES

INTRODUCTION

1. Testimony of Maj. Gen. Emmett O'Donnell, Jr., in U.S. Senate, 82d Congress, 1st Session, *Military Situation in the Far East: Hearings before the Committee on Armed Services and the Committee on Foreign Relations* (Washington, D.C.: USGPO, 1951), pt. 4, p. 3066.

2. Robert F. Futrell, *The United States Air Force in Korea 1950-1953*, rev. ed. (Washington, D.C.: USGPO, 1983), 63-66; letter, Maj. T. M. Sellers to his wife, 27 Nov 1952, furnished by Prof. Susan MacDonald, Illinois State University, Normal, Ill. The author of this book spent two years in Korea and still remembers his first winter field exercise, around Thanksgiving, where the nighttime temperature was sixteen degrees below zero Fahrenheit.

3. For a good short summary of LeMay's career, see Harry Borowski's entry in Roger J. Spiller, ed., *American Military Leaders* (New York: Praeger, 1989), 170-173. A good biography is Thomas M. Coffey's *Iron Eagle:The Turbulent Life of General Curtis LeMay* (New York: Crown, 1986). For more details on his World War II experience, see Conrad C. Crane, *Bombs, Cities, and Civilians: American Airpower Strategy in World War II* (Lawrence: University Press of Kansas, 1993), 125-137.

4. Wesley Frank Craven and James Lea Cate, eds., *The Army Air Forces in World War II*, vol. 2, *Europe: Torch to Pointblank, August 1942 to December 1943* (Chicago: University of Chicago Press, 1949), 478; Charles P. Cabell, *A Man of Intelligence: Memoirs of War, Peace, and the CIA* (Colorado Springs: Impavide Publications, 1997), 202-203.

5. Interview of Gen. Jacob E. Smart (ret.) by author, 2 Nov 1997, Arlington, Va., with changes provided by letter from General Smart on 29 Nov 1997, pp. 7-8, in possession of the author.

6. Futrell was the primary author for USAF Historical Studies No. 71, *United States Air Force Operations in the Korean Conflict, 25 June-1 November 1950*, No. 72, *United States Air Force Operations in the Korean Conflict, 1 November 1950-30 June 1952*, and No. 127, *United States Air Force Operations in the Korean Conflict, 1 July 1952-27 July 1953*, which cover all aspects of the Korean air war in great detail. He used them to produce his book *The United States Air Force in Korea 1950-1953*.

7. Richard Hallion, *The Naval Air War in Korea* (Baltimore: Nautical and Aviation Publishing Company of America, 1986).

8. Allan R. Millett provides the best coverage of the issues and techniques involved in close air support in the Korean War in his essay "Korea, 1950-1953," in *Case Studies in the Development of Close Air Support,* ed. Benjamin Franklin Cooling (Washington, D.C.: USGPO, 1990).

9. Interview of Gen. Jacob Smart by Lt. Col. Arthur McCant and Dr. James Hasdorff, 27-30 Nov 1978, pp. 188, 200, File K239.0512-1108, Air Force Historical Research Agency (AFHRA), Maxwell Air Force Base, Ala.

10. Cabell, *A Man of Intelligence,* 163.

11. David Rees, *Korea: The Limited War* (London: Macmillan and Company Limited, 1964), 460-461; Guenter Lewy, *America in Vietnam* (New York: Oxford University Press, 1978), 450; Bruce Cumings, *The Origins of the Korean War,* vol. 2, *The Roaring of the Cataract* (Princeton, N.J.: Princeton University Press, 1990), 748. Lewy argues that the proportion of civilian deaths to military ones in Korea is the highest of any war in the twentieth century. By his figures, 70 percent of those who died in the war were civilians. Documentation for any number is very sketchy, however. When I asked Bruce Cumings how he had computed his casualty totals, he told me that he got them from an encyclopedia.

12. Interview of Smart by author, pp. 5, 28.

CHAPTER 1. PRECEDENTS AND PRECONCEPTIONS

1. Letter, USAF Chief of Staff Carl Spaatz to Secretary of the Air Force Stuart Symington, 1947, Correspondence File, Declassified Documents, Box 4, Papers of Stuart Symington, Harry S. Truman Library, Independence, Mo.

2. Maj. Gen. Orville Anderson, "Air Warfare and Morality," *Air University Quarterly Review* 2 (winter 1949): 7. Anderson was the commandant of the Air War College at the time.

3. Air University lecture by Dan Dyer, "Horizontal Approach to Target Analysis," 12 Dec 1951, p. 7, File K239.716251-55, AFHRA, Maxwell Air Force Base, Ala. Dyer was the director of research of the Air Objectives Branch, Director of Intelligence, Headquarters, U.S. Air Force.

4. Interview of Thomas Power by Kenneth Leish, July 1960, Communications and Writings, Thomas S. Power Manuscript Collection, George Arents Research Library for Special Collections, Syracuse University, Syracuse, N.Y.; letter with attached report, Maj. Gen. Curtis LeMay to Gen. H. H. Arnold, 11 Mar 1945, File 312.1-2/59, 1945 AAG, Records of the Army Air Forces, Record Group 18, National Archives II, College Park, Md.

5. Kenneth P. Werrell, *Blankets of Fire: U.S. Bombers over Japan during World War II* (Washington, D.C.: Smithsonian, 1996), 152-154; Wesley Frank Craven and James Lea Cate, eds., *The Army Air Forces in World War II,* vol. 5, *The Pacific: Matterhorn to Nagasaki June 1944 to August 1945* (Chicago: University of Chicago Press, 1953), 750; for more details on the development of LeMay's incendiary tactics, see Conrad Crane, *Bombs, Cities, and Civilians: American Airpower Strategy in World War II* (Lawrence: University Press of Kansas, 1993), 120-136.

6. Foreword to Twenty-first Bomber Command Tactical Mission Report, Mission Number 40, Urban Area of Tokyo, 10 Mar 1945, prepared 15 Apr 1945, Box 26, Papers of Curtis LeMay, Manuscript Division, Library of Congress, Washington,

D.C.; Twentieth Air Force Mission Reports 297-302, 28-29 June 1945, File 760.331, AFHRA; Robert L. Gleason, "Psychological Operations and Air Power," *Air University Review* 22 (Mar-Apr 1971): 36-37.

7. Allied Translator and Interpreter Section, South West Pacific Area, Research Report No. 94, "Psychological Effect of Allied Bombing on the Japanese," 21 Sept 1944, Record Group 3, Reel 511, and Psychological Warfare Branch, U.S. Army Forces, Pacific Area, "Report on Psychological Warfare in the Southwest Pacific Area, 1944-1945," Record Group 4, Reel 617 of microfilm copy of Douglas MacArthur Archives at U.S. Military Academy Library, West Point, N.Y.; Craven and Cate, *Army Air Forces,* 5:696-699; for more on MacArthur's attitudes about bombing civilians, see Crane, *Bombs, Cities, and Civilians,* 122-123.

8. The plan was proposed in a letter from Laurence Kuter to Frederick Anderson, 15 Aug 1944, Operational Diary, Papers of Frederick L. Anderson, Hoover Institution on War, Revolution, and Peace, Stanford University, Stanford, Calif.: John D. Chappell, *Before the Bomb: How America Approached the End of the Pacific War* (Lexington: University Press of Kentucky, 1997), 194 n.86; Tami Davis Biddle, "British and American Approaches to Strategic Bombing: Their Origins and Implementation in the World War II Combined Bomber Offensive," *Journal of Strategic Studies* 18 (Mar 1995): 91, 117.

9. Msg 082328Z, Lauris Norstad to Carl Spaatz, 8 Aug 1945, Box 21, Papers of Carl Spaatz, Manuscript Division, Library of Congress.

10. Crane, *Bombs, Cities, and Civilians,* 136-142; the best new scholarship on the flaws of the bombing survey is Barton Bernstein, "Compelling Japan's Surrender without the A-bomb, Soviet Entry, or Invasion: Reconsidering the US Bombing Survey's Early Surrender Counterfactual," *Journal of Strategic Studies* 18 (June 1995): 101-148, along with Gian Peri Gentile's "A-Bombs, Budgets, and Morality: Using the Strategic Bombing Survey," *Air Power History* 44 (spring 1997): 18-31 and "Advocacy or Assessment? The United States Strategic Bombing Survey of Germany and Japan," *Pacific Historical Review* 66 (winter 1997): 53-79. Gentile has completed his dissertation on the survey at Stanford University. The Hansell quote is from Gentile's article in *Air Power History.*

11. Herman S. Wolk, *Planning and Organizing the Postwar Air Force 1943-1947* (Washington, D.C.: Office of Air Force History, 1984), 145-148; David R. Mets, *Master of Airpower: General Carl A. Spaatz* (Novato, Calif.: Presidio Press, 1988), 311-331; Walton S. Moody, *Building a Strategic Air Force* (Washington, D.C.: Air Force History and Museums Program, 1996), 329.

12. Robert F. Futrell, *Ideas, Concepts, Doctrine: Basic Thinking in the United States Air Force,* vol. 1, *1907-1960* (Maxwell Air Force Base, Ala.: Air University Press, 1989) 373-379; Anderson, "Air Warfare and Morality," 14; letter, Ira Eaker to Thomas Power, 6 May 1960, with 10 May reply and attached copy of Jerry Greene's "Capital Circus" newspaper column for 25 Apr 1960, Power Collection.

13. Futrell, *Ideas, Concepts, Doctrine,* 366-393.

14. Mets, *Master of Airpower,* 314-315; Futrell, *Ideas, Concepts, Doctrine,* 365-366; interview of Thomas Power by Kenneth Leish. For typical war plans see Steven T. Ross and David Alan Rosenberg, eds., *America's Plans for War against the Soviet Union, 1945-1950,* 15 vols. (New York: Garland, 1989); for more on the development of precision bombing doctrine, see Crane, *Bombs, Cities, and Civilians,* 12-27.

15. Dyer lecture; David Alan Rosenberg, "The Origins of Overkill: Nuclear

Weapons and American Strategy, 1945-1960," *International Security* 7 (spring 1983): 15; Fred Kaplan, *The Wizards of Armageddon* (New York: Simon and Schuster, 1983), 38-45; Futrell, *Ideas, Concepts, Doctrine,* 238. For more on Cabell's attitudes in World War II, see Crane, *Bombs, Cities, and Civilians,* 46, 106.

16. Barry H. Steiner, *Bernard Brodie and the Foundations of American Nuclear Strategy* (Lawrence: University Press of Kansas, 1991), 46-64, 269 n.11; "The Morale Factor in STRAP Planning," 5 Aug 1949, Box 11, Folder 17, Papers of Bernard Brodie, Special Collections Division, University Research Library, University of California at Los Angeles.

17. Kaplan, *Wizards of Armageddon,* 39-40, 45-49, 204-205; letter, Bernard Brodie to Thomas Power, 22 Dec 1950, Correspondence File, Dec 1950, Power Collection; RAND Corporation Social Sciences Division Research Memorandum 275, *The Warning of Target Populations in Air War: An Appendix of Working Papers* (Santa Monica, Calif.: RAND, Nov 1949), app. A and B (on Japan). The main report, RAND Progress Report R-167, 1 Nov 1949, is still classified.

18. Moody, *Building a Strategic Air Force,* 229-233, 255-264; Thomas M. Coffey, *Iron Eagle: The Turbulent Life of General Curtis LeMay* (New York: Crown, 1986), 270-344.

19. Futrell, *Ideas, Concepts, Doctrine,* 255; Moody, *Building a Strategic Air Force,* 105, 265-270; microfilm transcripts of hearings on *The Military Situation in the Far East and the Relief of General MacArthur* (Washington, D.C.: University Publications of America, 1977), p. 8082, reel 8. The transcripts are valuable because they include sections deleted from the published hearing records for security reasons.

20. Caroline F. Ziemke, "In the Shadow of the Giant: USAF Tactical Air Command in the Era of Strategic Bombing, 1945-1955" (Ph.D. diss., Ohio State University, 1989), 63-115; Jerome V. Martin, "Reforging the Sword: United States Air Force Tactical Air Forces, Air Power Doctrine, and National Security Policy, 1945-1956," Ph.D. diss., Ohio State University, 1988), 54-59.

21. Ziemke, "In the Shadow," 77-78; United States Army Combat Developments Command Institute of Special Studies, *A Short History of Close Air Support Issues,* July 1968, p. 35, copy furnished to the author by Allan Millett and Kelly Jordan; Futrell, *Ideas, Concepts, Doctrine,* 239, 250.

CHAPTER 2. OPENING MOVES

1. Msg, Ambassador Muccio to the Secretary of State, 25 June 1950, in U.S. Department of State, *Foreign Relations of the United States, 1950,* vol. 7, *Korea* (Washington, D.C.: USGPO, 1976), 133; hereafter, *FRUS.*

2. Testimony of Maj. Gen. Emmett J. O'Donnell, Jr., in U.S. Senate, 82d Congress, 1st Session, *Military Situation in the Far East: Hearings before the Committee on Armed Services and the Committee on Foreign Relations* (Washington, D.C.: USGPO, 1951), pt. 4, p. 3063.

3. Memoranda of conversation by Ambassador Jessup, 25 and 26 June 1950, in *FRUS, 1950,* 7:157-161, 178-183; USAF Historical Study No. 71, *United States Air Force Operations in the Korean Conflict, 25 June-1 November 1950* (Maxwell Air Force Base, Ala.: USAF Historical Division, 1 July 1952), 5-7; msg, GHQ ADCOM Korea to Dept. of the Army et al., 29 June 1950, General Decimal File, 1950-1951,

091 Korea, Box 121, Record Group 319, Army Operations, National Archives II, College Park, Md.

4. James F. Schnabel, *Policy and Direction: The First Year* (Washington, D.C.: USGPO, 1972), 76; memorandum of a meeting in the Office of the Under Secretary of State, 28 June 1950, and msg JCS 84681, JCS to MacArthur, 29 June 1950, in *FRUS, 1950,* 7:213, 240-241; USAF Historical Study No. 71, 9; Air Objective Section, A-2 Division, HQ FEAF, "Target Briefing—FEAF Area of Interest," 1 Aug 1949, File 720.328-1, AFHRA, Maxwell Air Force Base, Ala.; Philip S. Meilinger, *Hoyt S. Vandenberg: The Life of a General* (Bloomington: Indiana University Press, 1989), 163. Except for Seoul and southern ports, all key targets in Korea were in the more industrialized North.

5. USAF Historical Study No. 71, 16-17, 72; Robert F. Futrell, *The United States Air Force in Korea 1950-1953,* rev. ed. (Washington, D.C.: USGPO, 1983), 65; interview of Gen. Earle Partridge by Tom Sturm and Hugh Ahmann, 23-25 Apr 1974, p. 594, Oral History File K239.0512-729, AFHRA; interview of Gen. Jacob Smart by author, 2 Nov 1997, with additions provided by letter on 29 Nov 1997, pp. 13-14, in possession of author; memo, Col. W. A. Harris to Deputy Commandant, Subject: Reply to AFF Letter on Effectiveness of Close Air Support in Korea, 3 Nov 1952, with attachments, Edward M. Almond Papers, U.S. Army Military History Institute, Carlisle Barracks, Pa.; Allan R. Millett, "Korea, 1950-1953," in *Case Studies in the Development of Close Air Support,* ed. Benjamin Franklin Cooling (Washington, D.C.: USGPO, 1990), 363; Meilinger, *Vandenberg,* 172.

6. Msgs, HQ USAF to COMGENFEAF, 1 July 1950, and Norstad to Stratemeyer, 5 July 1950, Pacific I File, Box 56; msgs, Vandenberg to Stratemeyer, 19 July 1950, and Norstad to Stratemeyer, 24 July 1950, July 1950 Redline Files, Box 86; entry for 7 July 1950, Vandenberg Diary, Box 2, Papers of Hoyt Vandenberg, Manuscript Division, Library of Congress, Washington, D.C.

7. Curtis LeMay Diary #2, 1 July 1950 to 30 Dec 1950, entries for 1, 2, 4, 10, and 22 July, Box 103; letters, O'Donnell to LeMay, 11 July 1950, and Col. Charles Bondley to LeMay, 16 July 1950, File FEAF 1, Box 65, Papers of Curtis LeMay, Manuscript Division, Library of Congress; Futrell, *USAF in Korea,* 46-47, 71-74; Partridge interview, 656-657. During the war, USAF was transitioning between designating units as "groups" or "wings," and the terms are often used interchangeably.

8. Memorandum of teletype conference, 6 July 1950, in *FRUS, 1950,* 7:311; Universal International Newsreels, vol. 23, no. 367, 7 July 1950; no. 370, 18 July 1950; no. 371, 21 July 1950; no. 378, 14 Aug 1950; no. 380, 21 Aug 1950; no. 385, 7 Sept 1950; no. 386, 11 Sept 1950, no. 387, 14 Sept 1950, all in Record Group 200, National Archives II.

9. Entry for 10 July 1950, Stratemeyer Diary, File K720.13A, June-Oct 1950, AFHRA, Maxwell Air Force Base, Ala.; Futrell, *USAF in Korea,* 48-50. For the best coverage of the many disputes over close air support, see Millett, "Korea."

10. USAF Historical Study No. 71, 28-29; Commander in Chief, U.S. Pacific Fleet, Interim Evaluation Report No. 1, 25 June to 15 Nov 1950, Combat Operations Sections, Naval Air, pp. 282-285, 312, 321, Naval Historical Center, Washington, D.C.; Partridge interview, 605; James A. Winnefeld and Dana J. Johnson, *Joint Air Operations: Pursuit of Unity in Command and Control, 1942-1991* (Annapolis: Naval Institute Press, 1993), 42-43, 61.

11. USAF Historical Study No. 71, 29-31; msgs, V0193CG, Stratemeyer to

Norstad, 16 Aug 1950, and Norstad to Stratemeyer, 21 Aug 1950, Aug 1950 Redline Files, Box 86, Vandenberg Papers; interview of Partridge by Lieutenant Colonel Collins, Major Julian, and Major King, 12 Apr 1968, p. 13, File K239.0512-919, AFHRA.

12. Msg, CG FEAF to CG 5th AF, 29 July 1950; msgs, CG FEAF to COM NAVFE, 30 July and 3 Aug (2) 1950, File, FEAF In, 25 June-Aug 1950, Record Group 9, Radiograms, Douglas MacArthur Archives, reel 180 of microfilm copy in USMA Library, West Point, N.Y.

13. Redline msg, TS 1814, Vandenberg to Stratemeyer, 3 July 1950, LeMay Diary #2; Maj. Harold D. Jefferson, "Development of FEAF Bomber Command Target System," in *FEAF Bomber Command History, 4 Jul-31 Oct 1950,* vol. I, book I, File K713.01-1, AFHRA. SAC plans and JCS directives sometimes used different names for the same target grouping. Hungnam and Konan were interchangeable, as were Chongjin and Seishin.

14. Letter, O'Donnell to LeMay, 11 July 1950, File FEAF 1, Box 65, LeMay Papers; Thomas M. Coffey, *Iron Eagle: The Turbulent Life of General Curtis LeMay* (New York: Crown, 1986), 306. Before the meeting with MacArthur, O'Donnell had briefed Stratemeyer on SAC's bombing plans and received his support for them. The preference for overwhelming military force expressed by LeMay was echoed in the doctrine developed by Secretary of Defense Caspar Weinberger that helped shape our commitment to DESERT STORM.

15. HQ USAF, *An Evaluation of the Effectiveness of the United States Air Force in the Korean Campaign,* vol. V, *Psychological Warfare,* pp. 2, 107-108, File 168.041-1, AFHRA.

16. Transcript of telephone conversation between LeMay and General Ramey, 29 July 1950; memo, Subject: Mission Directive, Stratemeyer to O'Donnell, 11 July 1950, with message revising it; memo, Subject: Mission Priority Assigned This Command, O'Donnell to Stratemeyer, 19 July 1950; letter, O'Donnell to LeMay, 21 July 1950, all in LeMay Diary #2; letter, Col. Charles Bondley to LeMay, 16 July 1950, File FEAF 1, Box 65, LeMay Papers.

17. Futrell, *USAF in Korea,* 52-55; entries for 22 July through 8 Aug 1950, Weyland Diary, included with Stratemeyer Diary, File K720.13A; interview of Gen. Otto Weyland by Kenneth Leish, June 1960, pp. 44-45, File K146.34-105, AFHRA.

18. Entry 4631, Weyland, O. P., Facts on Demand, USAF Public Affairs Office.

19. Letter, Ramey to LeMay, 28 July 1950, TS Doc B-5972, Box 195, LeMay Papers; USAF Historical Study No. 71, 83; msgs, JCS 87522, JCS to CINCFE, 31 July 1950, and JCS 88806, JCS to CINCFE, 15 Aug 1950, Outgoing Messages, Box 9, 25 June 1950-29 Jan 1952, Records of the Joint Chiefs of Staff, Record Group 218, National Archives II; Jefferson, "Development of FEAF Bomber Command Target System."

20. Letters, Stratemeyer to LeMay, 12 Aug 1950, Stratemeyer File, Box 59, and O'Donnell to LeMay, 20 Aug 1950, File FEAF 1, Box 65, LeMay Papers; msg AX 5078, CG FEAF to subordinate commands, 15 Aug 1950, File FEAF In, 25 June-Aug 1950, Record Group 9, MacArthur Archives, reel 180 of microfilm version in USMA Library; 16 Aug entry, Stratemeyer Diary; Film 342-USAF-18478 and Universal International Newsreel, vol. 23, no. 380, 21 Aug 1950, Record Group 200, National Archives II; Gen. Paik Sun Yup, *From Pusan to Panmunjom* (New York: Brassey's, 1992), 39-40.

21. LeMay Diary #2, entries for 29 and 30 Jul 1950, including transcripts of telephone conversations between LeMay and General Ramey of the Air Staff, Box 103, LeMay Papers.

22. Ibid.; entries for 28 June and 9 July 1950, Folder, Historical Record Jan-July 50, Box 16, Matthew B. Ridgway Papers, U.S. Army Military History Institute, Carlisle Barracks, Pa. Bradley was always uneasy with those generals who had outranked him during World War II, and he would not handle MacArthur very well in the next few months. Calling in sick might have been a simple way to avoid dealing with Eisenhower, especially since he appeared to be filled with ideas about how to better prosecute the war.

23. Memo, Stefan Possony to Col. Walter Putnam, Subject: The Use of Atomic Bombs in Korea, 27 July 1950, with 2 Aug and 7 Aug 1950 transmittal memos by Col. O. L. Grover, File 385.2 Korea (28 July 1950), Box 906, Record Group 341, Records of Headquaters USAF; Joint War Plans Branch, G-3, summary sheet and attached report, "Employment of Atomic Bombs in Korea," 14 July 1950, General Decimal File, 1950-1951, 091 Korea, Box 34-A, Record Group 319, Army Operations, National Archives II.

24. Memo, MG Charles Bolte to General Gruenther, Subject: Use of the Atomic Bomb in Korea, 25 July 1950 (original and altered copies), and Memo, BG J. E. Moore to Asst Chief of Staff G-3, Subject: Use of Atom Bomb on Korea, 21 Aug 1950, General Decimal File, 1950-1951, 091 Korea, Box 34-A, Record Group 319.

25. J. Lawton Collins, *War in Peacetime: The History and Lessons of Korea* (Boston: Houghton Mifflin, 1969), 83; Roger Dingman, "Atomic Diplomacy during the Korean War," *International Security* 13 (winter 1988-89): 60-65; LeMay Diary #2, entries for 3-6 Aug, 13 Sept 1950, Box 103, LeMay Papers; msg, JCS 87570, JCS to MacArthur, 31 July 1950, Records of General Headquarters, FEC, SCAP, and UNC, Office of the Chief of Staff, Chief of Staff Subject File 1945-52, File TS Personal for 1949-1952, Box 3, Records of United States Army Commands, 1942-, Record Group 338, National Archives II. Robert F. Travis was the commander of the Ninth Bombardment Wing killed in the B-29 crash at Fairfield-Suisun Air Force Base, which was subsequently named in his honor.

26. Msgs, Norstad to Stratemeyer, 13 and 18 July 1950, July 1950 Redline Files; msg, Vandenberg to Stratemeyer, 21 Aug 1950, Aug 1950 Redline Files, Box 86, Vandenberg Papers; msg, JCS 87501, JCS to CINCFE, 30 July 1950, Outgoing Messages, Box 9, 25 June 1950-29 Jan 1952, Record Group 218.

27. Msgs, Vandenberg to Stratemeyer, 19 and 25 July 1950; msgs, Stratemeyer to Vandenberg, 23 and 26 July 1950, July 1950 Redline Files, Box 86, Vandenberg Papers.

CHAPTER 3. AIRPOWER GETS ITS CHANCE

1. Msg C68572, CINCFE to DA, 9 Nov 1950, Korea File #3, June 1950-Apr 1951, Record Group 6, Far East Command, Douglas MacArthur Archives, reel 624 of microfilm copy in USMA Library, West Point, N.Y.

2. Testimony of Gen. Douglas MacArthur in U.S. Senate, 82d Congress, 1st Session, *Military Situation in the Far East: Hearings before the Committee on Armed Services and the Committee on Foreign Relations* (Washington, D.C.: USGPO, 1951), pt. 1, p. 309.

3. USAF Historical Study No. 71, *United States Air Force Operations in the Korean Conflict, 25 June-1 November 1950* (Maxwell Air Force Base, Ala.: USAF Historical Division, 1 July 1952), 94-96.

4. Msg, AX 4143, CG FEAF to CG FEAF Bomber Command, 12 Aug 1950; msg AX 4169, CG FEAF to CG FEAF Bomber Command, 13 Aug 1950, File FEAF In, 25 June-Aug 1950, Record Group 9, MacArthur Archives, reel 180 of microfilm copy in USMA Library; testimony of Maj. Gen. Emmett O'Donnell, Jr., *Military Situation in the Far East,* pt. 4, p. 3092; USAF Historical Study No. 71, 84-89; msg, CG FEAF to HQ USAF, 25 Aug 1950, Redline Files, Aug 1950, Box 86, Papers of Hoyt Vandenberg, Manuscript Division, Library of Congress, Washington, D.C. SAC's Seishin grouping was called Chongjin in JCS directives, and Konan became Hungnam.

5. HQ 5th AF, *History of the Fifth Air Force, 25 June 1950-31 October 1950,* vol. I, pp. iv-v, File K730.01, AFHRA, Maxwell Air Force Base, Ala.; USAF Historical Study No. 71, 44-46; letter, Lt. Gen. George Stratemeyer to Vandenberg, 17 Sept 1950, Pacific I File, Box 56, Vandenberg Papers; Chester L. Blunk, *"Every Man a Tiger": The 731st USAF Night Intruders over Korea* (Manhattan, Kans.: Sunflower University Press, 1987), 14-27, 107.

6. Memorandum by the Under Secretary of State, 18 Aug 1950, and msg, Ambassador in India to Secretary of State, 5 Oct 1950, in U.S. Department of State, *Foreign Relations of the United States, 1950,* vol. 7, *Korea* (Washington, D.C.: USGPO, 1976), 599-600, 880-883 (hereafter, *FRUS*); msgs, Norstad to Stratemeyer, 21 Sept 1950, and Stratemeyer to Norstad, 22 Sept 1950, Redline Files, Sept 1950, Box 86, Vandenberg Papers; USAF Historical Study No. 71, 92-93; Gen. Paik Sun Yup, *From Pusan to Panmunjom* (New York: Brassey's, 1992), 78.

7. Letter, O'Donnell to LeMay, 9 Sept 1950, File B-7136, Box 196, and memo, Stratemeyer to O'Donnell, Subject: Emergency Use of B-29s, 3 Sept 1950, with 5 Sept endorsement from O'Donnell, Stratemeyer File, Box 65, Papers of Curtis LeMay, Manuscript Division, Library of Congress; msg AX-1393B, CG 5th AF to CG FEAF, 23 Sept 1950, in Hist. Off., HQ FEAF, *History of the Far East Air Forces, 25 June-31 Dec 1950,* vol. II, p. 91, File K720.01, and msg, CG FEAF to CG 5th AF, 20 Sept 1950, in HQ USAF, *An Evaluation of the Effectiveness of the United States Air Force in the Korean Campaign,* vol. I, pt. III, p. 235, File 168.041-1, AFHRA; for the viewpoint of British reporters, see Reginald Thompson, *Cry Korea* (London: MacDonald and Co., 1951), 94, and Rene Cutforth, *Korean Reporter* (London: Allan Wingate, 1952), 167, 173. One should be particularly wary of Thompson's opinions, as he is so virulently anti-American as to verge on being racist, but on the overuse of airpower, he has many corroborators. For examples of the many leaflets dropped to warn civilians, see Psychological Warfare, Korea Leaflets, Record Group 6, McArthur Archives, reel 629 of the microfilm copy at the USMA Library.

8. Msg, JCS 92658, JCS to MacArthur, 26 Sept 1950, Outgoing Messages, Box 9, 25 June 1950-29 Jan 1952, Records of the Joint Chiefs of Staff, Record Group 218, National Archives II, College Park, Md.; msg, CX63904, CINCFE to DA, 21 Sept 1950, File JCS Outgoing, July 1950-Apr 1951, Reel 186, and msg, AX 2607, CG FEAF to CG FEAF Bomber Command, 22 Oct 1950, File FEAF In, Oct 1950, Reel 180, Record Group 9, MacArthur Archives; USAF Historical Study No. 71, 94; Robert F. Futrell, *The United States Air Force in Korea 1950-1953,* rev. ed. (Washington, D.C.: USGPO, 1983), 188-194. For a detailed listing of the results of the strategic campaign, see USAF Historical Study No. 71, 87-89.

9. See documents in *FRUS, 1950,* 7:566-567, 573-577, 588-589, 593, 613-614, 660, 705-707, 721-722; msgs, TS 3297, HQ USAF to COMGENFEAF, 4 Aug 1950, TS 3532, CG FEAF to C/S USAF, 13 Aug 1950, TS 4016, Vandenberg to Stratemeyer, 31 Aug 1950, F51 Incident/Rashin Warnings File, Box 87, and msg, 52685, Vandenberg to Stratemeyer, Redline Files, Aug 1950, Box 86, Vandenberg Papers; letter, O'Donnell to LeMay with handwritten comments, 20 Aug 1950, File FEAF 1, Box 65, LeMay Papers; msgs, JCS 90734, JCS to CINCFE, 6 Sept 1950, JCS 90943, JCS to MacArthur, 8 Sept 1950, Outgoing Messages, Box 9, 25 June 1950-29 Jan 1952, and msg, CX 62348, CINCFE to COMGENARMYEIGHT, 7 Sept 1950, Incoming Messages, Box 1, 29 May 1950-3 Aug 1951, Record Group 218.

10. Msg, JCS 92986, JCS to MacArthur, 29 Sept 1950, Outgoing Messages, Box 9, 25 June 1950-29 Jan 1952, and msg, C 65036, MacArthur to JCS, 30 Sept 1950, Incoming Messages, Box 1, 29 May 1950-3 Aug 1951, Record Group 218; entries for 27, 28, and 30 Sept 1950, Stratemeyer Diary, File K720.13A, June-Oct 1950, and HQ USAF, *An Evaluation of the Effectiveness of the United States Air Force in the Korean Campaign,* vol. V, *Psychological Warfare,* pp. 108-109, File 168.041-1, AFHRA; testimony of Gen. J. Lawton Collins, *Military Situation in the Far East,* pt. 2, pp. 1362-1363.

11. See documents in *FRUS, 1950,* 7:916-917, 987, 991-992, 1025-1026, 1038, 1050-1051, 1074; msg, JCS 94799, JCS to CINCFE, 22 Oct 1950, File JCS Incoming, 30 June 1950-5 Apr 1951, Reel 186, Record Group 9, MacArthur Archives; Futrell, *USAF in Korea,* 198.

12. Conrad Crane, *Bombs, Cities, and Civilians: American Airpower Strategy in World War II* (Lawrence: University Press of Kansas, 1993), 122-123; "Fifth Report of the United Nations Command to the Security Council, United Nations, on the Course of Military Operations in Korea," 5 Oct 1950, in *Military Situation in the Far East,* appendices, p. 3409; msg, AX 4169, CG FEAF to CG Bomber Command, 13 Aug 1950, File, FEAF In, 25 June-Aug 1950, Reel 180, Record Group 9, MacArthur Archives; Douglas MacArthur, *Reminiscences* (New York: McGraw-Hill, 1964), 366; memorandum of teletype conference, 6 July 1950, in *FRUS, 1950,* 7:311.

13. *FEAF Bomber Command History, 1 Nov 1950-31 Jan 1951,* vol. I, book I, pp. 3-5, 35, File K713.01-9, and vol. II, book IV, Summaries of Missions No. 185, 186, and 188, File K713.01-10, AFHRA; msg, M22411, Stratemeyer to Vandenberg, 5 Nov 1950, Redline File, Nov 1950, Box 86, Vandenberg Papers; msgs, AX 3076, AX 3085, AX 3167, AX 5454, and AX 3325, Stratemeyer to O'Donnell and Maj. Gen. Earle Partridge, CG 5th Air Force, 5, 8, and 12 Nov 1950, File FEAF In, Nov-Dec 1950, Reel 180, Record Group 9, MacArthur Archives; *FRUS, 1950,* 7:1175; entry for 8 Nov 1950 at 1600, Weyland Diary of Korea, File 168.7104-3, and chart, "FEAF Bomber Command Bombs Expended," *FEAF Bomber Command Digest, Nov-Dec 1950,* File K168.041-1, vol. 13, pt. 2, AFHRA; see exchange of JCS-MacArthur messages in Incoming Messages, Box 1, 29 May 1950-3 Aug 1951, and Outgoing Messages, Box 9, 25 June 1950-29 Jan 1952, Record Group 218; msg, C68572, CINCFE to DA, 9 Nov 1950, Korea File #3, June 1950-Apr 1951, Reel 624, Record Group 6, Far East Command, MacArthur Archives; "U.S. Said to Weigh Power Dam Warning," *New York Times,* 6 Nov 1950, p. 1. For example of press coverage of Kanggye, see "New Army Facing the United Nations," *Times of London,* 6 Nov 1950, p. 4.

14. Entry for 2 Oct 1950, Partridge Diary of Korea, File 168.7104-1, AFHRA; letter, LeMay to Allan Davidson, 15 Jan 1952, Correspondence File, January 1952, Box 2, Thomas S. Power Manuscript Collection, George Arents Research Library for Special Collections, Syracuse University, Syracuse, N.Y.; msg, TS5400, Vandenberg to Stratemeyer, 7 Nov 1950, Redline File, Nov 1950, Vandenberg Papers.

15. Mark Andrew O'Neill, "The Other Side of the Yalu: Soviet Pilots in the Korean War, Phase I, 1 November 1950-12 April 1951" (Ph.D. diss., Florida State University, 1996), 13-51.

16. Ibid., 59-94, 118.

17. Phillip S. Meilinger, *Hoyt S. Vandenberg: The Life of a General* (Bloomington: Indiana University Press, 1989), 174-175, 180; Futrell, *USAF in Korea,* 220-223; MacArthur, *Reminiscences,* 368-372; msgs, JCS 95878 and 95949, JCS to CINCFE, 6 Nov 1950, Outgoing Messages, Box 9, 25 June 1950-29 Jan 1952, and msg, C-68396, CINCFE to DEPTAR, 6 Nov 1950, Incoming Messages, Box 1, 29 May 1950-3 Aug 1951, Record Group 218; msg, AX 31123, CG FEAF to CG 5th AF et al., 6 Nov 1950, File FEAF In, Nov-Dec 1950, Record Group 9, MacArthur Archives, reel 180 of microfilm copy in USMA Library.

18. Meilinger, *Vandenberg,* 180; Futrell, *USAF in Korea,* 222-223; O'Neill, "Other Side of the Yalu," 63; "Ninth Report of the United Nations Command to the Security Council, United Nations, on the Course of Military Operations in Korea," 27 Dec 1950, in *Military Situation in the Far East,* appendices, pp. 3433-3434.

19. Interview of Gen. Jacob Smart (Ret.) by author, 2 Nov 1997, Arlington, Va., with changes provided by letter from Smart on 29 Nov 1997, in possession of author; testimony of Gen. Hoyt Vandenberg, in *Military Situation in the Far East,* pt. 2, pp. 1377, 1467, 1486.

20. Appendix no. 4, "The Collection of Air Technical Intelligence in Korea," in Concepts Division, Aerospace Studies Institute, *Guerrilla Warfare and Airpower in Korea, 1950-53* (Maxwell Air Force Base, Ala.: Air University, Jan 1964), 228-232.

21. Interview of Gen. Earle Partridge by Tom Sturm and Hugh Ahmann, 23-25 Apr 1974, p. 568, Oral History K239.0512-729, AFHRA; Futrell, *USAF in Korea,* 6, 29, 34, 502; *Guerrilla Warfare and Airpower in Korea,* 73-80. In his autobiography *How Many Times Can I Die?* (Brooksville, Fla.: Brownsville Printing, 1981), Nichols even claims that he procured a copy of the plans for the NKPA invasion, but his superiors did not believe his reports that war was coming. He retired from service as a colonel in 1962.

22. Partridge interview, p. 568; msg, O. P. Weyland to Vandenberg, 21 July 1951, Redlines, June 1951 to . . . , Folder 1, Box 86, Vandenberg Papers; Ministry of National Defense, Republic of Korea, *The History of the United Nations Forces in the Korean War,* vol. 2 (Seoul: ROK Ministry of National Defense, 1973), 694-695; "Britons Still Argue over U.S. MIG Bribe," *New York Times,* 14 May 1953, p. 3; USAF Historical Study No. 127, *United States Air Force Operations in the Korean Conflict, 1 July 1952-27 July 1953* (Maxwell Air Force Base, Ala.: Air University, 1 July 1956), 62-63. Some have claimed that Communist leaders restricted the flights of their planes because of MOOLAH out of fear that pilots would defect, but after a thorough analysis, FEAF concluded in late 1953, "No positive information has been made available to substantiate the conclusion that the announcement of the $100,000 offer was responsible for any variation in Communist air activity."

23. Partridge interview, p. 568; testimony of Gen. Hoyt Vandenberg, in *Military*

Situation in the Far East, pt. 2, pp. 1463, 1641; msg, White to Weyland, 23 Feb 1952, Redlines, Nov 1951 to . . . , Folder 1, Box 87, and "Tabular Comparison of Aircraft of the U.S. and the U.S.S.R.," 1 May 1952, File 13, Box 84, Vandenberg Papers; interview of Lt. Gen. James T. Stewart by Col. Charles Andrean, 1986, p. 182, James T. Stewart Papers, U.S. Army Military History Institute, Carlisle Barracks, Pa. After the war, American test pilots on Okinawa got to fly the MiG-15 that the defector had brought out. They liked it but wanted to modify it by adding the missing systems they were used to. Stewart added up their suggested modifications and figured that the result would be just as heavy as an F-86 and fly the same way. Mark O'Neill says that Soviet fliers also had complaints about the MiG-15: the framed double-paned glass panels of the canopy sometimes allowed moisture to become trapped between the panes and freeze, pilots lacked G-suits and good helmets, they had to breathe pure oxygen at high altitudes, and the plane had poor air brakes and was not very maneuverable in the horizontal plane.

24. Memoranda by the Director of the Policy Planning Staff, 4 Nov 1950, and by the Planning Adviser, Bureau of Far Eastern Affairs, 8 Nov 1950, in *FRUS, 1950,* 7:1041-1042, 1098-1100; JCS 2173, note by the Secretaries to the JCS on Possible Employment of Atomic Bombs in Korea, 21 Nov 1950, and memo, G-3 to Chief of Staff, US Army, Subject: Possible Employment of Atomic Bombs in Korea, 16 Nov 1950, General Decimal File, 1950-1951, 091 Korea, Box 34-A, Record Group 319, Army Operations, National Archives II.

25. Msg, C69808, MacArthur to JCS, 25 Nov 1950, Incoming Messages, Box 1, 29 May 1950-3 Aug 1951, Record Group 218; J. Lawton Collins, *War in Peacetime: The History and Lessons of Korea* (Boston: Houghton Mifflin, 1969), 215-216. Stratemeyer admired MacArthur so much and considered him such a friend of the Air Force that the FEAF chief thought that CINCFE deserved another Medal of Honor. Vandenberg and Finletter told Stratemeyer that they supported his proposal but wanted the recommendation to come from someone other than an Air Force officer. Otherwise, it might look like USAF was trying to influence MacArthur's testimony in congressional hearings on tactical air support that were expected to begin shortly. See letter, Stratemeyer to Vandenberg, 13 Nov 1950, with reply, Pacific I File, Box 56, Vandenberg Papers.

26. Shu Guang Zhang, *Mao's Military Romanticism: China and the Korean War, 1950-1953* (Lawrence: University Press of Kansas, 1995), 82-84; Chen Jian, *China's Road to the Korean War* (New York: Columbia University Press, 1994), 175-177, 199-209. In October 1950, two Soviet air divisions turned over their 231 aircraft to the Communist Chinese Air Force, and during the next two months, the Soviet air force sent nine fighter divisions, three attack aircraft divisions, and a bomber division to China for defensive purposes only. Periodic intelligence reports about these aircraft would raise fears in the Far East Command about a possible surprise Soviet air attack on UN forces in Korea. New releases from Soviet archives are changing the views of the actual course of events leading to Chinese intervention in 1950, but they have also reinforced the importance of the issue of Soviet air cover in Chinese decision making. See Alexandre Y. Mansourov, "Stalin, Mao, Kim, and China's Decision to Enter the Korean War, September 16-October 15, 1950: New Evidence from the Russian Archives," *Cold War International History Project Bulletin* (winter 1995-1996): 94-119, and Shen Zhihua, "The Discrepancy between the Russian and Chinese Versions of Mao's 2 October Message to Stalin on Chinese Entry into the

Korean War: A Chinese Scholar's Reply," *Cold War International History Project Bulletin* (winter 1996-1997): 237-242.

CHAPTER 4. CHOOSING NEW TARGETS AND RESTORING THE BALANCE

1. Testimony of Maj. Gen. Emmett O'Donnell, Jr., in U.S. Senate, 82d Congress, 1st Session, *Military Situation in the Far East: Hearings before the Committee on Armed Services and the Committee on Foreign Relations* (Washington, D.C.: USGPO, 1951), pt. 4, p. 3091.

2. Testimony of Gen. Hoyt Vandenberg, *Military Situation in the Far East,* pt. 2, pp. 1378-1379.

3. U.S. Department of State, *Foreign Relations of the United States, 1950,* vol. 7, *Korea* (Washington, D.C.: USGPO, 1976), 1242-1248, 1263-1264, 1276-1281, 1291-1295 (hereafter, *FRUS*); memorandum, Col. Noel Parrish to General McKee, 5 Dec 1950, OPD 381 Korea (9 May 1947), Sec. 12, Box 894, Record Group 341, Records of Headquarters, USAF, National Archives II, College Park, Md. In reality, American intelligence had overestimated the number of bombers available to Communist forces in Manchuria and did not know that Stalin had given strict orders to all Soviet bomber and ground-attack units to stay out of Korean airspace. See Mark A. O'Neill, "The Other Side of the Yalu: Soviet Pilots in the Korean War, Phase One, 1 November 1950-12 April 1951" (Ph.D. diss., Florida State University, 1996), 125-126.

4. Memorandum, Gen. J. Lawton Collins to the JCS, Subject: Report on Visit to FECOM and Korea, 4-7 Dec 1950, 8 Dec 1950, on reel IX of the microfilm collection, *Records of the Joint Chiefs of Staff,* pt. 2, *1946-53, The Far East* (Washington, D.C.: University Publications of America, 1979).

5. Gen. Omar N. Bradley, Memoranda of Activities Leading up to the Relief of Gen. Douglas MacArthur, 24 Apr 1951, with handwritten corrections, Box, Papers Declassified in June 1981, Omar N. Bradley Papers, U.S. Army Military History Institute, Carlisle Barracks, Pa.

6. Memorandum, Maj. Gen. R. C. Wilson to Lt. Gen. Edwards, 1 Dec 1950, File 385.2 Korea (28 July 1950), Box 906, Record Group 341; msg, CG9939, LeMay to Vandenberg, 2 Dec 1950, File B8552, Box 196, and diary entry, 26 Jan 1951, LeMay Diary #3, 1951, Box 103, Papers of Curtis LeMay, Manuscript Division, Library of Congress, Washington, D.C.

7. *FRUS, 1950,* 7:1261-1262, 1300; *FRUS, 1951,* vol. 7, *Korea and China* (Washington, D.C.: USGPO, 1983), pt. 1, p. 101; William Stueck, *The Korean War: An International History* (Princeton, N.J.: Princeton University Press, 1995), 131-132. As a result of the earlier incidents, Secretary of the Navy Francis Matthews lost his position and was appointed ambassador to Ireland, and Gen. Orville Anderson was forced to retire.

8. Dean Acheson, *The Korean War* (New York: W. W. Norton, 1971), 84-91; JCS 2173/3, "Use of Atomic Bomb," 4 Dec 1950, General Decimal File, 1950-1951, 091 Korea, Box 34-A, Record Group 319, Army Operations, National Archives II. The Canadian prime minister was referring to an incident in 1932 when Japan had retaliated for the death of one of its monks in the streets of Shanghai by bombing the Chapei section of the city. By the time international pressure brought an end to

fighting weeks later, Chapei had been reduced to ashes, and the world was outraged by accounts of Japanese aggression and the suffering of Chinese civilians.

9. Memorandum of telephone conversation by Mildred Asbjornson and memorandum of conversation by Lucius D. Battle, 12 Jan 1951, in *FRUS, 1951,* vol. 7, pt. 7, pp. 67-68.

10. Entry for 6 Jan 1951, LeMay Diary #3, Box 103, LeMay Papers; introduction to *FEAF Bomber Command History, 4 Jul-31 Oct 1950,* vol. I, book I, File K713.01-1, AFHRA; testimony of Maj. Gen Emmett O'Donnell, Jr., in *Military Situation in the Far East,* pt. 4, p. 3066.

11. Msg, Norstad to Johnson, 14 Aug 1950, Redline Files, Aug 1950, and msg, Norstad to Stratemeyer, 21 Sept 1950, Redline Files, Sept 1950, Box 86, Papers of Hoyt Vandenberg, Manuscript Division, Library of Congress; Charles P. Cabell, *A Man of Intelligence: Memoirs of War, Peace, and the CIA* (Colorado Springs: Impavide Publications, 1997), 37; memo, Col. Donovan to Maj. Gen. Landon, Subject: Mr. McCone's Inquiry Concerning a USSBS in North Korea, 19 Jul 1950, File OPD 384.5 Korea (22 Jul 1950), Box 904, Record Group 341; letter, O. P. Weyland to Vandenberg, 12 Oct 1950, in History Office, HQ FEAF, *History of the Far East Air Forces, 25 June-31 Dec 1950,* vol. II, p. 19, File K720.01, AFHRA; Allan R. Millett, "Korea, 1950-1953," in *Case Studies in the Development of Close Air Support,* ed. Benjamin Franklin Cooling (Washington, D.C.: USGPO), 371-372; memorandum for record by Gen. Nathan Twining, Subject: Functions of Dr. Stearns, General Barcus, and General White, 17 Nov 1950, File, Korean Evaluation Project 1950-51, Box 119, Papers of Nathan Twining, Manuscript Division, Library of Congress; Headquarters X Corps, *Army Tactical Air Support Requirements,* 25 Dec 1950, and William A. Gunn, *A Study of the Effectiveness of Air Support Operations in Korea,* Technical Memorandum ORO-T-13(FEC), 26 Sept 1951, copies at U.S. Army Military History Institute (USAMHI), Carlisle Barracks, Pa.

12. Letter, Twining to LeMay, with attached extracts of Stearns's evaluation, 24 Jan 1951, File B9476, Box 197, LeMay Papers; HQ USAF, *Summary of an Evaluation of the United States Air Force in Korea* (Barcus Report), File 160.041-1, AFHRA.

13. Memorandum from W. Barton Leach, Subject: Status of "Korean Evaluation Project," 9 Jan 1951, File, Korean Evaluation Project 1950-51, Box 119, Twining Papers; letter, Maj. Gen. Edward Almond to Gen. Collins, 23 Jan 1951 and Collins reply, 1 Feb 1951, Folder, Air Support for Ground Operations 1950-1951, Box, Korean War Tactical Air Support Studies 1950-1951, Edward M. Almond Papers, USAMHI. Almond's papers contain many examples of the critical studies of USAF CAS he conducted at the Army War College.

14. Appendix B, "A Comparison of Air Force and Marine Air Support," in Operations Research Office, Far East Command, "Close Air Support Operations in Korea: Preliminary Evaluation," Feb 1951, Report ORO-R-3, AFHRA, copy furnished to the author by Allan Millett and Kelly Jordan; HQ USAF, *An Evaluation of the Effectiveness of the United States Air Force in the Korean Campaign* (Barcus Report), vol. III, pp. 24-45, and Summary Report, pp. 8-13, File 168.041-1, AFHRA.

15. *An Evaluation of the Effectiveness of the United States Air Force in the Korean Campaign* (Barcus Report), vol. III, pp. 57-69, File 168.041-1, AFHRA.

16. *FEAF Report on the Korean War, 25 Jun 1950-27 Jul 1953,* p. 3, File K720.04D, and entries for 29 Dec 1950-1 Jan 1951, Weyland Handwritten Diary, File 168.7104-3, 50/07/14-51/04/12, AFHRA; Robert F. Futrell, *The United States*

Air Force in Korea 1950-1953, rev. ed. (Washington, D.C.: USGPO, 1983) 278; advanced press releases 586, 593, 600, 601, 602, FEAF Operational Summaries, Jan-Apr 1951, Record Group 6, MacArthur Archives, reel 625 of microfilm copy in U.S. Military Academy Library, West Point, N.Y.; memorandum for the record, 13 Feb 1951, in *FRUS, 1951,* vol. 7, pt. 1, pp. 174-177.

17. General Headquarters, Far East Command, *Special Report No. 39, Electric Power Resources, Northern Korea,* 6 Nov 1950, Record Group 6, MacArthur Archives, reel 697 of microfilm copy; memo, Col. R. D. Wentworth to Col. Musgrave, 18 Jan 1951, Subject: Bombing of the Chanjin-Pusan-Yalu River Power Complex (PM-2058), with tabs, and memo, BG Dudley Hale to General Smith, Subject: Bombing of the Changjin-Pujon-Yalu River Complex (JSPC 853/84), 2 Mar 1951, with tabs, File OPD 384.5 Korea (22 Jul 1950), Box 904, Record Group 341; memorandum of telephone conversation, 1 Mar 1951, in *FRUS, 1951,* vol. 7, pt. 1, p. 201. The changes in place names between the different JCS studies indicate the problems Americans had with Korean words. This often caused confusion, as towns with similar names, such as Pusan and Pujon, were often very far apart. The same difficulty occurred with tactical maps, creating significant targeting problems.

18. Msgs, CX55610, 15 Feb 1951, and C55830, 18 Feb 1951, MacArthur to JCS, Incoming Messages, Box 1, 29 May 1950-3 Aug 1951, and msgs, JCS 83773, 17 Feb 1951, and JC84026, 21 Feb 1951, Outgoing Messages, Box 9, 25 June 1950-29 Jan 1952, Records of the Joint Chiefs of Staff, Record Group 218; memos, Maj. Gen. Maxwell Taylor to Chief of Staff, U.S. Army, Subject: Instructions to the Commander-in-Chief, Far East Command Respecting the Bombing of Rashin (Najin-dong), 15 and 18 Feb 1951, General Decimal Files, 1950-51, 091 Korea, Box 37, Record Group 319; memo, Joseph Smith to Gen. Vandenberg, Subject: Removal of Restriction against Attacks on Najin, 2 Aug 1951, OPD 381 Korea (9 May 1947), Sec. 11, Box 894, Record Group 341.

19. HQ FEAF, Advance Release No. 588, 25 Feb 1951, FEAF Operational Summaries, Jan-Apr 1951, Record Group 6, MacArthur Archives, reel 625 of microfilm copy; O'Neill, "Other Side of the Yalu," 154, 193; Gunn, *Study of the Effectiveness of Air Support Operations in Korea;* E. J. Kahn, Jr., *The Peculiar War: Impressions of a Reporter in Korea* (New York: Random House, 1952), 132; Lt. Bruce D. Gamble, ed., "Time Flies: The Oral History of Lt. Col. John F. Bolt, USMC (Ret.)," *Foundation* (fall 1993): 97.

20. John Darrell Sherwood, *Officers in Flight Suits: The Story of American Air Force Fighter Pilots in the Korean War* (New York: New York University Press, 1996), 102-105; Rene Cutforth, *Korean Reporter* (London: Allan Wingate, 1952), 173-176.

21. Memo, Commanding General EUSAK to subordinate commanders, Subject: Demolition Policy in South Korea, 2 Jan 1951, Special File, Dec 1950-Mar 1951, Box 20, and letters with enclosures, Almond to Ridgway, 16 and 25 Jan 1951, File, Korea Correspondence, A-C, Box 17, Korean War, Eighth Army Correspondence, Dec 1950-Apr 1951, Matthew B. Ridgway Papers, USAMHI; Billy C. Mossman, *Ebb and Flow: November 1950-July 1951* (Washington, D.C.: USGPO, 1990), 226; Bruce Cumings, *The Origins of the Korean War,* vol. 2, *The Roaring of the Cataract 1947-1950* (Princeton, N.J.: Princeton University Press, 1990), 754-755.

22. Letter, MacArthur to Ridgway, 7 Jan 1951, and diary entry for 6 Mar 1951, Special File, Dec 1950-Mar 1951, Box 20; msg, Ridgway to Hickey, 30 Jan 1951, Historical Record Folder, Dec 1950-Jan 1951, Box 22; msg, Ridgway to CINCFE,

23 Jan 1951, M-R Korean Correspondence File, Box 17; letter with P.S., Ridgway to Lt. Gen. James Van Fleet, 4 July 1951, T-Z Folder, CINCFE Correspondence, Box 19, Ridgway Papers; msgs, CX 62673, CINCFE to JCS, 16 May 1951, and JCS 91612, JCS to CINCFE, 18 May 1951, "Pertinent Papers Concerning the Conduct of and Limitations Surrounding Operations of the Eighth Army," 1 Apr 53, vol. I, File 381 Korea (9 May 1947), Sec. 23, Appendix, Box 897, Record Group 341; USAF Historical Study No. 72, *United States Air Force Operations in the Korean Conflict, 1 November 1950-30 June 1952* (Maxwell Air Force Base, Ala.: Air University, 1 July 1953), 217.

23. Futrell, *USAF in Korea,* 293–312; Department of Defense Office of Public Information, press release no. 128-51, 23 Jan 1951 and letter, O'Donnell to Vandenberg, 26 Jan 1951, File FEAF I, Box 65; letters, Stratemeyer to LeMay, 16 Feb 1951, and LeMay reply, 6 Mar 1951, Stratemeyer File, Box 59, LeMay Papers; msg, AX 4966, CG FEAF to CG 5th AF et al., 24 Dec 1950, File FEAF In, Nov–Dec 1950, Radiograms, Record Group 9, MacArthur Archives, reel 180 of microfilm copy; O'Neill, "Other Side of the Yalu," 142, 146, 154, 166, 234. The JCS had considered employing B-36s in Korea in July 1950 but had agreed to defer consideration of that matter indefinitely. See Memorandum for Record, Subject: JCS 1952/12 (Suggestion for Employment of B-36 Airplanes in Korean Operations), 24 July 1950, on microfilm in *Records of the Joint Chiefs of Staff,* pt. 2, *1946-53, Meetings of the JCS* (Frederick, Md.: University Publications of America, 1980), reel 1.

24. O'Neill, "Other Side of the Yalu," 273–274; Rogen Dingman, "Atomic Diplomacy during the Korean War," *International Security* 13 (winter 1988–89): 69–79; Roger M. Anders, "The Atomic Bomb and the Korean War: Gordon Dean and the Issue of Civilian Control," *Military Affairs* (Jan 1988): 1–3; Phillip S. Meilinger, *Hoyt S. Vandenberg: The Life of a General* (Bloomington: Indiana University Press, 1989), 175; msg, C-58676, CINCFE to CG ARMY EIGHT, 27 Mar 1951, Records of General Headquarters, FEC, SCAP, and UNC, Office of the Chief of Staff, Chief of Staff Subject File 1945-52, TS Personal File for 1949-1952, Box 3, Records of United States Army Commands, 1942-, Record Group 338, National Archives II; entries for 5, 7, and 24 Apr and 7, 8, and 9 May 1951, LeMay Diary #3, Box 103, letter, LeMay to Stratemeyer, 27 Nov 1951, File B14692, Box B198, and letter, BG Richard Carmichael to CG FEAF, 25 June 1953, File B28370, Box B203, LeMay Papers; Lt. Col. Crocker, Operations Division, "Action to Conclude Operations in Korea," 5 July 1951, General Decimal File, 1950-51, 091 Korea, Box 38-A, Record Group 319; HQ USAF, Staff Study on Use of Atomic Weapons in Korea, 23 May 1952, File 385.2 Korea (28 July 1950), Sec. 2, Box 907, Record Group 341; interview of Lt. Gen. James T. Stewart by Col. Charles Andrean, 1986, James T. Stewart Papers, USAMHI. Dingman is correct that the Ninth Bomb Wing returned to the United States in the summer, but it was replaced by the Forty-third Wing, which conducted the first missions for HUDSON HARBOR. Some historians speculate that this first transfer of atomic weapons from civilian to military control was an attempt by Truman to bribe the JCS into supporting his relief of MacArthur, but there is no good evidence to support that claim. If MacArthur's relief had anything to do with the decision, it was to make the situation in the Far East look even more precarious.

25. Msg, SAC X-RAY to SAC, 2 May 1951, File B-10856, along with Files B-10951, 10952, and 10953, Box B197, and letter, Ridgway to LeMay, 7 Nov 1951, File B-14389, Box B198, and entries for 28 and 31 Aug and 12-14 Sept 1951,

LeMay Diary #3, Box 103, LeMay Papers; Lt. Col. Crocker, Operations Division, "Action to Conclude Operations in Korea," 5 July 1951, General Decimal File, 1950-51, 091 Korea, Box 38-A, Record Group 319; memo for Vandenberg by Maj. Gen. Joseph Smith, Subject: CINCFE Exercise "Hudson Harbor" (JCS 2173/9), 21 Sept 1951, msg, DOSPC 0289, CGSAC to CGUSAF, 27 Sept 1951, memorandum for record by Col. J. S. Samuel, 5 Oct 1951, and memo, MG Ramey to Director of Plans, Subject: (Top Secret) Use of Atomic Weapons in Korea, 20 May 1952, File 385.2 Korea (28 July 1950), Sec. 2, Box 907, Record Group 341. Contrary to the assertions of historians such as Bruce Cumings, there is no indication that these operations were designed to send any message to the enemy, and it seems unlikely from the cover story and flight paths that the Communists could have presumed the missions' intent.

26. Cabell, *Man of Intelligence,* 264-265; Laurence Jolidon, "Soviet Interrogation of U.S. POWs in the Korean War," *Cold War International History Project Bulletin* (winter 1995-1996): 124; O'Neill, "Other Side of the Yalu," 135-136; msgs, CINCFE to JCS, TSW 242, 27 Apr 1951, and CX 63075, 22 May 1951, Incoming Messages, Box 1, 29 May 1950-3 Aug 1951, Record Group 218; msg, Weyland to Vandenberg and LeMay, 8 June 1951, File B-11501, letter, Col. Winton Close to MG Thomas Power, 6 June 1951, File B-11651, letter, BG Robert Terrill to Power, 16 Aug 1951, File B-12789, Box B198, LeMay Papers; msg, Redline 298, Weyland to Twining, 5 July 1951, Redline Messages, 1 May-31 Dec 1951, Folder 2, Box 86, and Tab 1 to aide-mémoire for General Vandenberg, Subject: U.S. Courses of Action in Korea, 1 Nov 1951, File 19, Box 85, Vandenberg Papers; interview with Gen. Jacob E. Smart (Ret.) by author, 2 Nov 1997, Arlington, Va., with changes provided by letter from Smart on 29 Nov 1997, in possession of author. The 1 Nov 1951 report also contains detailed information on Operation STINKER, a plan for the mining of Chinese ports and inland waterways by two B-29 wings.

27. Smart interview, pp. 16-18; memorandum by the Joint Chiefs of Staff to the Secretary of Defense, Subject: USSR Diplomatic Note Concerning Violation of USSR Asiatic Border by U.S. Plane, 23 Nov 1951, and memorandum by Walworth Barbour, Subject: Bomber Shot Down by Soviet Union, 17 Dec 1951, in *FRUS, 1951,* vol. 7, pt. 1, pp. 1163-1165, 1353-1354. For more detail on the air intelligence effort against the Soviet Union during the war, see John Thomas Farquhar, "A Need to Know: The Role of Air Force Reconnaissance in War Planning, 1945-1953" (Ph.D. diss., Ohio State University, 1991), 149-183.

28. Msg, CX 57735, CINCFE to JCS, 25 Oct 1952, Incoming Messages, 1 July 1952-10 Feb 1953, Box 6, Record Group 218; letter, First Secretary John Steeves to Commander-in-Chief, Far East, 20 Nov 1952, with attached telegram; memo, PIO to Chief of Staff, Subject: Public Information Plan in Event of Future Aerial Border Violations, 16 Dec 1952; letters, Col. K. A. Damke to Col. Larsen and Mr. Turner, 19 Nov 1952; exchange of letters between Generals Clark and Weyland, 24 Dec 1952, Chief of Staff 1952 Correspondence File, Box 4, and msg, VC 0395 CG, Weyland to Twining, 27 Oct 1952, Records of General Headquarters, FEC, SCAP, and UNC, Office of the Chief of Staff, Chief of Staff Subject File 1945-52, TS Personal File for 1949-1952, Box 3, Record Group 338; Richard Hallion, *The Naval Air War in Korea* (Baltimore: Nautical and Aviation Publishing Company of America, 1986), 160-163.

29. Memo, Maj. Gen. L. C. Craigie to Chief of Staff USAF, Subject: War-Gaming

of Initial Emergency War Plan, 11 June 1951, with attached staff study and summary, File OPD 370.2 Korea (30 Aug 1950), Sec. 3, Box 886, Record Group 341; Matthew B. Ridgway, *The Korean War* (New York: Da Capo, 1986), 168-169.

30. *Military Situation in the Far East,* pt. 1, pp. 19-20, 309; pt. 2, pp. 1010, 1379, 1453-1454, 1493; pt. 4, pp. 3067, 3075, 3091. The eight reels of microfilm transcripts of the hearings published by University Publications of America in 1977, which include sections deleted from the published record for security reasons, further emphasize the senators' concerns about the U.S. ability to counter Soviet air strength. Many questions were asked about actual numbers of operational Soviet aircraft and their involvement in Korea. Vandenberg also had to defend the performance of his jets in close air support to Chairman Richard Russell of the Senate Armed Services Committee. See, for example, pp. 3690-3691, 3763-3772, reel 4.

CHAPTER 5. TALKING AND DYING

1. Msg, C 67877, CINCUNC to DEPTAR for JCS, 28 July 1951, File 383.21 Korea (3-19-45), Sec. 55, Box 33, Geographic File 1951-53, Records of the Joint Chiefs of Staff, Record Group 218, National Archives II, College Park, Md.

2. Letter, Gen. Curtis LeMay to BG Joe Kelly, 28 Nov 1951, File B14698, Box B198, Papers of Curtis Lemay, Manuscript Division, Library of Congress, Washington, D.C.

3. Msg, CX 60410, CINCFE to subordinate commands, 19 Apr 1951, Sec. 45, and msg, C 61367, 30 Apr 1951, Sec. 46, Box 31; msg, C 67474, 21 July 1951, Sec. 54, Box 33, Geographic File 1951-53, 383.21 Korea (3-19-45), Record Group 218; memo, Weyland to Ridgway, Subject: Armistice Negotiations, 3 July 1951, T-Z Folder, CINCFE Corespondence, Box 19, Matthew B. Ridgway Papers, U.S. Army Military History Institute, Carlisle Barracks, Pa.; msg, UNC-071, Ridgway to Hickey, 13 July 1951, File K720.1622, 1950-1951, AFHRA, Maxwell Air Force Base, Ala.

4. Msgs, C 67474, CINCFE to JCS, 21 July 1951, JCS 96938, 21 July 1951, and C 67520, CINCFE to JCS, 23 July 1951, Sec. 54, Box 33; JCS 1776/240, "United States Course of Action in Korea," 13 July 1951, with attachments, Sec. 53, Box 32; memorandum for the JCS with attachments, Subject: Joint Chiefs of Staff Meeting, for item 10 on agenda, 25 July 1951, Sec. 55, Box 33, Geographic File 1951-53, 383.21 Korea (3-19-45), Record Group 218; msgs, CX 67652, CINCFE to JCS, and JCS 97223, JCS to CINCFE, 25 July 1951, in *Pertinent Papers Concerning the Conduct of and Limitations Surrounding Operations of the Eighth Army,* vol. I, 1 Apr 1953, File 381 Korea (9 May 1947), Sec. 23 appendix, Box 897, Records of Headquarters USAF, Record Group 341, National Archives II.

5. Msg, C 68064, CINCFE to JCS, 31 July 1951, Box 1, Incoming Messages, 29 May 1950-3 Aug 1951, Record Group 218; letter, Terrill to Power, 16 Aug 1951, File B-12789, Box B198, LeMay Papers; notes on conference with General Weyland, 30 Aug 1951, Folder, Special File Apr 1951-Jan 1952, Box 20, Ridgway Papers.

6. JCS 1776/244 with enclosures, "Removal of Restriction against Attacks on Najin (Rashin)," 10 Aug 1951, Sec. 57, Box 33, Geographic File 1951-53, 383.21 Korea (3-19-45), Record Group 218; memo, Joseph Smith to Gen. Vandenberg, Subject: Removal of Restriction against Attacks on Najin (Rashin), File OPD 381 Korea (9 May 1947), Sec. 12, Box 894, Record Group 341; USAF Historical Study No. 72,

United States Air Force Operations in the Korean Conflict, 1 November 1950–30 June 1952 (Maxwell Air Force Base, Ala.: USAF Historical Division, 1 July 1955), 145.

7. Msgs, HNU 8-3, CINCUNC (ADV) to CINCFE, C 68927, CINCUNC to DEPTAR for G3 and JCS, 14 Aug 1951, and C 68959, CINCUNC to DEPTAR for JCS, 15 Aug 1951, Geographic File 1951–53, 383.21 Korea (3-19-45), Sec. 58, Box 33, Record Group 218; memo, R. A. Grussendorf to Col. Murphy, Aug 1951, File 3C, Box 88, Papers of Hoyt Vandenberg, Manuscripts Division, Library of Congress.

8. Eduard Mark, *Aerial Interdiction: Air Power and the Land Battle in Three American Wars: A Historical Analysis* (Washington, D.C.: Center for Air Force History, 1994), 289–319; letter, M. B. Ridgway to Col. Paul Carter, 15 Dec 1976, Folder C, 1964–1983, Post Retirement A-G, Box 34B, Ridgway Papers; Matthew B. Ridgway, *The Korean War* (New York: Da Capo, 1986), 191, 244.

9. Richard H. Kohn and Joseph P. Harahan, eds., *Air Interdiction in World War II, Korea, and Vietnam* (Washington, D.C.: Office of Air Force History, 1986), 15–16, 51; Ridgway, *The Korean War,* 192, 217–218.

10. Mark, *Aerial Interdiction;* Mark A. O'Neill, "The Other Side of the Yalu: Soviet Pilots in the Korean War, Phase One, 1 November 1950–12 April 1951" (Ph.D. diss., Florida State University, 1996), 281–285; Commander in Chief, U.S. Pacific Fleet, *Interim Third Evaluation Report, 1 May–31 December 1951,* pp. 10-45–10-46, U.S. Naval Historical Center, Washington, D.C.; *FEAF Report on the Korean War, 25 June 1950–27 July 1953,* book I, p. 77, File K720.04D; "The Aerial War during Operation Strangle," vol. I, pp. 12–17, and "Notes on Use of the Term 'Operation Strangle,'" vol. III, app. 2, in *History of the Fifth Air Force, 1 July–31 December 1951,* File K730.01, AFHRA.

11. Maj. Gen. William F. Dean, *General Dean's Story* (New York: Viking Press, 1954), 272–273; J. Lawton Collins, *War in Peacetime: The History and Lessons of Korea* (Boston: Houghton Mifflin, 1969), 313; Mark, *Aerial Interdiction,* 312–314; Shu Guang Zhang, *Mao's Military Romanticism: China and the Korean War, 1950–1953* (Lawrence: University Press of Kansas, 1995), 176–181; Robert F. Futrell, *The United States Air Force in Korea 1950–1953,* rev. ed. (Washington, D.C.: USGPO, 1983), 401–405; aide-mémoire for General Vandenberg, Subject: U.S. Courses of Action in Korea, with maps, 1 Nov 1951, File 19, Box 85, Vandenberg Papers; memorandum of conversation by Frank P. Lockhart, 28 Sept 1951, in U.S. Department of State, *Foreign Relations of the United States, 1951,* vol. 7, *Korea and China* (Washington, D.C.: USGPO, 1983), pt. 1, pp. 966–968; hereafter *FRUS.*

12. USAF Historical Study No. 72, 132–137; msgs, RL 275, Vandenberg to Weyland, 22 June 1951, RL 354, HQ USAF to CG FEAF, 15 Oct 1951, V 0450 CG, Weyland to Vandenberg, 17 Oct 1951, and RL 389, Twining to Weyland, 6 Dec 1951, Redline File, May–Dec 1951, Folder 1, Box 86, Vandenberg Papers; msg, V 0488 D/O, CG FEAF to C/S USAF, 9 Nov 1951, OPD 381 Korea (9 May 1947), Sec. 13, Box 895, Record Group 341; Allan R. Millett, "Korea, 1950–1953," in *Case Studies in the Development of Close Air Support,* ed. Benjamin Franklin Cooling (Washington, D.C.: USGPO, 1990), 381–383; memo for record by Gen. James A. Van Fleet, 30 Oct 1951, Folder 1, Box 82, Papers of James A. Van Fleet, George C. Marshall Research Library, Lexington, Va.

13. Memorandum for the Secretary, Subject: Report on Trip to Japan and Korea with General Bradley, 4 Oct 1951, Memorandum for General Vandenberg, Subject: General Bradley's Notes on His Trip to Japan and Korea, 10 Oct 1951, and msgs,

AFODC TS 2188, Burns to Weyland, 20 Oct 1951, V 0462 CG, Weyland to Burns, 22 Oct 1951, and V0465 CG, Weyland to Vandenberg, 23 Oct 1951, File OPD 381 Korea (9 May 1947), Sec. 13, Box 895; msg, CX 51897, CINCFE to JCS, 30 Sept 1951, and memo, JCS to the Secretary of Defense, Subject: United States Courses of Action in Korea, 3 Nov 1951, "Pertinent Papers Concerning the Conduct of and Limitations Surrounding Operations of the Eighth Army," 1 Apr 1953, vol. I, File 381 Korea (9 May 1947), Sec. 23 appendix, Box 897, Record Group 341; Ridgway Record of Conversation with General Bradley and Charles Bohlen, 29 Sept 1951, Folder, Special File Apr 1951–Jan 1952, Box 20, Ridgway Papers; letter, Maj. Gen. F. F. Everest to Vandenberg, 7 Oct 1951, Pacific IV File, Box 56, Vandenberg Papers.

14. Letters, BG Joe Kelly to LeMay, 29 Oct 1951 and 7 Nov 1951, File FEAF 1, Box 65, LeMay Papers; O'Neill, "Other Side of the Yalu," 287.

15. Ibid.; Flt. Lt. B. Lyman, *The Significance of Australian Air Operations in Korea* (Fairbairn: RAAF Air Power Studies Centre, March 1992), 43–49; memo by BG James Ferguson, Subject: Air Operations in Korea against the MIG-15, 9 Nov 1951, document attached to Lt. Col. Bruce Hinton, "MIG-15 versus F-86 in Korea," 25 July 1951, Document AF383279, Air University Library, Maxwell Air Force Base, Ala.; Futrell, *USAF in Korea,* 410–411. Where there are discrepancies between Futrell's aircraft figures and the official letters and reports, I relied on the latter. The Meteor was also plagued by a very short range. It was easily identifiable, however, and could be used for close escort without fear of being mistaken for a MiG. Even Sabre pilots had a hard time differentiating between a MiG-15 and an F-86 at a distance.

16. Ibid. Mark O'Neill notes in his dissertation that the Soviet pilots were indeed instructed to avoid capture, and this would have contributed to their reluctance to pursue over water.

17. Ibid.; msg, RL 362, Weyland to Vandenberg, 24 Oct 1951, Redlines, June 1951 to . . . , Folder 1, Box 86, Vandenberg Papers; analysis of the Russian–Chinese–North Korean Ground Control Intercept Net Transmissions, 15–31 May 1952, File B-18859, LeMay Papers; Universal International Newsreels, vol. 24, no. 511, 22 Nov 1951, Record Group 200, National Archives II. When Vandenberg mentioned in an October press conference that Russians were flying against the Sabres in MiG Alley, USAF and FEAF headquarters reacted quickly to emphasize that there was still no conclusive proof of Soviet participation. This was in keeping with official policy to deflect attention away from direct Soviet involvement in the war. See Michael J. McCarthy, "Uncertain Enemies: Soviet Pilots in the Korean War," *Air Power History* 44 (spring 1997): 42–43.

18. Aide-mémoire for General Vandenberg, Subject: U.S. Courses of Action in Korea, 1 Nov 1951, File 19, Box 85; msg, RL 347, White to Weyland, 22 Feb 1952, Redlines, Nov 1951 to . . . , Folder 1, Box 87; memorandum for the secretary of the Air Force on the military outlook in Korea, File 3, and memo of FEAF forces, Dec 1951, File 3D, Box 88, Vandenberg Papers; memorandum for Asst. Vice Chief of Air Staff, Subject: Additional F-86s for Korea, 10 Dec 1951, with enclosures, and memorandum for General Vandenberg, Subject: CINCFE's Message on Situation in Korea, 11 Dec 1951, File OPD 381 Korea (9 May 1947), Sec. 14, Box 895, Record Group 341; memorandum on the substance of discussions at a Department of State–JCS meeting, 25 Sept 1951, in *FRUS, 1951,* vol. 7, pt. 1, p. 943; C. P. Trussell, "Plane Output Lag Is Menace to Nation, Senators Declare," *New York Times,* 29 Aug 1952, p. 1.

19. Dept. of Defense Office of Public Information Press Release No. 274-51, 21

Nov 1951, with attached examples of newspaper coverage from the *New York Times, New York Herald Tribune,* and *Philadelphia Inquirer,* File 4D, Box 83, Vandenberg Papers.

20. Letter, LeMay to Kelly, 28 Nov 1951, File B-14698, Box B198; letter, LeMay to Weyland, 3 Jan 1952, with enclosure, and letter, Weyland to LeMay, 9 Feb 1952, with enclosure, Weyland File, Box B61; letter, Kelly to LeMay, 9 Jan 1952, with attached memorandum, Subject: Comment on the SAC Staff Study on Employment of SAC War Plan Tactics and Techniques in Korea, File B-15528, Box B199, LeMay Papers. News of the effectiveness of the MiGs prompted one article in *Aviation Week* in February 1952 that questioned the ability of SAC to carry out its atomic attacks. See O'Neill, "Other Side of the Yalu," 183.

21. Letter, LeMay to O'Donnell, 16 Dec 1950, File B-8797, Box B196, and memorandum for General Weyland, Subject: Initial Operations in the Outbreak of War between the United States and the USSR and China, 14 Feb 1951, File B-9919, Box B197, LeMay Papers; USAF Historical Study No. 72, 179–185; USAF Historical Study No. 92, *Development of Night Air Operations 1941–1952* (Maxwell Air Force Base, Ala.: USAF Historical Division, 1953), 203–211; Daniel T. Kuehl, "Refighting the Last War: Electronic Warfare and U.S. Air Force B-29 Operations in the Korean War, 1950–53," *Journal of Military History* 56 (Jan 1992): 87–111; HQ 5th AF Operations Analysis Office, "Analysis of Shoran Bombing Operations by B-29 Aircraft in Korea," 27 Jan 1952, File K730.3101-17; memo from Col. Lewis, Subject: Review of Operations Analysis Memorandum "Analysis of Shoran Bombing Operations by B-29 Aircraft in Korea," 12 May 1952, File K730.310-1, 52/01/27; *FEAF Bomber Command History July–December 1951,* vol. I, pp. 164–190, File K713.01-20; *FEAF Bomber Command History January–June 1952,* vol. I, pp. 24–28, File K713.01-27, AFHRA; memo, BG John Gerhart to Director of Plans, Subject: Review of Operations Analysis Memorandum "B-26 Night Intruder Rail Cutting Program," 28 July 1952, File OPD 384.5 Korea (22 July 1950), Sec. 2, Box 904, Record Group 341. CEP was a measurement of bombing accuracy expressed as the radius of a circle within which 50 percent of bombs dropped could be expected to hit.

22. Memorandum for General Vandenberg by BG John Gerhart, Subject: USAF Aircraft Utilization in FEAF, 18 Apr 1952, annex II of memorandum, Subject: Impact of the Korean War, Box 87, Vandenberg Papers; letter, Twining to Lt. Gen. Edwin Rawlings, 18 Apr 1952, Reading File, Apr 1952, Box 56, Papers of Nathan Twining, Manuscript Division, Library of Congress; entry for 8 Feb 1952, Weyland memoranda for record, vol. II, File 168.7104-5, 51/12/01–52/05/31, AFHRA. By the end of the war, logistics had improved enough to support eighteen B-29 sorties a day.

CHAPTER 6. MANNING AND INSPIRING THE FORCE

1. Memo, Col. Emmett Cassady to Gen. Grussendorf, Subject: Personal Views on Problem Presented by Major Connor in his study of Fear of Flying and Lack of Motivation to Learn to Fly, 25 Mar 1952, File 15, Box 84, Papers of Hoyt Vandenberg, Manuscript Division, Library of Congress, Washington, D.C.

2. Notes on Fear of Flying Policy, 28 Mar 1952, Curtis LeMay Diary #4, 1952, Box 103, Papers of Curtis LeMay, Manuscript Division, Library of Congress.

3. Letter, Col. P. D. Fleming to Gen. Thomas Power, 2 Aug 1953, Correspon-

dence Folder, Aug 1953, Box 3, Thomas S. Power Manuscript Collection, George Arents Research Library for Special Collections, Syracuse University, Syracuse, N.Y.

4. Robert F. Futrell, *The United States Air Force in Korea 1950-1953* (Washington, D.C.: USGPO, 1983), 709.

5. USAF Historical Study No. 71, *United States Air Force Operations in the Korean Conflict, 25 June-1 November 1950* (Maxwell Air Force Base, Ala.: USAF Historical Division, 1 July 1952), 9, 83; Futrell, *USAF in Korea,* 46-47, 72-74; msg AX 2607, CG FEAF to CG FEAF Bomber Command, 22 Oct 1950, File FEAF In, Oct 1950, Reel 180, microfilm of MacArthur Archives in USMA Library, West Point, N.Y.; LeMay Diary #2, 1 July 1950-30 Dec 1950, entries for 22 and 29 July, Box 103, LeMay Papers.

6. Summary sheet on Redline Messages, Stratemeyer to Twining, 2 Dec 1950, and Vandenberg to Stratemeyer, 4 Dec 1950; summary sheet on messages between Vandenberg and Weyland on rotation of jet aces, Feb 1952, File 4, Box 83, Vandenberg Papers.

7. Air University Human Resources Research Institute, Report No. MM-1, "Human Factors Affecting the War Effort," Dec 1951, copy in Air University Library, Maxwell Air Force Base, Ala.

8. Chester L. Blunk, *"Every Man a Tiger": The 731st USAF Night Intruders over Korea* (Manhattan, Kans.: Sunflower University Press, 1987), 14-16; msg, Redline 248, Maj. Gen. Earle Partridge to Vandenberg, 21 May 1951, Redline Messages, 1 May 1951-31 Dec 1951, Folder 2, Box 86, Vandenberg Papers; Futrell, *USAF in Korea,* 75.

9. Entry for 6 Jan 1951, LeMay Diary #3, Box 103; letter, BG James Briggs to LeMay, 16 Mar 1951, File FEAF 1, Box 65; letter, Lt. Gen. George Stratemeyer to LeMay, 16 Feb 1951, Stratemeyer File, Box 59, LeMay Papers; Vance O. Mitchell, *Air Force Officers Personnel Policy Development 1944-1974* (Washington, D.C.: USGPO, 1996), 86-87.

10. Letters, Briggs to LeMay, 16 and 18 Mar 1951, File FEAF 1, Box 65, and entry for 9 Jan 1951, LeMay Diary #3, Box 103, LeMay Papers; msg, Redline 377, Vandenberg to Twining, 13 Dec 1951, Redline Messages 1 May 1951-31 Dec 1951, Folder 2, Box 86, Vandenberg Papers; letter, Lt. Gen. Thomas Power to Joe Brovich, 24 Feb 1951, Correspondence File, Feb 1951, Box 2, Power Manuscript Collection; letter, Paul Carter to Gen. Matthew Ridgway, 27 Nov 1976, Folder C, 1964-1983, Post Retirement A-G, Box 34B, Matthew B. Ridgway Papers, U.S. Army Military History Institute, Carlisle Barracks, Pa.

11. John Darrell Sherwood, *Officers in Flight Suits: The Story of American Air Force Fighter Pilots in the Korean War* (New York: New York University Press, 1996), 53-54; Maj. Donald W. Hastings et al., *Psychiatric Experiences of the Eighth Air Force: First Year of Combat (July 4, 1942-July 4, 1943)* (New York: Josiah Macy, Jr., Foundation, 1944), 28-32; Mark K. Wells, *Courage and Air Warfare: The Allied Aircrew Experience in the Second World War* (London: Frank Cass, 1995), 171-173; Kenneth P. Werrell, *Blankets of Fire: U.S. Bombers over Japan during World War II* (Washington, D.C.: Smithsonian, 1996), 206.

12. *History of the Air Training Command, January-June 1952,* pp. 105-106, File K220.01, AFHRA, Maxwell Air Force Base, Ala.

13. Ibid., 107, 110, 119; Mitchell, *Air Force Officers,* 90-91.

14. *History of the Air Training Command,* 110; "Fear of Flying," notes for Com-

manders' Conference, 7 Nov 1951, Box 101, LeMay Papers. B-29 names mentioned can be spotted in USAF film footage of Korea. See "B-29 Mission to Konan," NWDNM(m)-342-USAF-18472, and "Air Force Operations in Japan and Korea," NWDNM(m)-342-USAF-18648, Record Group 342, National Archives II, College Park, Md.

15. *History of the Air Training Command,* 111–114; letter, MG James Powell to LTG Laurence Kuter, 7 Mar 1952, "Summary of Fear of Flying Cases" File, Box 84, Vandenberg Papers.

16. Maj. Joseph Connor, Jr., Staff Study, Subject: Fear of Flying and Lack of Motivation to Fly, 5 Mar 1952; memo, Col. Emmett Cassady to General Grussen-dorf, Subject: Personal Views on Problems Presented by Major Connor in His Study of Fear of Flying and Lack of Motivation to Learn to Fly, 25 Mar 1952, File 15, Box 84, Vandenberg Papers; Joseph J. Corn, *The Winged Gospel: America's Romance with Aviation, 1900–1950* (New York: Oxford University Press, 1983), 132–133. Cassady proposed that Milton Caniff's comic strip "Steve Canyon" be subsidized to cover aviation cadet life and appeal to the seventeen-to-nineteen-year-old age group. The comic did do much to promote a positive image of the Air Force, as did the television show that derived from it.

17. Transcript of telephone conversation between LeMay and Gen. E. S. Wetzel, 26 Mar 1952, LeMay Diary #4, 1952, Box 103, LeMay Papers.

18. Msg, AFPDC 57499, Vandenberg to All Commanders, 16 Apr 1952, File 15, Box 84, Vandenberg Papers; msg, CG FEAF to All Commanders, 25 Apr 1952, copy in HQ FEAF, *History of the Far East Air Forces, Jan–Jun 1952,* vol. III, File 720.01, AFHRA.

19. LTC Robert Valimont, memo, Subject: Hearings on Flying and Other Incentive Pay and Overseas Allowances, 18 Apr 1952; memo, LTG Kuter for BG Robert Landry, 18 Apr 1952; Randolph Air Force Base Public Information Office Release, 21 Apr 1952; statement by General Vandenberg, San Antonio, Tex., 21 Apr 1952, "Summary of Fear of Flying Cases" File, Box 84, Vandenberg Papers; Mitchell, *Air Force Officers,* 97.

20. *History of the Air Training Command,* 117, 137.

21. "Percentage of Reserves and Regulars Assigned to Units," "Summary of Fear of Flying Cases" File, Box 84, Vandenberg Papers; *History of the Far East Air Forces, 1 July–31 December 1952,* vol. I, pp. 248–249, File K720.01, and *Report of the FEAF Surgeon, January–June 1953,* p. 18, File K720.740, AFHRA.

22. Sherwood, *Officers in Flight Suits,* 108–110; letter, Sherwood to author, 18 May 1998. Most pilots who received a monthly ration of USAF "rotgut" stashed the bottles in their quarters and preferred the cold beer and ten-cent whiskey of higher quality at the officers' club. The mission whiskey tradition was a carryover from World War II that also appeared to a limited extent during the Vietnam War.

23. Letter, Maj. T. M. Sellers to his wife, 22 Jan 1953, furnished by Prof. Susan MacDonald, Illinois State University, Normal, Ill. Sellers wrote, "I used to like the song, but now its meaning and thoughts bring back too many unpleasant memories."

24. Entry for 28 Mar 1952 with attached "Notes on Fear of Flying Policy"; entries for 21 July and 1 Nov 1952, LeMay Diary #4, 1952, Box 103, LeMay Papers.

25. Entry for 2 Dec 1952, Weyland memoranda for record, vol. III, File 168-7104-6, 52/06/01–52/12/31, and entry for 8 May 1953, Weyland memoranda for record, vol. IV, File 168.7104-7, 53/01/01–53/07/31, AFHRA; msg, BC8147,

Fisher to LeMay, 4 Dec 1952; memo, Director of Personnel to Command Section, Subject: Proposed Policy Governing Combat Tour for FEAF Bomb Crews, 8 Dec 1952; msg, LeMay to Fisher, 13 Dec 1952, FEAF 2 Folder, Box 65, and letter, Fisher to LeMay, 8 Apr 1953, FEAF Folder, Box B84, LeMay Papers.

26. Fleming letter, Power Collection.

27. Entry for 13-18 July 1953, LeMay Diary #5, 1953, Box 104a, LeMay Papers; Mitchell, *Air Force Officers,* 103-107; Document M-550, press releases on the AFA Hollywood Bowl Program, 24 Aug 1951, and Document M-492, Letter, Robert Denton to LTC Clair Towne, Re: *Strategic Air Command,* 16 Feb 1953, with attached story outline from Beirne Lay, Jr., in David Culbert, ed., *Film and Propaganda in America: A Documentary History,* vol. 5, *Microfiche Supplement, 1939-1979* (Westport, CT: Greenwood Press, 1993), frames 3390-3393, 3586-3587. At the Hollywood Bowl, Jimmy Stewart and Bob Hope served as masters of ceremonies, and other entertainment was provided by Dean Martin and Jerry Lewis, Dinah Shore, Kathryn Grayson, and Marge and Gower Champion. The spectacle climaxed with a flyover by one of SAC's B-36 bombers. For more on Stewart's combat flying record in World War II, see Conrad Crane, *Bombs, Cities, and Civilians: American Airpower Strategy in World War II* (Lawrence: University Press of Kansas, 1993), 54-55.

28. Msg by Gen. James A. Van Fleet for release to all news media, 5 Apr 1952 and letter, General Van Fleet to Gen. Matthew Ridgway, 9 Apr 1952, Folder T-Z, CINCFE Correspondence, Box 19, Ridgway Papers.

CHAPTER 7. APPLYING AIR PRESSURE

1. Col. R. L. Randolph and Lt. Col. B. I. Mayo, Staff Study for Deputy for Operations, FEAF, "The Application of FEAF Effort in Korea," 12 Apr 1952, in FEAF Historical Division, *FEAF Operations Policy, Korea, Mid-1952,* Mar 1955, File K720.01, 1952 (addendum), AFHRA, Maxwell Air Force Base, Ala.

2. Memo, BG E. K. Wright to the Chief of Staff, Subject; Close Air Support, 15 Jan 1952, with handwritten annotations, Folder, Special File Jan-Apr 1952, Box 20, Matthew B. Ridgway Papers, U.S. Army Military History Institute, Carlisle Barracks, Pa.

3. Letter, Gen. James Van Fleet to Commander in Chief, Far East Command, Subject: Close Air Support, 20 Dec 1951, attached to memo, Subject: Close Air Support, 15 Jan 1952, Folder, Special File Jan-Apr 1952, Ridgway Papers.

4. Interview of Gen. Jacob Smart by Lt. Col. Arthur McCant and Dr. James Hasdorff, 27-30 Nov 1978, pp. 188-193, File K239.0512-1108, AFHRA; interview of General Smart by author, 2 Nov 1997, with changes provided by letter on 29 Nov 1997, pp. 18-20, in possession of author.

5. Memorandum of conversation with Lt. Gen. O. P. Weyland by Gen. Matthew Ridgway and memorandum for record by BG Edwin Wright, 31 Dec 1951, Folder, Special File Apr 1951-Jan 1952; memo, Weyland to Ridgway, Subject: General Van Fleet's Letter dated 20 Dec 1951, Subject: "Close Air Support," 12 Jan 1952, memo of conversation with General Weyland by Ridgway, 13 Jan 1952, and memo, BG E. K. Wright to the Chief of Staff, Subject: Close Air Support, 15 Jan 1952, with handwritten annotations, Folder, Special File Jan-Apr 1952, Box 20, Ridgway Papers; Matthew B. Ridgway, *The Korean War* (New York: Da Capo, 1986), 103-104.

6. Memo for record by Ridgway, 4 Apr 1952, Folder, Special File Jan-Apr 1952,

Box 20, Ridgway Papers; Ridgway, *The Korean War,* 238–239.

7. Smart interview by author, pp. 35–36, 40; Commander in Chief, U.S. Pacific Fleet, *Interim Evaluation Report No. 4, 1 January 1952-30 June 1952,* chap. 3, Carrier Operations, p. 3–91, Naval Historical Center, Washington, D.C.

8. Commander in Chief, U.S. Pacific Fleet, *Interim Third Evaluation Report, 1 May-31 December 1951,* chap. 10, Interdiction, pp. 10-41-10-42; *Interim Evaluation Report No. 4,* chap. 3, pp. 3-62-3-63, 3-69; letter, Maj. T. M. Sellers to his wife, 24 Mar 1953, furnished by Prof. Sharon MacDonald, Illinois State University, Normal, Ill.

9. Smart interview with author, pp. 1–2; "The Application of FEAF Effort in Korea."

10. "The Application of FEAF Effort in Korea"; Smart interview with author, p. 5.

11. Ridgway, *The Korean War,* 200, 202, 244; Gen. Mark W. Clark, *From the Danube to the Yalu* (Blue Ridge Summit, Pa.: Tab Books, 1988), 3; letter, Weyland to Vandenberg, 15 Sept 1952, Box 56, Papers of Hoyt Vandenberg, Manuscript Division, Library of Congress, Washington, D.C. For more on interdiction operations in Italy and northwestern Europe in World War II, see Eduard Mark, *Aerial Interdiction: Air Power and the Land Battle in Three American Wars: A Historical Analysis* (Washington, D.C.: Center for Air Force History, 1994), 141–257.

12. Extracts from FEAF Target Committee meeting minutes, 1952, in *FEAF Operations Policy, Korea, Mid-1952.*

13. Fifth Air Force Air Attack Program, in *5th AF Intelligence Summary, 16-31 July 1952,* File K730.607, AFHRA. There is some confusion on the actual date of the directive; some sources attribute it to 10 July, others two days later.

14. *History of the Far East Air Forces, January-June 1952,* vol. I, pp. 41–48, File K720.01, AFHRA; msg, VCO 118 CG, FEAF to HQ USAF, 29 Apr 1952, Sec. 96, msg, JCS 908100, JCS to CINCFE, 6 May 1952, Sec. 97, Box 39, and JCS 1776/297 with attachments, 19 June 1952, Sec. 104, Box 40, Geographic File, 1951-53, 383.21 Korea (3-19-45), Records of the Joint Chiefs of Staff, Record Group 218, National Archives II, College Park, Md.; msg, CG FEAF to CG FEAF BOMCOM, 10 Apr 1952, with 16 Apr reply, File B-17961, Box B200, Papers of Curtis LeMay, Manuscript Division, Library of Congress; msg, JCS 95977, JCS to CINCUNC, 10 July 1951, in U.S. Dept. of State, *Foreign Relations of the United States, 1951,* vol. 7, *Korea and China* (Washington, D.C.: USGPO, 1983), pt. 1, pp. 646–647; hereafter *FRUS.*

15. Entry for 11 June 1952, Weyland memoranda for record, 52/06/01-52/12/31, File 168.7104-6, AFHRA; Smart interview with author, pp. 3–5.

16. Memo, Operations Evaluation Group Representative to Commander Task Force 77, Subject: The Suiho Power Plant Attack 23 June 1952, 13 Aug 1952, in *Interim Evaluation Report No. 4,* chap. 3, pp. 3-122-3-126; Robert F. Futrell, *The United States Air Force in Korea 1950-1953* (Washington, D.C.: USGPO, 1983), 487–489; Maj. Gen. William F. Dean, *General Dean's Story* (New York: Viking Press, 1954), 263; "Labour Protests at Bombing on the Yalu River: Mr. Churchill Denies Change of Policy," *Times of London,* 25 June 1952, p. 2; also see continued coverage of parliamentary debates the next day: "Speculation Links Raid to Truce Talks" and "New Initiative in Korea," *New York Times,* 24 June 1952, pp. 3, 28; Austin Stevens, "Lovett Says the Joint Chiefs Authorized Air Blow at Yalu," *New York Times,* 25 June 1952, pp. 1, 3.

17. Entry for 1 July 1952, LeMay Diary #4, Box 103, letter, BG Wiley Ganey to LeMay, 2 July 1952, File FEAF 1, and letter, Ganey to LeMay, 28 July 1952, File FEAF 2, Box 65, LeMay Papers.

18. Letter, Ganey to LeMay, 2 July 1952, File FEAF 1, Box 65, LeMay Papers;

USAF Director of Plans, "Staff Study on Use of Atomic Weapons in Korea," 23 May 1952, File 385.2 Korea (28 July 1950), Sec. 2, Box 907, Record Group 341, Records of Headquarters USAF, National Archives II; entries for 9 and 10 June 1952, Weyland memoranda for record, 52/06/01-52/12/31, File 168.7104-6, AFHRA; memo, Clark to Army Chief of Staff for JCS, Subject: Fighter-Borne Atomic Capability, 23 June 1952, TS Personal File for 1949-1952, Box 3, and approved draft of FEC Emergency War Plan 1-52, 1 Mar 1952 with "Report on Wargaming of Emergency War Plan CINCFE1-52," 10 June 1952, 2 vols., in Boxes 7 and 8 of Records of General Headquarters FEC, SCAP, and UNC, Office of the Chief of Staff, Chief of Staff Subject Files 1945-52, Records of United States Army Commands, 1942-, Record Group 338, National Archives II; JCS 1776/300, 1 July 1952, Sec. 105, and JCS 1776/302, 9 July 1952, Sec. 106, Box 40, Geographic File, 1951-53, Korea 383.21 (3-19-45), Record Group 218; H. Goldhamer, Research Memorandum 903, *Communist Reaction in Korea to American Possession of the A-Bomb and Its Significance for U.S. Political and Psychological Warfare* (Santa Monica, Calif.: RAND Corporation, 1 Aug 1952).

19. See documents in *FRUS, 1952-1954,* vol. 15, *Korea* (Washington, D.C.: USGPO, 1984), pt. 1, pp. 120, 128-130, 356-357; Dean Acheson, *The Korean War* (New York: W. W. Norton, 1971), 135-136.

20. Memo, MG Herbert Thatcher to Gen. Nathan Twining, 1 July 1952, with attachments, File OPD 384.5 Korea (22 July 1950), Sec. 2, Box 904, Record Group 341; Futrell, *USAF in Korea,* 516-517, 525; Stephen E. Pease, *Psywar: Psychological Warfare in Korea, 1950-53* (Harrisburg, Pa.: Stackpole Books, 1992), 82-84; entry for 25 June 1952, Weyland memoranda for record, File 168.7104-6, 52/06/01-52/12/31; memo, BG Jacob Smart to CG, 5th AF, Subject: Targets in Pyongyang, *History of the Far East Air Forces, 1 July-31 December 1952,* vol. II, File K720.01; minutes of FEAF Target Committee meetings for 12 Aug and 21 Aug 1952, File K720.151A, 22 July-16 Dec 1952, AFHRA.

21. "Chinese Accuse US Pilots: Raid across Yalu Reported," and "Korean Negotiations," *Times of London,* 14 July 1952, pp. 6-7; "Asians in UN Fear Raids Harm Truce," *New York Times,* 12 July 1952, p. 2; telegram, Holmes to Dept. of State, 23 July 1952, in *FRUS, 1952-1954,* vol. 15, pt. 1, p. 419; Lindesay Parrott, "Long UN Air Raid Pounds Pyongyang and Reds' Build-up," *New York Times,* 12 July 1952, pp. 1-2; Lindesay Parrott, "Heaviest Air Blow of War Smashes Red Korea Capital," *New York Times,* 30 Aug 1952, pp. 1-2; Universal International Newsreels, vol. 25, no. 582, 28 July 1952, Record Group 200, National Archives II; "New Initiative in Korea," *New York Times,* 24 June 1953, p. 28.

22. Intelligence summaries for 16-31 July 1952, pp. 57, 74-76, and for 1-15 Aug 1952, containing copies of the STRIKE leaflets, *Fifth Air Force Intelligence Summaries,* File K730.607, and *History of 3rd Bombardment Wing, 1 July 1952-31 December 1952,* pp. 5-10, File KWG-3-HI, AFHRA; Commander in Chief, US Pacific Fleet, *Evaluation Report No. 5, Interim, 1 July 1952-31 January 1953,* pp. 3-93-3-95, U.S. Naval Historical Center; Pease, *Psywar,* 82-84; Universal International Newsreels, vol. 25, no. 596, 15 Sept 1952, lead story, Record Group 200; *USAF in Korea,* Futrell, 518-519; entries for 28 July and 7 Aug 1952, Weyland memoranda for record, 52/06/01-52/12/31, File 168.7104-6, AFHRA.

23. Entries for 14-22 Sept 1952, LeMay Diary #4, Box 103, and letter, BG W. P. Fisher to LeMay, 6 Mar 1953, FEAF Folder, Box B84, LeMay Papers; msg, CG

1583, LeMay to Clark, 30 Aug 1952, Records of General Headquarters FEC, SCAP, and UNC, Office of the Chief of Staff, Chief of Staff Subject Files 1945–52, TS Personal File for 1949–1952, Box 3, Record Group 338.

24. Entries for 24 and 28 July and 1 Aug 1952, Weyland memoranda for record, File 168.7104-6, 52/06/01–52/12/31, AFHRA. Weyland and Clark lost interest in Rashin after detailed target analysis showed that its rail lines and port facilities were now little used and there were no apparent military installations in the city.

25. Memorandum by the Chief of Staff, USAF for the JCS, Subject: Air Operations on the Chinese Mainland and Manchuria, 4 Aug 1952, and Joint Strategic Plans Committee, "Future Courses of Action in Connection with the Situation in Korea," 18 Aug 1952, File OPD 381 Korea (9 May 1947), Sec. 16, Box 895, Record Group 341.

26. Memo, Banfill to Deputy for Operations, Subject: Utilization of Air Power in Korea, 29 Aug 1952, *FEAF Operations Policy, Korea, Mid-1952.*

27. Memo, Smart to Deputy for Intelligence, Subject: Utilization of Air Power in Korea, 16 Sept 1952, *FEAF Operations Policy, Korea, Mid-1952.*

28. Letter, Weyland to Vandenberg, 15 Sept 1952, Box 56, Vandenberg Papers; entries for 1, 7, 11 Aug 1952, Weyland memoranda for record, File 168.7104-6, 52/06/01–52/12/31, AFHRA.

29. Letter, Weyland to Vandenberg, 15 Sept 1952, Box 56, Vandenberg Papers; entries for 1 Aug and 2 Oct 1952, Weyland memoranda for record, File 168.7104-6, 52/06/01–52/12/31, AFHRA; msgs, DA 912775, Chief of Staff US Army to Clark, 3 July 1952, and C 59373, Clark to Lovett, 23 Nov 1952, Records of General Headquarters FEC, SCAP, and UNC, Office of the Chief of Staff, Chief of Staff Subject Files 1945–52, TS Personal File for 1949–1952, Box 3, Record Group 338.

30. Richard Hallion, *The Naval Air War in Korea* (Baltimore: Nautical and Aviation Publishing Company of America, 1986), 135–136; memorandum of conversation by Allison, Subject: General Clark's Request to Bomb Targets in Korea near Manchurian and Soviet Borders, 26 Aug 1952, in *FRUS, 1952–1954,* vol. 15, pt. 1, pp. 458–459.

31. See documents in *FRUS, 1952–1954,* vol. 15, pt. 1, pp. 39, 436–442, 470, 527–528, 575, 650; Shu Guang Zhang, *Mao's Military Romanticism: China and the Korean War, 1950–1953* (Lawrence: University Press of Kansas, 1995), 180–181.

32. *FRUS, 1952–1954,* vol. 15, pt. 1, pp. 466–469, 475, 514–519; minutes of FEAF Target Committee meeting, 24 Sept 1952, File K720.151A, 22 July–16 Dec 1952, AFHRA.

CHAPTER 8. THE QUEST FOR BETTER BOMBS AND BOMBING

1. Letter, BG Wiley D. Ganey to Gen. Curtis LeMay, 7 May 1952, File FEAF 1, Box 65, Papers of Curtis LeMay, Manuscript Division, Library of Congress, Washington, D.C.

2. Memo, MG Howard Bunker to LTG T. D. White, Subject: Air Force Program for Biological and Chemical Warfare, 22 Apr 1953, BW-CW General Decimal Files, 1953, Box 1, Record Group 341, Records of Headquarters, USAF, National Archives II, College Park, Md.

3. For a more thorough discussion of the development of American precision bombing doctrine, see Conrad Crane, *Bombs, Cities, and Civilians: American Airpower*

Strategy in World War II (Lawrence: University Press of Kansas, 1993), 12-27.

4. Ibid., 86-87.

5. USAF Historical Study No. 71, *United States Air Force Operations in the Korean Conflict, 25 June-1 November 1950* (Maxwell Air Force Base, Ala.: USAF Historical Division, 1 July 1952), 46; USAF Historical Study No. 72, *United States Air Force Operations in the Korean Conflict, 1 November 1950-30 June 1952* (Maxwell Air Force Base, Ala.: USAF Historical Division, 1 July 1955), 141.

6. USAF Historical Study No. 72, 141-142; memo, MG William McKee to Gen. Hoyt Vandenberg, Subject: FEAF Tarzon-Razon Program, 1 Nov 1951, Pacific IV File, Box 56, Papers of Hoyt Vandenberg, Manuscript Division, Library of Congress, Washington, D.C.; USAF Historical Study No. 127, *United States Air Force Operations in the Korean Conflict, 1 July 1952-27 July 1953* (Maxwell Air Force Base, Ala.: USAF Historical Division, 1 July 1956), 131; Universal International Newsreels, vol. 25, no. 570, 16 June 1952, Record Group 200, National Archives II.

7. Commander in Chief, U.S. Pacific Fleet, *Evaluation Report No. 5, Interim, 1 July 1952-31 January 1953,* chap. 3, Carrier Operations, pp. 3-49-3-50, Naval Historical Center, Washington, D.C.; Universal International Newsreels, vol. 25, no. 598, 22 Sept 1952, Record Group 200. For more on the War-Weary bombers of World War II, see Crane, *Bombs, Cities, and Civilians,* 78-85.

8. Ezra Bowen, *Knights of the Air* (Alexandria, Va.: Time-Life Books, 1980), 53; USAF Historical Study No. 72, 185, 217-218; USAF Historical Study No. 127, 73.

9. Commander in Chief, U.S. Pacific Fleet, *Evaluation Report No. 6, Interim, 1 February 1953-27 July 1953,* chap. 3, Carrier Operations, pp. 3-48-3-51, Naval Historical Center; USAF Historical Study No. 72, 219.

10. Robert F. Futrell, *The United States Air Force in Korea 1950-1953* (Washington, D.C.: USGPO, 1983), 519-520; 5th AF Operations Analysis Office Memo 62, "Approximation of Force Requirements for Fighter Bombers," 16 Jan 1953, p. 4, File K720.3101-62; Capt. M. J. McCarthy, "Fifth Air Force Status of Bombing Accuracy," in HQ 5th AF, *History of the Fifth Air Force, 1 July-31 December 1952,* vol. II, app. 5, File K730.01, 1 July-31 Dec 1952, and summaries of OA Memoranda Nos. 68 and 69, in HQ 5th AF, *History of the Fifth Air Force, 1 July-31 December 1953,* pp. 370-371, File K730.01, July-Dec 1953, AFHRA, Maxwell Air Force Base, Ala.; Commander in Chief, U.S. Pacific Fleet, *Interim Evaluation Report No. 4, 1 January 1952-30 June 1952,* chap. 3, Carrier Operations, pp. 3-88-3-89, Naval Historical Center.

11. USAF Historical Study No. 72, 85-86, 175-176; "Fifth Air Force Status of Bombing Accuracy"; *Interim Evaluation Report No. 4,* pp. 3-69-3-72; *Evaluation Report No. 5, Interim,* p. 3-3; interview with Gen. Jacob Smart (Ret.), by author, 2 Nov 1997, Arlington, Va., with changes provided by letter on 29 Nov 1997, pp. 23-24, in possession of author; Richard H. Kohn and Joseph P. Harahan, eds., *Air Interdiction in World War II, Korea, and Vietnam* (Washington, D.C.: Office of Air Force History, 1986), 56-58; Futrell, *USAF in Korea,* 490-492.

12. Louis W. Davis, "How Korean Cliff Dwellers Called the Shots," in *Bombs Away! True Stories of Strategic Airpower from World War I to the Present,* ed. Stanley Ulanoff (Garden City, N.Y.: Doubleday, 1971), 484-493; USAF Historical Study No. 92, *Development of Night Air Operations 1941-1952* (Maxwell Air Force Base, Ala.: USAF Historical Division, 1953), 211-217; Smart interview, p. 37; 5th AF Operations Analysis Office, Memo. No. 78, "An Assessment of B-29 Close Support Blind Bombing Accuracy during the Korean War," 12 June 1954, File K720.3101-

78; summary of OA Memorandum No. 70, in HQ 5th AF, *History of the Fifth Air Force, 1 July-31 December 1953,* p. 371, File K730.01, July–Dec 1953, AFHRA.

13. Interview with Maj. James W. Miller, 30 Nov 1950, in Recorded Interviews, B-29s, in HQ USAF, *An Evaluation of the Effectiveness of the United States Air Force in the Korean Campaign,* general appendix, book III, pp. 62–72, File 168.041-1, AFHRA. For data on World War II bombing accuracy, see Crane, *Bombs, Cities, and Civilians,* 38, 63–77.

14. USAF Historical Study No. 92, 191–192, 199–205; letter, BG Robert Terrill to Gen. Curtis LeMay, 20 June 1951 letter, BG Joe Kelly to LeMay, 2 Nov 1951, and letter, BG Wiley Ganey to LeMay, 7 May 1952, File FEAF 1, Box 65, LeMay Papers; Walton S. Moody, *Building a Strategic Air Force* (Washington, D.C.: Air Force History and Museums Program, 1996), 403; JCS 2220/19, Joint Strategic Plans Committee, "Revision of Information for General Ridgway on Availability of Atomic Weapons," 6 May 1953, on microfilm, *Records of the Joint Chiefs of Staff,* part 2, *1946-1953, Strategic Issues, Section I, Atomic Weapons* (Frederick, Md.: University Publications of America, 1980), reel 4. The JCS planning figure for dive or toss bombing from fighter-bombers was 600 feet. The 600-foot and 1,500-foot CEP figures were used as standards in figuring munitions requirements for Korean contingency plans. See, for example, Joint Strategic Plans Committee, "Future Courses of Action in Connection with the Situation in Korea," 18 Aug 1952, File OPD 381 Korea (9 May 1947), Sec. 16, Box 895, Record Group 341.

15. USAF Historical Study No. 72, 184–185; USAF Historical Study No. 127, 72–81.

16. W. Kendall et al., *FEC Psychological Warfare Operations: Leaflets* (Baltimore: Operations Research Office, Johns Hopkins University, 31 Mar 1952). One of the complaints of the analysts about Far East Command leaflet drops was that some of them were wasted on cities that had already been leveled.

17. FECOM Psychological Warfare Section, Divisive Bomb Warning, Serial No. 1123, 24 Nov 1951, in *Fifth Air Force Intelligence Summary, 16–30 June 1952,* File K730.607, AFHRA.

18. Jean Hungerford, Research Memorandum No. 925, *Reactions of Civilian Populations to Air Attacks by Friendly Forces* (Santa Monica, Calif.: RAND Corporation, 2 Sept 1952), iii, 36.

19. Msg, CG FEAF to Subordinate Commands, Subject: Cal .22 Soft Nose Hornet Ammunition, in HQ FEAF, *History of the Far East Air Forces, 1 January-30 June 1952,* vol. II, p. 71, File K720.01, AFHRA.

20. Summary of Communist Bacteriological and Chemical Warfare Charges, in *Fifth Air Force Intelligence Summary, 16-30 June 1952,* p. 65, File K730.607, AFHRA; "Germ-Carrying Rats Bred in North Korea," *New York Times,* 6 Nov 1950, p. 3.

21. Summary of Communist Bacteriological and Chemical Warfare Charges, pp. 65–66; msg, C 50261, CINCFE to JCS, 16 June 1952, File 383.21 Korea, Geographic Files 1951-53, Sec. 103, Box 39, Record Group 218, Records of the Joint Chiefs of Staff, National Archives II.

22. Summary of Communist Bacteriological and Chemical Warfare Charges; Psychological Strategy Board Staff Study D-25b, "Preliminary Analysis of the Communist BW Propaganda Campaign, with Recommendations," 7 Aug 1952, and memo, MG Robert Lee to Gen. Vandenberg, Subject: Chinese Communist Threat, 14 Mar 1952, File OPD 383.6 Korea (12 July 1951), Sec. 3, Box 903, Record Group 341;

Milton Leitenberg, *The Korean War Biological Warfare Allegations Resolved,* Occasional Paper 36 (Stockholm: Center for Pacific Asia Studies at Stockholm University, May 1998), 5-6, 27-28.

23. Psychological Strategy Board Staff Study D-25b; JCS 1776/282 and JCS 1776/283, 12 Mar 1952, both with enclosures, File OPD 383.6 Korea (12 July 1951), Box 903, Record Group 341; JCS 1776/293, 12 June 1952, with enclosures, File 383.21 Korea, Geographic Files 1951-53, Sec. 103, Box 39; msgs, JCS 903457, JCS to CINCFE, 14 Mar 1952, and JCS 903780, 17 Mar 1952, Outgoing Messages, 2 Mar 1952-21 July 1953, Box 10; msg, C 69794, CINCFE to DEPTAR, 7 June 1952, Incoming Messages, 26 Apr 1952-30 June 1952, Box 5, Record Group 218, Records of the Joint Chiefs of Staff, National Archives II; "U.S. Proposes Investigation of Bacteriological Warfare Charges," *Department of State Bulletin* 27 (7 July 1952): 32-37, and "Security Council Statement of July 3," *Department of State Bulletin* 27 (28 July 1952):159; memorandum for the Secretary of Defense from the Secretary of the Air Force, 23 Apr 1952, BW-CW General Decimal Files, 1952, Box 2, Record Group 341.

24. Memo, George Morgan to David K. E. Bruce, et al., Subject: Staff Study—Preliminary Analysis of the Communist BW Propaganda Campaign with Recommendations, 25 July 1952, with attached Psychological Strategy Board Staff Study D-25b, File OPD 383.6 Korea (12 July 1951), Sec. 3, Box 903, Record Group 341. The Psychological Strategy Board had been established by presidential directive on 4 Apr 1951 "to accomplish nationally consistent and cumulative results from coordinated psychological operations." Memorandum for the Joint Chiefs of Staff, Subject: Establishment of the Psychological Strategy Board, 9 Apr 1951, in microfilm, *Records of the Joint Chiefs of Staff, part 2, 1946-53, Meetings of the Joint Chiefs of Staff* (Washington, D.C.: University Publications of America, 1980), reel 2.

25. Memorandum by the Asst. Scty. of State for UN Affairs to the Deputy Under Scty. of State, 20 May 1952, pp. 210-212, and Editorial Note, pp. 343-344, in U.S. Department of State, *Foreign Relations of the United States, 1952-1954,* vol. 15, *Korea* (Washington, D.C.: USGPO, 1984), pt. 1; "U.S. Proposes Investigation of Bacteriological Warfare Charges" and "Security Council Statement of July 3"; Thomas J. Hamilton, "Malik Blocks U.N. Vote on Inquiry into Red Charges of Germ Warfare," *New York Times,* 24 June 1952, p. 1; lead story, Universal International Newsreels, vol. 25, no. 571, 19 June 1952, Record Group 200, National Archives II.

26. State Department Intelligence Reports, "The Effect of the Bacteriological Warfare Campaign," 7 Oct and 7 Nov 1952, on reel 5 of microfilm collection, *OSS/State Department Intelligence and Research Reports,* vol. 8, *Japan, Korea, Southeast Asia, and the Far East Generally: 1950-1961 Supplement* (Washington, D.C.: University Publications of America, 1979); Shu Guang Zhang, *Mao's Military Romanticism: China and the Korean War, 1950-1953* (Lawrence: University Press of Kansas, 1995), 182-183, 186. The new revelations are covered in Kathryn Weathersby, "Deceiving the Deceivers: Moscow, Beijing, Pyongyang, and the Allegations of Bacteriological Weapons Use in Korea," and Milton Leitenberg, "New Russian Evidence on the Korean War Biological Warfare Allegations: Background and Analysis," *Cold War International History Project Bulletin* (winter 1998): 176-199. Despite this new evidence, there are still some who argue that the BW allegations are valid. The most recent example of such a position is Stephen Endicott and Edward Hagerman, *The United States and Biological Warfare: Secrets from the Early Cold War and Korea* (Bloomington: Indiana University Press, 1998). They admit, "Clear and

identifiable direct evidence that the United States experimented with biological weapons in the Korean war is not available in the U.S. archives as they presently exist for public scrutiny." However, they weave a complicated tangle of circumstantial evidence that indicts the U.S. Air Force, U.S. Army, Far East Command, Far East Air Forces, Joint Chiefs of Staff, and Central Intelligence Agency, among others. They are correct about the increased American emphasis on BW and evolving plans for its use in the era of the Korean War, but they do not understand the course of the air war nor the conduct of intelligence or psychological operations. For instance, they claim that F-86s were rushed to Korea to conduct BW, instead of to counter the threat of MiG-15s. Their work reinforces a Leitenberg quote from John Ellis van Courtland Moon on BW charges: "Once an allegation is made, it is impossible to disprove it completely, since the nature of the weapon makes it almost invisible. If it is difficult to prove that it has been used, it is impossible to prove that it has not been used."

27. Zhang, *Mao's Military Romanticism,* 181-186; Maj. Gen. William F. Dean, *General Dean's Story* (New York: Viking Press, 1954), 275-278; entry for 28 Apr 1953, Weyland memoranda for record, vol. IV, 53/01/01-53/07/31, File 168.7104-7, AFHRA.

28. Msg, 59755, HQ USAF to CG FEAF, 16 May 1952, and JCS 1776/293, 12 June 1952, p. 1562, and memo, BG Charles Banfill to Chief of Staff, USAF, Subject: Investigation of Allegations Regarding a Use of Bacteriological Warfare by UN, 26 June 1952, Sec. 2; memo, Psychological Warfare Division to Directorate of Intelligence, USAF, Subject: Bacteriological Warfare Charges by Communists, 5 Nov 1952, with 6 Nov 1952 endorsement from Directorate of Intelligence, Sec. 3; memo from HQ USAF, Subject: Investigation into Communist Allegations of USAF Participation in Biological Warfare in Korea, 27 Mar 1953, Sec. 5; memorandum for the Secretary of Defense by the Secretary of the Air Force, 18 Mar 1953, Sec. 4; memo, Secretary of Defense to Secretary of the Air Force and Commandant, U.S. Marine Corps, Subject: Statements Regarding Biological Warfare by Members of the US Air Force and the US Marine Corps, 15 Sept 1953, Sec. 7, File OPD 383.6 Korea (12 July 1951), Box 903, Record Group 341; Army Security Center, "U.S. Prisoners of War in the Korean Operation: A Study of Their Treatment and Handling by the North Korean Army and the Chinese Communist Forces," Nov 1954, copy furnished by Allan Millett.

29. Entry for 28 Apr 1953, Weyland memoranda for record, vol. IV, 53/01/01-53/07/31, File 168.7104-7; FBIB GRNC W171847, transmission from Peking, 17 June 1952, in HQ FEAF, *History of the Far East Air Forces, 1 January-30 June 1952,* vol. II, File K720.01, AFHRA; memo, Directorate of Intelligence to Directorate of Plans, Subject: Affidavit of 1st Lt V. E. Tharp—Special Inquiry, 30 Jan 1953, memo, Col. John Hutchison to MG Lee, Subject: Germ Warfare Charges, 26 Jan 1953, and memo, Chaplain (Maj.) Harry McKnight, Jr., to Col. J. W. Anderson, Subject: Report of Chaplain's Visit with Mrs. John S. Quinn, 20 Apr 1953, Sec. 4, File OPD 383.6 Korea (12 July 1951), Box 903, Record Group 341.

30. Henry R. Lieberman, "Freed American Tells of Drugging with 'Truth Medicine' in China," *New York Times,* 12 July 1952, p. 1; memo, MG Lee to LTG White, Subject: Air Force Council Showing of Psychological Warfare Movie, 5 Nov 1952, Sec. 3; memo, Col. Hutchison to MG Lee, Subject: Germ Warfare Charges, 26 Jan 1953, Sec. 4; msg, DA 945519, DA G2 to CINCFE J2, 6 Aug 1953, Sec. 5, File

OPD 383.6 Korea (12 July 1951), Box 903, Record Group 341.

31. Memorandum for record by LTC Floyd Robinson, with attached memorandum from Gen. G. B. Erskine (Ret.) and statements of POWs, 12 Oct 1953, Sec. 7, File OPD 383.6 Korea (12 July 1951), Box 903, Record Group 341; Universal International Newsreels, vol. 26, no. 513, 29 Oct 1953, Record Group 200, National Archives II. The actual film footage of the September POW interviews is available in Record Group 342 at the National Archives II, entries NWDNM(m)-342-USAF-34921 and NWDNM(m)-342-USAF-35833. Endicott and Hagerman, in *The U.S. and Biological Warfare,* argue that since the airmen were not really subjected to much abuse in the POW camps but were pressured strongly to deny the BW allegations when they were repatriated, the recantations are actually less believable than the original confessions.

32. Sworn Statement by Col. Walker M. Mahurin, USAF, "Communist Way: Case History of a Confession," *New York Times,* 1 Nov 1953, p. E3.

33. Msg, V0222 CG, Weyland to White, 26 Mar 1953, Sec. 4, File OPD 383.6 Korea (12 July 1951), Box 903, Record Group 341.

34. JCS 1837/5, Note by the Joint Secretaries, "Special Biological Warfare Operations," with attachments, 9 Feb 1949, and "Report of the Secretary of Defense's ad hoc Committee on Biological Warfare," 11 July 1949, in microfilm, *Records of the JCS, Part 2, 1946–53, Strategic Issues, Section I, Atomic Weapons,* reel 4; memo, MG McKee to Mr. Burden, Subject: BW Policy, 19 Dec 1951, BW Munitions Folder, BW-CW Decimal Files, 1951, Box 1; memo, Col. Frank Seilor to MG Bunker, Subject: Briefing for LTG Partridge, 24 June 1953, with enclosure, and Resume of the USAF BW-CW Program from 1951 to Present, 7 Aug 1953, BW-CW General Decimal Files, 1953, Box 2, Record Group 341.

35. Discrepancies Noted in IG Six-Month Progress Report on BW-CW Program, Dated 16 May 1951, 7 June 1951; memorandum for Commanding General, Air University, Subject: Biological and Chemical Warfare, 7 June 1951; Staff Study, BW-CW Program in USAF, 11 June 1951; memo, MG D. L. Putt to Chairman of the Research and Development Board, Subject: Request for Supplemental Funds for Air Force Biological and Chemical Munitions, 15 Nov 1951; memo, Col. W. M. Canterbury to DCS/Operations, Subject: Memorandum for Secretary of the Air Force on BW and CW, 27 Nov 1951, BW-CW Decimal Files, 1952, Box 1; memorandum for personal files, LTG White to Secretary Finletter, 7 Nov 1951, and memorandum for record by LTC Karl Retzer, Subject: Informal RCAF-USAF Discussion on BW-CW Test Areas, 2 Nov 1951, BW-CW General Decimal Files, 1951, Box 1, Record Group 341. At the time, the Soviet Union was projected to possess 500,000 tons of World War II CW stocks and 16,000 tons of new nerve agents.

36. Letter, LeMay to White, 17 June 1952, File B-18635, Box B201, LeMay Papers; memo, LTC Seth Mize to Col. James Totten, Subject: Recent BW-CW Developments, 14 Apr 1952, and memo, Psychological Warfare Division to Director of Operations, Subject: BW Plans for SAC Operations, 20 Mar 1952, BW-CW General Decimal Files, 1952, Box 4; briefings for Commanding General, Air Material Command, and Commanding General, Strategic Air Command, 21 May 1952, letter, Col. Erlath Zuehl to USAF Chief of Staff, 14 Apr 1952, and memo, Col. Totten to MG Donald Yates, Subject: Review of Advanced Copy of RAND Report on BW, 27 June 1952, BW-CW General Decimal Files, 1952, Box 2.

37. Memo, Col. Totten to MG Donald Yates, Subject: Review of Advanced Copy

of RAND Report on BW, 27 June 1952, and memorandum for record, Subject: Interim Report on Symposium on BW Agents, 23 Apr 1952, with enclosures, BW-CW General Decimal Files, 1952, Box 2; memoranda for General Bunker, Subject: Proposed Air Force Agenda for BW Inter-Service Coordinating Committee, 5 May 1952, and Subject: BW-CW Inter-Service Coordinating Committee, 29 May 1952, and memorandum for Secretary Pace from Finletter, 7 Nov 1952, BW-CW General Decimal Files, 1952, Box 4, Record Group 341. For more on Doolittle, see Crane, *Bombs, Cities, and Civilians*, 39–40, 107–108.

38. Entry for 31 May 1952, Weyland memoranda for record, vol. II, 51/12/01–52/05/31, File 168.7104-5, AFHRA; memoranda for record by LTC R. F. Garner, Subject: FEAF Preparedness of BW-CW, 21 July 1952, Subject: FEAF Chemical Warfare Capability, 29 July 1952, Subject: FEAF Preparedness for BW-CW, 8 Aug 1952, and Subject: Typical Working Plan for Employment of CW in FEAF, 17 Nov 1952; msg CX 59022, CINCFE to DEPTAR, 19 Nov 1952, BW-CW General Decimal Files, 1952, Box 4; proposed amendments to memorandum of the Vice Chief of Staff, 15 Jan 1952, USAF Biological and Chemical Warfare Program, 18 Apr 1952, with 3 July 1952 approval, BW-CW General Decimal Files, 1952, Box 2, Record Group 341.

39. Memo, MG Robert Burns to Deputy Chief of Staff for Plans and Research, Subject: Army Requirements for Mustard, 2 Oct 1952, and memo, MG Howard Bunker to Chief Chemical Officer, DA, Subject: Protective Equipment of Enemy Forces in North Korea, 30 Jan 1953, with 1st endorsement from MG E. F. Bullene, BW-CW General Decimal Files, 1953, Box 1; memorandum for record by LTC Karl Retzer, Subject: Visit by FEAF Representatives, 21 May 1953, memo, Col. Frank Seiler to MG Bunker, Subject: Briefing for LTG Partridge, 24 June 1953, with enclosure, and memorandum for record by LTC Francis Bodine, Subject: FEAF Stockpiling of CW Munitions, 20 Aug 1953, BW-CW General Decimal Files, 1953, Box 2, Record Group 341; JCS 1837/48, "Overseas Deployment of Toxic Chemicals," 16 Apr 1953, in microfilm, *Records of the JCS, Part 2, 1946–53, Strategic Issues, Section I, Atomic Weapons,* reel 4.

40. Memo, MG Howard Bunker to LTG T. D. White, Subject: Air Force Program for Biological and Chemical Warfare, 22 Apr 1953, BW-CW General Decimal Files, 1953, Box 1; memo, Col. Frank Seiler to MG Bunker, Subject: Briefing for LTG Partridge, 24 June 1953, with enclosure, BW-CW General Decimal Files, 1953, Box 2; memo, Col. Guthrie to BW-CW Division, Asst for Atomic Energy, Subject: Military Characteristics for a Biological Bomb for Balloon Delivery, 29 Jan 1953, letter, MG Yates to Commander, Air Research and Development Command, Subject: Development of the Balloon System for Delivery of Anti-Crop BW Munitions, 13 Nov 1953, and memo, BG J. C. Jensen to Asst for Atomic Energy, Subject: Requirements for Coordinated Staff Action on E77 (Biological Bomb for Balloon Delivery), 18 Dec 1953, BW-CW General Decimal Files, 1953, Box 6, Record Group 341; JSPC 954/29, Joint Strategic Plans Committee, "Chemical (Toxic) and Biological Warfare Readiness," 13 Aug 1953, in microfilm, *Records of the JCS,* part 2, *1946–53, Strategic Issues, Section I, Atomic Weapons,* reel 4. On the Japanese use of balloon bombs in World War II, see Crane, *Bombs, Cities, and Civilians,* 122. Army Air Forces commanding general "Hap" Arnold feared that the enemy was going to use them for biological warfare.

CHAPTER 9. THE FINAL ACTS

1. Msg, C-54277, CINCFE to DEPTAR, 27 Aug 1952, File 383.21 Korea (3-19-45), Geographic Files, 1951–53, Sec. 110, Box 40, Record Group 218, Records of the Joint Chiefs of Staff, National Archives II, College Park, Md.

2. HQ, UNC, Operation Plan CINCUNC No. 8-52, 15 Oct 1952, File 383.21 Korea (3-19-45), Gepgraphic File 1951–1953, Box 47, Record Group 218.

3. "Staff Study of Intelligence Requirements by Commander, FEAF, for the Present and the Future," in *History of the Far East Air Forces, January–December 1953,* vol. III, pt. 1, p. 5, File K720.01, AFHRA, Maxwell Air Force Base, Ala.

4. Operation Plan CINCUNC No. 8-52, 15 Oct 1952, Box 47, Geographic File, 1951–53, Korea 383.21 (3-19-45), Record Group 218; memo, Director of Plans to Director of Intelligence, Subject: Study on the Use of Atomic Weapons in the Far East, 3 Dec 1952, File OPD 381 Korea (9 May 1947), Sec. 18, Box 896, Record Group 341, Records of Headquarters, USAF, National Archives II.

5. Transcript of briefing on Oplan 8-52 with briefing charts, Nov 1952, File 091 Korea, General Decimal File 1952, Box 20, Record Group 319, Army Operations, National Archives II; memo, MG Sanford to LTG White, Subject: Analaysis and Implications of the Communist IL-28 Threat and Proposed Counter Action, 10 Feb 1953; memo, MG Lee for Chief of Staff, USAF, Subject: Air Operations against Chinese Communist Air Bases in Manchuria, 10 Feb 1953; memo, R. M. Ramey to Chief, War Plans Division, Subject: Future Courses of Action in Connection with the Situation in Korea, 18 Feb 1953; memo, MG Lee to DCS/Operations, Subject: Vulnerability of UN Air Forces in Korea to the CCAF, 25 Feb 1953, with enclosures, File OPD 381 Korea (9 May 1947), Sec. 20, Box 895, Record Group 341; Commander in Chief, U.S. Pacific Fleet, *Evaluation Report No. 5, Interim, 1 July 1952-31 January 1953,* chap. 3, Carrier Operations, p. 3-118, Naval Historical Center, Washington, D.C.

6. Entry for 13 Nov 1952, Weyland memoranda for record, 52/06/01–52/12/31, File 168.7104-6, AFHRA. In one of his last communications as president, Truman reaffirmed his continued aversion to the employment of nuclear weapons. On 19 Jan 1953 he wrote to the chairman of the Atomic Energy Commission that the use of the atomic bomb was "far worse than gas and biological warfare because it affects the civilian population and murders them by the wholesale." Letter, Truman to Thomas Murray, 19 Jan 1953, General File-A/bomb Folder, Box 112, President's Secretary's Files, Papers of Harry S. Truman, Harry S. Truman Library, Independence, Mo.

7. Msg, V0017, Weyland to White, 9 Jan 1953, memo, Director of Plans to Director of Intelligence, Subject: Study on the Use of Atomic Weapons in the Far East, 3 Dec 1952, with attachments, memo, CINCUNC to Chief of Staff, Dept. of the Army, Subject: Operation Plan CINCUNC No. 8-52, 16 Oct 1952, Sec. 18, Box 896, supplemental memorandum for the Chief of Staff, Subject: Future Courses of Action in Connection with the Situation in Korea (Analysis), 13 May 1953, Sec. 24, Box 898, and summary sheet, Subject: Course of Action in Connection with Korea, 30 June 1953, Sec. 25, Box 898, File OPD 381 Korea (9 May 1947), Record Group 341; Roger Dingman, "Atomic Diplomacy in the Korean War," *International Security* 13 (winter 1988-1989): 82-85.

8. Memorandum by the Joint Chiefs of Staff to the Secretary of Defense, Subject: Courses of Action in Connection with the Situation in Korea, 19 May 1953, and memorandum of discussion at the 145th meeting of the National Security Council, Wed., 20 May 1953, in U.S. Department of State, *Foreign Relations of the United States, 1952-1954,* vol. 15, *Korea* (Washington, D.C.: USGPO, 1984), pt. 1, pp. 1059-1068 (hereafter *FRUS*); Shu Guang Zhang, *Mao's Military Romanticism: China and the Korean War, 1950-1953* (Lawrence: University Press of Kansas, 1995), 257; memo, MG Robert Lee to MG John Samford, Subject: The Possible Employment of Atomic Weapons in Connection with Korea, 8 June 1953, with enclosures, Sec. 24, and memo, MG Lee to DCS/O, Subject: Course of Action in Connection with Korea, 30 June 1953, with enclosures, Sec. 25, Box 898, File OPD 381 Korea (9 May 1947), Record Group 341. Security about the atomic recommendations dealing with the plan, JCS 1776/372, was so tight that each service had to compile a list of everyone who was aware of them.

9. "Staff Study of Intelligence Requirements by Cdr, FEAF for the Present and the Future," in *History of the Far East Air Forces, January-December 1953,* vol. III, pt. 1, p. 5, File K720.01, AFHRA; memo by Maj. Gen. Lee, 4 May 1953, and summary sheet by Lt. Col. Kidd, 28 Apr 1953, Subject: Air Attacks against Targets in Korea Near the Manchurian Border, with attachments, File OPD 384.5 Korea (22 July 1950), Sec. 3, Box 906, Record Group 341; msg, JCS 915579, JCS to CINCFE, 8 Aug 1952, Geographic File, 1951-53, 383.21 Korea (3-19-45), Sec. 109, Box 40, and msg, C 62275, CINCFE to JCS, 6 May 1953, with attached memo for General Bradley, Incoming Messages, 11 Feb.-31 May 1953, Box 7, Record Group 218.

10. Commander in Chief, U.S. Pacific Fleet, *Interim Evaluation Report No. 2, 16 November 1950 to 30 April 1951,* vol. II, p. 766, Naval Historical Center; minutes of the FEAF Formal Target Committee meeting for 24 Mar 1953, with enclosure, in *FEAF Bomber Command History, January-27 July 1953,* vol. III, File K713.01-39, AFHRA; msg, C62419, Clark to JCS, 14 May 1953, Incoming Messages, 11 Feb-31 May 1953, Box 7, Record Group 218.

11. Minutes of the FEAF Formal Target Committee meetings for 7 Apr, 12 May, and 26 May 1953, in *FEAF Bomber Command History, January-27 July 1953,* vol. III, File K713.01-39, and entries for 7 and 8 May 1953, Weyland memoranda for record, vol. IV, 53/01/01-53/07/31, File 168.7104-7, AFHRA; msg, 62451, Clark to JCS, 16 May 1953, Incoming Messages, 11 Feb-31 May 1953, Box 7, Record Group 218.

12. Msg, CX 62662, Clark to JCS, 27 May 1953, Incoming Messages, 11 Feb-31 May 1953, Box 7, Record Group 218; msg, CX 62983, Clark to JCS, 11 June 1953, with JCS reply, JCS 941184, 11 June 1953, Sec. 130, Box 44, Geographic File, 383.21 Korea (3-19-45), Record Group 218; interview of Gen. Jacob Smart (Ret.) by author, 2 Nov 1997, Arlington, Va., incorporating changes provided by letter from Smart on 29 Nov 1997, in possession of author; msgs, Clark to JCS, CX 62901, 8 June 1953, CX 62960, 10 June 1953, and CX 63033, 13 June 1953, Incoming Messages, 1 June-31 July 1953, Box 8, Record Group 218.

13. As an example of the McConnell-Fernandez coverage, see Robert Alden, "Sabre Jets Score 12 Mig Bag in Day," *New York Times,* 19 May 1953, p. 3. For press releases by both sides on the dam attacks, see the official reports of Korean action that were always on p. 2 of the *New York Times,* 15, 17, 18, and 23 May 1953.

14. USAF Historical Study No. 127, *United States Air Force Operations in the*

Korean Conflict, 1 July 1952-27 July 1953 (Maxwell Air Force Base, Ala.: USAF Historical Division, 1 July 1956), 157-160; summary of OA Memorandum No. 68, in HQ 5th AF, *History of the Fifth Air Force, 1 July-31 December 1953,* pp. 370-371, File K730.01, July-Dec 1953, AFHRA.

15. Minutes of FEAF Formal Target Committee meetings for 23 June and 22 July 1953, in *FEAF Bomber Command History, January-27 July 1953,* vol. III, File K713.01-39, AFHRA; memo, MG Lee to DCS/Operations, Subject: Carrier Forces versus Land Based Forces, 13 Feb 1953, with enclosures; memorandum for General Vandenberg from W. Barton Leach, 11 Mar 1953, with enclosures; memo, Col. Wallace Barrett to Leach, Subject: Carrier Operations in Korea, 30 Mar 1953; memorandum for General Vandenberg from Leach, 31 Mar 1953, Folder 7C, Box 84, Papers of Hoyt S. Vandenberg, Manuscript Division, Library of Congress, Washington, D.C.

16. Minutes of FEAF Formal Target Committee meeting for 26 May 1953, in *FEAF Bomber Command History, January-27 July 1953,* vol. III, File K713.01-39, AFHRA; entries for 21 May, 26 May, and 16 June 1953, Weyland memoranda for record, vol. IV; Quarterly Review Staff Study, "The Attack on the Irrigation Dams in North Korea," *Air University Quarterly Review* 4 (winter 1953-1954): 40-61.

17. "U.S. Troops Smash New Red Attacks," and Austin Stevens, "Arms Chiefs Tell President of Plans for Global Defense," *New York Times,* 26 July 1953, p. 1; memorandum of discussion at the 156th meeting of the National Security Council, 23 Jul 1953, in *FRUS, 1952-1954,* vol. 15, pt. 2, 1420-1423; entry for 23-26 July 1953, LeMay Diary #5, 1953, Box 104a, Papers of Curtis LeMay, Manuscript Division, Library of Congress.

18. William Stueck, *The Korean War: An International History* (Princeton, N.J.: Princeton University Press, 1995), 326-330, 341-342, letter to author from BG Theo. C. Mataxis, 12 May 98. After the war, Eisenhower did become convinced that his threats had been successful. In early 1965, President Lyndon Johnson discussed the growing problem in Vietnam with Eisenhower, and the general remarked that he had ended the war in Korea by having the word passed through three different channels "telling the Chinese that they must agree to an armistice quickly, since he had decided to remove the restrictions of area and weapons if the war had to be continued." Notes by Andrew Goodpaster of a meeting between Johnson and Eisenhower, 17 Feb 1965, from the LBJ Library, copy furnished by Charles F. Brower IV.

19. Draft msg, JCS to CINCFE, undated but probably from early March, Sec. 21, Box 897, File OPD 381 Korea (9 May 1947), Record Group 341; msg, CX 61455, CINCFE to JCS, 9 Mar 1953, Geographic File, 1951-53, 383.21 Korea (3-19-45), Sec. 124, Box 43, Record Group 218; Michael J. McCarthy, "Uncertain Enemies: Soviet Pilots in the Korean War," *Air Power History* 44 (spring 1997): 39; Gen. O. P. Weyland, "The First Jet Air War," p. 12, advance copy of article to be published in HQ USAF, *Air Intelligence Digest,* provided to director of intelligence, Air University, Sept 1953, in Air University Library, Maxwell Air Force Base, Ala., Robert F. Futrell, *The United States Air Force in Korea 1950-1953,* rev. ed. (Washington, D.C.: USGPO, 1983) 654-655.

20. Futrell, *USAF in Korea,* 656. Letters and documents concerning the last mission of Maj. Thomas Sellers are in possession of his daughter, Prof. Sharon MacDonald, at Illinois State University, Normal, Ill. She has devoted considerable effort to tracking down the truth about her father's death, and the author is extremely grateful that she made available the results of her extensive research.

21. Lt. Bruce D. Gamble, ed., "Time Flies: The Oral History of Lt. Col. John F. Bolt, USMC," *Foundation* (fall 1993): 101.

22. Letters, Maj. T. M. Sellers to his wife, 4, 13, 29 May, 5, 11, 29, June, and 17 July 1953, furnished by Prof. MacDonald.

23. Weyland, "The First Jet Air War"; Mark A. O'Neill, "The Other Side of the Yalu: Soviet Pilots in the Korean War, Phase One, 1 November 1950-12 April 1951" (Ph.D. diss., Florida State University, 1996), 292; Gamble, "Time Flies," 102; Xiaoming Zhang, "China and the Air War in Korea, 1950-1953," *Journal of Military History* 62 (Apr 1998): 366-369; 548th RTS, "Bomb Damage Assessment of Major North Korean Cities," app. B, tab 1, File K720.323A, AFHRA. Even with such great American success, if the war had been extended into 1954, projections for normal jet combat attrition would have required the deferral of activation of ten fighter wings to keep FEAF up to strength. JCS 1776/360, Approval of Study by Permanent Logistics Reviewing Committee, 13 Mar 1953, Geographic File, 1951-53, 383.21 Korea (3-19-45), Sec. 124, Box 43, Record Group 218.

24. "Compilation of Destruction Achieved by FEAF Bomber Command—13 July 1950 to 26 July 1953," in *FEAF Bomber Command History, January-27 July 1953,* vol. V, File K713.01-41, AFHRA; Maj. Gen. William F. Dean, *General Dean's Story* (New York: Viking Press, 1954), 129, 272-273, 283; Futrell, *USAF in Korea,* 628-629.

25. Msg, White to LeMay, 5 Aug 1953, File B29051, Box B203, LeMay Papers; Bill McWilliams, A Return to Glory: The Untold Story of Honor, Dishonor, and Triumph at the United States Military Academy, 1950-1953, unpublished manuscript, 830-845; Walton S. Moody, *Building a Strategic Air Force* (Washington, D.C.: Air Force History and Museums Program, 1996), 399; USAF Historical Study No. 127, 122-140; Earl H. Tilford, Jr., *Crosswinds: The Air Force's Setup in Vietnam* (College Station: Texas A&M University Press, 1993), 12-30.

CHAPTER 10. LEGACIES AND CONCLUSIONS

1. Msg, V0022, Gen. O. P. Weyland to Gen. Earle Partridge, 19 Jan 1954, Weyland Official Correspondence, 50/00/00-53/00/00, File 168.7104-50, AFHRA, Maxwell Air Force Base, Ala.

2. Gen. O. P. Weyland, "The Air Campaign in Korea," *Air University Quarterly Review* 6 (fall 1953): 27-28.

3. Partridge interview by Tom Sturm and Hugh Ahmann, 23-25 Apr 1974, Oral History K239.0512-729, AFHRA.

4. Weyland, "The Air Campaign in Korea." Weyland was far ahead of his time in his observation that the strict delineations between the tactical, strategic, and later operational levels of war were blurring for airpower. The issue would not be widely discussed by military observers until after Desert Storm.

5. Gen. O. P. Weyland, "The First Jet Air War," advance copy of article to be published in HQ USAF, *Air Intelligence Digest,* provided to director of intelligence, Air University, Sept 1953, in Air University Library, Maxwell Air Force Base, Ala.; Earl H. Tilford, Jr., *Crosswinds: The Air Force's Setup in Vietnam* (College Station: Texas A&M University Press, 1993), 25. For two thorough analyses of TAC's transformation after the Korean War, see Jerome V. Martin, "Reforging the Sword: United States Air Force Tactical Air Forces, Air Power Doctrine, and National Secu-

rity Policy, 1945–1956" (Ph.D. diss., Ohio State University, 1988), 201–357, and Caroline F. Ziemke, "In the Shadow of the Giant: USAF Tactical Air Command in the Era of Strategic Bombing, 1945–1955" (Ph.D. diss., Ohio State University, 1989), 239–309.

6. Msg, V0022, Weyland to Partridge, 19 Jan 1954, Weyland Official Correspondence, 50/00/00–53/00/00, File 168.7104-50, AFHRA.

7. Interview of Lt. Gen. James T. Stewart by Col. Charles Andrean, 1986, pp. 191–193, U.S. Army Military History Institute Senior Officer Oral History Program, James T. Stewart Papers, U.S. Army Military History Institute, Carlisle Barracks, Pa.; James T. Stewart, ed., *Airpower, the Decisive Force in Korea* (Princeton, N.J.: Van Nostrand, 1957); Robert F. Futrell, *The United States Air Force in Korea 1950–1953,* rev. ed. (Washington, D.C.: USGPO, 1983).

8. Ziemke, "In the Shadow," 270–309.

9. Prof. Dennis M. Drew, "Air Theory, Air Force, and Low Intensity Conflict: A Short Journey to Confusion," in *The Paths of Heaven: The Evolution of Airpower Theory,* ed. Col. Phillip S. Meilinger (Maxwell Air Force Base, Ala.: Air University Press, 1997); Mark Clodfelter, *The Limits of Airpower: The American Bombing of North Vietnam* (New York: Free Press, 1989), 30–33; Robert B. Johnson, "RAND Studies of Air Power in Limited Wars," 21 May 1957, File K720.3102-7, AFHRA.

10. Clodfelter, *Limits of Airpower,* 29; interview of Gen. Jacob Smart by Dr. Edgar Puryear, 10 June 1980, pp. 2, 17, File K239.0512-1497, AFHRA; Document M-501, interview with Curtis LeMay, 17 Aug 1975, in David Culbert, ed., *Film and Propaganda in America: A Documentary History,* vol. 5, *Microfiche Supplement, 1939–1979* (Westport, Conn.: Greenwood Press, 1993). LeMay thought that *Gathering of Eagles* came closest to showing a true picture of SAC, though he did not particularly like any of Hollywood's depictions. Information on Power, including the draft of his book, can be found in the Thomas S. Power Manuscript Collection, George Arents Research Library for Special Collections, Syracuse University, Syracuse, N.Y.

11. Richard Hallion, *The Naval Air War in Korea* (Baltimore: The Nautical and Aviation Publishing Company of America, 1986), 188–209; Allan R. Millett and Peter Maslowski, *For the Common Defense: A Military History of the United States,* rev. ed. (New York: Free Press, 1994), 539–540.

12. A. J. Bacevich, *The Pentomic Era: The U.S. Army between Korea and Vietnam* (Washington, D.C.: National Defense University Press, 1986); letter from BG Theo. C. Mataxis to author, 12 May 1998; Student Reference, *Deviations between US Army and US Air Force Doctrine* (Carlisle Barracks, Pa.: U.S. Army War College, 1954–1955), copy at U.S. Army Military History Institute; United States Army Combat Developments Command Institute of Special Studies, *A Short History of Close Air Support Issues,* July 1968, copy provided by Kelly Jordan and Allan Millett; summary of OA Memorandum No. 69, in HQ 5th AF, *History of the Fifth Air Force, 1 July–31 December 1953,* pp. 370–371, File K730.01, July–Dec 1953, AFHRA; Millett and Maslowski, *For the Common Defense,* 552; Allan R. Millett, "Korea, 1950–1953," in *Case Studies in the Development of Close Air Support,* ed. Benjamin Franklin Cooling (Washington, D.C.: USGPO, 1990), 398–399. The Marines were not interested in the CAS potential of the helicopter because they were satisfied with their current fixed-wing capabilities.

13. Ziemke, "In the Shadow," 303; Drew, "Air Theory," 334; J. Lawton Collins, *War in Peacetime: The History and Lessons of Korea* (Boston: Houghton Mifflin, 1969),

313; Partridge interview, pp. 543–544; James A. Winnefeld and Dana J. Johnson, *Joint Air Operations: Pursuit of Unity in Command and Control, 1942–1991* (Annapolis: Naval Institute Press, 1993), 63–82; HQ USAF, *Summary of an Evaluation of the United States Air Force in Korea,* pp. 1–2, File 160.041-1, AFHRA. For an insightful analysis of the way the Korean experience shaped the actions of American civilian leaders early in the Vietnam War, see Yuen Foong Khong, *Analogies at War: Korea, Munich, Dien Bien Phu, and the Vietnam Decisions of 1965* (Princeton, N.J.: Princeton University Press, 1992), 97–147.

14. Matthew B. Ridgway, *The Korean War* (New York: Da Capo, 1986), viii; Matthew B. Ridgway with Harold H. Martin, *Soldier: The Memoirs of Matthew B. Ridgway* (New York: Harper and Brothers, 1956), 277.

15. Ronald H. Spector, *Advice and Support: The Early Years, 1941–1960* (New York: Free Press, 1985), 205–206. In late March, Eisenhower had mused about a single American strike in unmarked planes, but he was not convinced it would be decisive and knew "we'd have to deny it forever." George C, Herring, *America's Longest War: The United States and Vietnam 1950–1975,* 2d ed. (New York: McGraw-Hill, 1986), 31.

16. Memorandum of conversation by Ridgway, 22 Mar 1954; memoranda for the Secretary of Defense by Radford, 31 Mar and 22 Apr 1954; memoranda for JCS by Ridgway, 2 and 6 Apr 1954; memoranda for record by Ridgway, 28 Apr and 17 May 1954, Folder, Historical Record Jan–June 1954, Box 30, Matthew B. Ridgway Papers, USAMHI; George C. Herring and Richard H. Immerman, "Eisenhower, Dulles, and Dienbienphu: 'The Day We Didn't Go to War' Revisited," *Journal of American History* 71 (Sept 1984): 346–363; Ridgway, *Soldier,* 278. Herring and Immerman believe that Eisenhower was more willing to intervene than he later admitted in his memoirs, *The White House Years,* vol. 1, *Mandate for Change, 1953–1956* (Garden City, N.Y.: Doubleday, 1963). However, Melanie Billings-Yun argues in *Decision against War: Eisenhower and Dien Bien Phu, 1954* (New York: Columbia University Press, 1988) that Eisenhower never wanted to intervene militarily but could not afford to take that position openly without threatening French motivation to win the war and bringing into question America's commitment to the security of Southeast Asia.

17. Interview of Gen. Jacob Smart (Ret.) by author, 2 Nov 1997, Arlington, Va., with changes provided by letter on 29 Nov 1997, in possession of author; transcript of *Meet the Press,* 21 Mar 1965, vol. 9, no. 10, Communications and Writings: Interviews and Meet the Press Folder, Box 9, Power Collection; Clodfelter, *Limits of Airpower,* 206–210.

18. Letter, BG W. P. Fisher to LeMay, 8 June 1953, with enclosed Report of General Inspection of Bomber Command, FEAF Folder, Box B84, Papers of Curtis LeMay, Manuscript Division, Library of Congress, Washington, D.C.

19. Smart interview by author.

20. Document M-490, letter, Rear Adm. W. S. Parsons to LTC Walter Ott, 14 Dec 1951 and Document M-491, Letter, N. Panama and W. Frank to Parsons, 15 Jan 1952, in Culbert, *Film and Propaganda in America.* For an example of such a Gulf War comparison, see Yasuo Kurata, "Americans Are Insensitive to Casualties Because Their Country Hasn't Been Bombed," *Kansas City Star,* 5 May 1991, p. K-2. Kurata is a political commentator for the *Tokyo Shimbun,* where the article originally appeared.

SELECT BIBLIOGRAPHY

MANUSCRIPT SOURCES

Air Force Historical Research Agency of the United States Air Force, Maxwell Air Force Base, Ala.
  Special Collections
  Unit Histories
Air University Library, Maxwell Air Force Base, Ala.
  Documents Section
George Arents Research Library for Special Collections, Syracuse University, Syracuse, N.Y.
  Thomas S. Power Manuscript Collection
George C. Marshall Research Library, Virginia Military Institute, Lexington, Va.
  Papers of George C. Marshall
  Papers of James A. Van Fleet
Harry S. Truman Library, Independence, Mo.
  Papers of Harry S. Truman
  Papers of Stuart Symington
Hoover Institution on War, Revolution, and Peace, Stanford University, Stanford, Calif.
  Papers of Frederick L. Anderson
Library of Congress, Manuscript Division, Washington, D.C.
  Papers of Curtis E. LeMay
  Papers of Carl A. Spaatz
  Papers of Nathan F. Twining
  Papers of Hoyt S. Vandenberg
National Archives at College Park (Archives II), College Park, Md.
  Record Group 18, Army Air Forces
  Record Group 200, Universal International Newsreels
  Record Group 218, Joint Chiefs of Staff
  Record Group 319, Army Operations
  Record Group 338, United States Army Commands, 1942-
  Record Group 341, Headquarters, U.S. Air Force
  Record Group 342, USAF Films and Photographs
Naval Historical Center, Washington, D.C.

Commander in Chief, U.S. Pacific Fleet, Interim Reports
Thomas M. Sellers Papers, in the possession of Prof. Sharon MacDonald, Illinois
State University, Normal, Ill.
United States Army Military History Institute, Carlisle Barracks, Pa.
Papers of Edward M. Almond
Papers of James T. Stewart
Papers of Matthew B. Ridgway
Papers of Omar N. Bradley
United States Military Academy Library, West Point, N.Y.
Douglas MacArthur Archives (microfilm copy)
Special Collections
University Research Library, Special Collections Division, University of California at
Los Angeles
Papers of Bernard Brodie

AUTHOR INTERVIEWS AND CORRESPONDENCE

Bolt, Lt. Col. John F. (Ret.). Marine pilot in Korea, 1952–1953. Correspondence,
30 May 1998.
MacDonald, Sharon S. Daughter of Maj. Thomas Sellers, last Sabre pilot shot down
in the Korean War. Correspondence, 7 May 1998.
Mataxis, Brig. Gen. Theo. C. (Ret.). Deputy G-2 Eighth Army and Regimental
Commander in Korea, 1952–1953. Correspondence, 12 May 98.
Smart, Gen. Jacob S. (Ret.). FEAF Deputy Commander for Operations, 1951–1953.
Interview, Arlington, Va., 2 Nov 1997.
———. Correspondence. 29 November 1997.

PUBLISHED MICROFORM COLLECTIONS

Culbert, David, ed. *Film and Propaganda in America: A Documentary History.* Vol. 5.
Microfiche Supplement, 1939–1979. Westport, Conn.: Greenwood Press, 1993.
The Military Situation in the Far East and the Relief of General MacArthur. Washing-
ton, D.C.: University Publications of America, 1977. (microfilm)
OSS/State Department Intelligence and Research Reports. Vol. 8. *Japan, Korea, Southeast
Asia and the Far East Generally: 1950–1961 Supplement.* Washington, D.C.: Univer-
sity Publications of America, 1979. (microfilm)
Records of the Joint Chiefs of Staff. Part 2. *1946–53, The Far East.* Washington, D.C.:
University Publications of America, 1979. (microfilm)
Records of the Joint Chiefs of Staff. Part 2. *1946–53, Meetings of the JCS.* Frederick, Md.:
University Publications of America, 1980. (microfilm)
Records of the Joint Chiefs of Staff. Part 2. *1946–53, Strategic Issues, Section I, Atomic
Weapons.* Frederick, Md.: University Publications of America, 1980. (microfilm)

BOOKS AND DOCUMENTS

Acheson, Dean. *The Korean War.* New York: W. W. Norton, 1971.

Air University Human Resources Research Institute. *Human Factors Affecting the Air War Effort*. Maxwell Air Force Base, Ala.: Air University, December 1951.

Appleman, Roy E. *South to the Naktong, North to the Yalu*. Washington, D.C.: USGPO, 1961.

Bacevich, A. J. *The Pentomic Era: The U.S. Army between Korea and Vietnam*. Washington, D.C.: National Defense University Press, 1986.

Billings-Yun, Melanie. *Decision against War: Eisenhower and Dien Bien Phu, 1954*. New York: Columbia University Press, 1988.

Blair, Clay. *The Forgotten War: America in Korea, 1950-1953*. New York: Anchor Books, 1989.

Blunk, Chester L. *"Every Man a Tiger": The 731st USAF Night Intruders over Korea*. Manhattan, Kans.: Sunflower University Press, 1987.

Bowen, Ezra. *Knights of the Air*. Alexandria, Va.: Time-Life Books, 1980.

Cabell, Charles P. *A Man of Intelligence: Memoirs of War, Peace, and the CIA*. Colorado Springs: Impavide Publications, 1997.

Chapell, John D. *Before the Bomb: How America Approached the End of the Pacific War*. Lexington: University Press of Kentucky, 1997.

Clark, Mark W. *From the Danube to the Yalu*. Blue Ridge Summit, Pa.: Tab Books, 1988.

Clodfelter, Mark. *The Limits of Airpower: The American Bombing of North Vietnam*. New York: Free Press, 1989.

Coffey, Thomas M. *Iron Eagle: The Turbulent Life of General Curtis LeMay*. New York: Crown, 1986.

Collins, J. Lawton. *War in Peacetime: The History and Lessons of Korea*. Boston: Houghton Mifflin, 1969.

Concepts Division, Aerospace Studies Institute. *Guerrilla Warfare and Airpower in Korea*. Maxwell Air Force Base, Ala.: Air University, January 1964.

Cooling, Benjamin Franklin, ed. *Case Studies in the Development of Close Air Support*. Washington, D.C.: USGPO, 1990.

Corn, Joseph J. *The Winged Gospel: America's Romance with Aviation, 1900-1950*. New York: Oxford University Press, 1983.

Crane, Conrad C. *Bombs, Cities, and Civilians: American Airpower Strategy in World War II*. Lawrence: University Press of Kansas, 1993.

Craven, Wesley Frank, and James Lea Cate, eds. *The Army Air Forces in World War II*. 7 vols. Chicago: University of Chicago Press, 1948-1953.

Cumings, Bruce. *The Origins of the Korean War*. Vol. 2. *The Roaring of the Cataract*. Princeton, N.J.: Princeton University Press, 1990.

Cutforth, Rene. *Korean Reporter*. London: Allan Wingate, 1952.

Dean, Maj. Gen. William F. *General Dean's Story*. New York: Viking Press, 1954.

Dews, Edmund, and Felix Kozaczka. *Air Interdiction: Lessons from Past Campaigns*. Santa Monica, Calif.: RAND Corporation, September 1981.

Eisenhower, Dwight David. *The White House Years*. Vol. 1. *Mandate for Change, 1953-1956*. New York: Doubleday, 1963.

Endicott, Stephen, and Edward Hagerman. *The United States and Biological Warfare: Secrets from the Early Cold War and Korea*. Bloomington: Indiana University Press, 1998.

Futrell, Robert F. *Ideas, Concepts, Doctrine: Basic Thinking in the United States Air Force*. 2 vols. Maxwell Air Force Base, Ala.: Air University Press, 1989.

———. *The United States Air Force in Korea 1950-1953*. Rev. ed. Washington, D.C.: USGPO, 1983.

Goldhamer, H. *Communist Reaction in Korea to American Possession of the A-Bomb and Its Significance for U.S. Political and Psychological Warfare*. Santa Monica, Calif.: RAND Corporation, 1 August 1952.

Gunn, William A. *A Study of the Effectiveness of Air Support Operations in Korea*. Baltimore: Operations Research Office, Johns Hopkins University, 26 September 1951.

Hallion, Richard. *The Naval Air War in Korea*. Baltimore: Nautical and Aviation Publishing Company of America, 1986.

Hastings, Maj. Donald W., et al. *Psychiatric Experiences of the Eighth Air Force: First Year of Combat (July 4, 1942–July 4, 1943)*. New York: Josiah Macy, Jr., Foundation, August 1944.

Hastings, Max. *The Korean War*. New York: Touchstone, 1988.

Hermes, Walter G. *Truce Tent and Fighting Front*. Washington, D.C.: USGPO, 1966.

Herring, George C. *America's Longest War: The United States and Vietnam, 1950–1975*. 2d ed. New York: McGraw-Hill, 1986.

Hose, Peter M. *Effectiveness of Radar Controlled Night Bombing*. Baltimore: Operations Research Office, Johns Hopkins University, 5 July 1952.

Hungerford, Jean. *Reactions of Civilian Populations to Air Attacks by Friendly Forces*. Santa Monica, Calif.: RAND Corporation, 2 September 1952.

Hyatt, Joan. *Korean War, 1950–1953: Selected References*. Maxwell Air Force Base, Ala.: Air University Library, December 1995.

Jian, Chen. *China's Road to the Korean War*. New York: Columbia University Press, 1994.

Kahn, E. J., Jr. *The Peculiar War: Impressions of a Reporter in Korea*. New York: Random House, 1952.

Kaplan, Fred. *The Wizards of Armageddon*. New York: Simon and Schuster, 1983.

Kendall, W., et al. *FEC Psychological Warfare Operations: Leaflets*. Baltimore: Operations Research Office, Johns Hopkins University, 31 March 1952.

Khong, Yuen Foong. *Analogies at War: Korea, Munich, Dien Bien Phu, and the Vietnam Decisions of 1965*. Princeton, N.J.: Princeton University Press, 1992.

Kohn, Richard H., and Joseph P. Harahan, eds. *Air Interdiction in World War II, Korea, and Vietnam*. Washington, D.C.: Office of Air Force History, 1986.

Leitenberg, Milton. *The Korean War Biological Warfare Allegations Resolved*. Occasional Paper 36. Stockholm: Center for Pacific Asia Studies at Stockholm University, May 1998.

Lewy, Guenter. *America in Vietnam*. New York: Oxford University Press, 1978.

Lyman, Flt. Lt. B. *The Significance of Australian Air Operations in Korea*. Fairbairn: Royal Australian Air Force Air Power Studies Centre, March 1992.

MacArthur, Douglas. *Reminiscences*. New York: McGraw-Hill, 1964.

Mark, Eduard. *Aerial Interdiction: Air Power and the Land Battle in Three American Wars: A Historical Analysis*. Washington, D.C.: Center for Air Force History, 1994.

Meilinger, Phillip S. *Hoyt S. Vandenberg: The Life of a General*. Bloomington: Indiana University Press, 1989.

Meilinger, Col. Phillip S., ed. *The Paths of Heaven: The Evolution of Airpower Theory*. Maxwell Air Force Base, Ala.: Air University Press, 1997.

Mets, David R. *Master of Airpower: General Carl A. Spaatz*. Novato, Calif.: Presidio Press, 1988.

Millett, Allan R., and Peter Maslowski. *For the Common Defense: A Military History of the United States*. Rev. ed. New York: Free Press, 1994.

Ministry of National Defense, Republic of Korea. *The History of the United Nations Forces in the Korean War*. Seoul: ROK Ministry of National Defense, 1973.

Mitchell, Vance O. *Air Force Officers Personnel Policy Development 1944-1974*. Washington, D.C.: USGPO, 1996.

Momyer, Gen. William. *Air Power in Three Wars*. Washington, D.C.: USGPO, 1978.

Moody, Walton S. *Building a Strategic Air Force*. Washington, D.C.: Air Force History and Museums Program, 1996.

Mossman, Billy C. *Ebb and Flow: November 1950-July 1951*. Washington, D.C.: USGPO, 1990.

Nichols, Donald. *How Many Times Can I Die?* Brooksville, Fla: Brownsville Printing, 1981.

Paik Sun Yup, Gen. *From Pusan to Panmunjom*. New York: Brassey's, 1992.

Pease, Stephen E. *Psywar: Psychological Warfare in Korea, 1950-53*. Harrisburg, Pa.: Stackpole Books, 1992.

RAND Corporation Social Sciences Division Progress Report R-167. *The Warning of Target Populations in Air War*. Santa Monica, Calif.: RAND Corporation, 1 November 1949 (classified).

RAND Corporation Social Sciences Division Research Memorandum 275. *The Warning of Target Populations in Air War: An Appendix of Working Papers*. Santa Monica, Calif.: RAND Corporation, November 1949.

Rees, David. *Korea: The Limited War*. London: Macmillan and Company Limited, 1964.

Ridgway, Matthew B. *The Korean War*. New York: Da Capo, 1986.

Ridway, Matthew B., with Harold H. Martin. *Soldier: The Memoirs of Matthew B. Ridgway*. New York: Harper and Brothers, 1956.

Ross, Steven T., and David Alan Rosenberg, eds. *America's Plans for War against the Soviet Union, 1945-1950*. 15 vols. New York: Garland, 1989.

Schnabel, James F. *Policy and Direction: The First Year*. Washington, D.C.: USGPO, 1972.

Schnabel, James F., and Robert J. Watson. *The Joint Chiefs of Staff and National Policy*. Vol. 3. *The Korean War*. Washington, D.C.: Historical Division, Joint Secretariat, JCS, 12 April 1978.

Sherwood, John Darrell. *Officers in Flight Suits: The Story of American Air Force Fighter Pilots in the Korean War*. New York: New York University Press, 1996.

Spiller, Roger J., ed. *American Military Leaders*. New York: Praeger, 1989.

Steiner, Barry H. *Bernard Brodie and the Foundations of American Nuclear Strategy*. Lawrence: University Press of Kansas, 1991.

Stewart, James T., ed. *Airpower, The Decisive Force in Korea*. Princeton, N.J.: Van Nostrand, 1957.

Stueck, William. *The Korean War: An International History*. Princeton, N.J.: Princeton University Press, 1995.

Sunderland, Riley. *Evolution of Command and Control Doctrine for Close Air Support*. Washington, D.C.: Office of Air Force History, March 1973.

Thompson, Reginald. *Cry Korea*. London: MacDonald and Co., 1951.

Tilford, Earl H., Jr. *Crosswinds: The Air Force's Setup in Vietnam*. College Station: Texas A&M University Press, 1993.

Ulanoff, Stanley, ed. *Bombs Away! True Stories of Strategic Airpower from World War I to the Present*. Garden City, N.Y.: Doubleday, 1971.

United States Air Force Historical Study No. 71. *United States Air Force Operations in the Korean Conflict, 25 June-1 November 1950.* Maxwell Air Force Base, Ala.: USAF Historical Division, Air University, 1 July 1952.

United States Air Force Historical Study No. 72. *United States Air Force Operations in the Korean Conflict, 1 November 1950-30 June 1952.* Maxwell Air Force Base, Ala.: USAF Historical Division, Air University, 1 July 1953.

United States Air Force Historical Study No. 88. *The Employment of Strategic Bombers in a Tactical Role 1941-1951.* Maxwell Air Force Base, Ala.: USAF Historical Division, Air University, April 1954.

United States Air Force Historical Study No. 92. *Development of Night Air Operations 1941-1952.* Maxwell Air Force Base, Ala.: USAF Historical Division, Air University, 1953.

United States Air Force Historical Study No. 127. *United States Air Force Operations in the Korean Conflict, 1 July 1952-27 July 1953.* Maxwell Air Force Base, Ala.: USAF Historical Division, Air University, 1 Jul 1956.

United States Department of State. *Foreign Relations of the United States, 1950.* Vol. 7. *Korea.* Washington, D.C.: USGPO, 1976.

United States Department of State. *Foreign Relations of the United States, 1951.* Vol. 7. *Korea and China.* Washington, D.C.: USGPO, 1983.

United States Department of State. *Foreign Relations of the United States, 1952-1954.* Vol. 15. *Korea.* 2 parts. Washington, D.C.: USGPO, 1984.

United States Senate, 82d Congress, 1st Session. *Military Situation in the Far East: Hearings before the Committee on Armed Services and the Committee on Foreign Relations.* Washington, D.C.: USGPO, 1951.

Wells, Mark K. *Courage and Air Warfare: The Allied Aircrew Experience in the Second World War.* London: Frank Cass, 1995.

Werrell, Kenneth P. *Blankets of Fire: U.S. Bombers over Japan during World War II.* Washington, D.C.: Smithsonian, 1996.

Winnefeld, James A., and Dana J. Johnson. *Joint Air Operations: Pursuit of Unity in Command and Control, 1942-1991.* Annapolis: Naval Institute Press, 1993.

Wolk, Herman S. *Planning and Organizing the Postwar Air Force 1943-1947.* Washington, D.C.: Office of Air Force History, 1984.

Zhang, Shu Guang. *Mao's Military Romanticism: China and the Korean War, 1950-1953.* Lawrence: University Press of Kansas, 1995.

DISSERTATIONS

Farquhar, John Thomas. "A Need to Know: The Role of Air Force Reconnaissance in War Planning, 1945-1953." Ph.D. diss., Ohio State University, 1991.

Gentile, Gian Peri. "Advocacy or Assessment? The United States Strategic Bombing Survey of Germany and Japan." Ph.D. diss., Stanford University, 1998.

Martin, Jerome V. "Reforging the Sword: United States Air Force Tactical Air Forces, Air Power Doctrine, and National Security Policy, 1945-1956." Ph.D. diss., Ohio State University, 1988.

O'Neill, Mark Andrew. "The Other Side of the Yalu: Soviet Pilots in the Korean war, Phase One, 1 November 1950-12 April 1951." Ph.D. diss., Florida State University, 1996.

Ziemke, Caroline F. "In the Shadow of the Giant: USAF Tactical Air Command in the Era of Strategic Bombing, 1945-1955." Ph.D. diss., Ohio State University, 1989.

ARTICLES

Anders, Roger M. "The Atomic Bomb and the Korean War: Gordon Dean and the Issue of Civilian Control." *Military Affairs* (January 1988): 1-6.

Anderson, Maj. Gen. Orville. "Air Warfare and Morality." *Air University Quarterly Review* 2 (winter 1949): 5-14.

Bernstein, Barton. "Compelling Japan's Surrender without the A-bomb, Soviet Entry, or Invasion: Reconsidering the US Bombing Survey's Early Surrender Counterfactual." *Journal of Strategic Studies* 18 (June 1995): 101-148.

Biddle, Tami Davis. "British and American Approaches to Strategic Bombing: Their Origins and Implementation in the World War II Combined Bomber Offensive." *Journal of Strategic Studies* 18 (March 1995): 91-144.

Dingman, Roger. "Atomic Diplomacy during the Korean War." *International Security* 13 (winter 1988-1989): 50-112.

Gamble, Lt. Bruce D., ed. "Time Flies: The Oral History of Lt. Col. John F. Bolt, USMC (Ret)." *Foundation* (fall 1993): 94-104.

Gentile, Gian Peri. "A-bombs, Budgets, and Morality: Using the Strategic Bombing Survey." *Air Power History* 44 (spring 1997): 18-31.

———. "Advocacy or Assessment? The United States Strategic Bombing Survey of Germany and Japan." *Pacific Historical Review* 66 (winter 1997): 53-79.

Gleason, Robert L. "Psychological Operations and Air Power." *Air University Review* 22 (March–April 1971): 35-41.

Herring, George C., and Richard H. Immerman. "Eisenhower, Dulles, and Dienbienphu: 'The Day We Didn't Go to War' Revisited." *Journal of American History* 71 (September 1984): 343-363.

Kuehl, Daniel T. "Refighting the Last War: Electronic Warfare and U.S. Air Force B-29 Operations in the Korean War, 1950-53." *Journal of Military History* 56 (January 1992): 87-111.

Jolidon, Laurence. "Soviet Interrogation of U.S. POWs in the Korean War." *Cold War International History Project Bulletin* (winter 1995-1996): 123-125.

Leitenberg, Milton. "New Russian Evidence on the Korean War Biological Warfare Allegations: Background and Analysis." *Cold War International History Project Bulletin* (winter 1998): 185-199.

Mahurin, Walker M. "Communist Way: Case History of a Confession." *New York Times,* 1 November 1953.

Mansourov, Alexandre Y. "Stalin, Mao, Kim, and China's Decision to Enter the Korean War, September 16-October 15, 1950: New Evidence from the Russian Archives." *Cold War International History Project Bulletin* (winter 1995-1996): 94-119.

McCarthy, Michael J. "Uncertain Enemies: Soviet Pilots in the Korean War." *Air Power History* 44 (spring 1997): 32-45.

Quarterly Review Staff Study. "The Attack on the Irrigation Dams in North Korea." *Air University Quarterly Review* 6 (winter 1953-1954): 40-61.

Rosenberg, David Alan. "The Origins of Overkill: Nuclear Weapons and American Strategy, 1945-1960." *International Security* 7 (spring 1983): 3-71.

Shen Zhihua. "The Discrepancy between the Russian and Chinese Versions of Mao's 2 October Message to Stalin on Chinese Entry into the Korean War: A Chinese Scholar's Reply." *Cold War International History Project Bulletin* (winter 1996/ 1997): 237–242.

"U.S. Proposes Investigation of Bacteriological Warfare Charges." *Department of State Bulletin* 27 (7 July 1952): 32–37.

Weathersby, Kathryn. "Deceiving the Deceivers: Moscow, Beijing, Pyongyang, and the Allegations of Bacteriological Weapons Use in Korea." *Cold War International History Project Bulletin* (winter 1998): 176–185.

Weyland, Gen. O. P. "The Air Campaign in Korea." *Air University Quarterly Review* 6 (fall 1953): 3–28.

Zhang, Xiaoming. "China and the Air War in Korea, 1950 1953." *Journal of Military History* 62 (April 1998): 335–370.

INDEX